LEWIE

Lewis R. Donelson, III

Published by Rhodes College,
2000 North Parkway,
Memphis, Tennessee 38112-1690

ISBN: 978-0-615-56752-5
LCCN: 2011943380

PRINTED IN THE UNITED STATES OF AMERICA

CONTENTS

INTRODUCTION

I was born in Memphis, October 9, 1917. My parents lived on Harbert, east of Bellevue, then a gravel road. Bellevue Junior High had not been built. My parents were Memphians. My father, Lewis Randolph Donelson, Jr., was born October 15, 1881; my mother, Katharine Loring Campbell, January 30, 1889. Both had strong family backgrounds in Tennessee.

As I look back, my life has been blessed with many privileges and opportunities that enabled me to achieve success. One major influence was a strong sense of my heritage; therefore, it seems appropriate to outline that heritage.

When I began these memoirs, I was faced with a choice: Should I research my ancestors and establish the details and events in my own life? I realized it would take me forever to do that. What I truly wanted to write about were things I remember. My memories of my family history are based upon stories told to me, primarily by my two grandmothers, along with letters, books, and articles. After some consideration, I decided to tell the story as I remember it; even with factual errors, wrong dates, and perhaps confusion of characters, it would be better than a researched historical version. I apologize for any errors, but this is what I remember. I hope it is not too far from the facts.

ONE

MY DONELSON LEGACY

My Donelson ancestors came to this country around 1700. Patrick Donelson, the first in my line to arrive in the colonies, settled in Snow Hill, Maryland, on the eastern shore of the Chesapeake Bay. When his will was probated in 1720, he was a landowner and listed on the tax rolls of the county. Some investigations I have undertaken indicate he came from a small settlement, now gone, near Carrickfergus in Ulster. Carrickfergus is a port town on the Irish Sea.

Patrick Donelson had two children, a son and a daughter. The son John became a ship captain. Property records in Snow Hill indicate he owned several different ships, but no more than one at a time. We also found records that John Donelson was an executor in Maryland for a wealthy citizen of Barbados, and there are records of his efforts to settle that person's affairs. Records indicate that John Donelson, after 1735, "returned to port no more." His wife, Catherine Davis Donelson, survived him by a couple of years. Catherine Davis was a daughter of Sam Davis, the first minister of the first Presbyterian church in the colonies.

Presbyterians tended to settle on the Eastern Shore of the Chesapeake Bay in Maryland because Maryland had religious freedom. In the latter part of the 17th century, the official church in Massachusetts was Congregationalist; in Connecticut, Baptist; and in New York and

Virginia, Anglican. Only in Pennsylvania, Maryland, Delaware, and New Jersey was there religious freedom. Lord Baltimore, the founder of the Maryland colony, a Catholic, had been persecuted for his religion in England. William Penn, a Quaker, likewise, had been persecuted. Both of them required religious freedom in their colonies and this influence extended into Delaware and New Jersey. After a number of Presbyterians settled in these areas, they wrote to their presbytery in Ulster asking for ministers. The presbytery enlisted Francis Macamey to come to the colonies and found churches. He brought with him about a dozen young ministers and founded churches at Snow Hill, Maryland, and a total of 12 places in Delaware, New Jersey, the Eastern Shore of Maryland, and the Eastern Shore of Virginia. The church in Snow Hill, Maryland, was founded in 1683.

In 1704, when the Presbyterian Church had its first General Assembly in the colonies, Francis Macamey announced that the first church established was Snow Hill, and that was officially ratified by the General Assembly. Catherine Davis' father, Sam Davis, had come to the colonies in 1683, one of the Presbyterian preachers led by Macamey. He became the first minister of the Snow Hill Presbyterian Church and thus the first minister of the Presbyterian Church in the colonies.

One of Francis Macamey's accomplishments was his successful fight for religious freedom. Macamey went to New York to start Presbyterian churches and was arrested for preaching without a license. Being a Presbyterian, he couldn't get a license. He then brought suit and hired a high-powered Edinburgh lawyer to represent him alleging that the action of New York violated the Act of Religious Tolerance passed during the reign of Queen Anne in England. The case went to the House of Lords, which held that the Act of Religious Tolerance applied in all the colonies, opening up every colony to religious freedom. This historic event changed the entire nature of religious freedom in the colonies.

John Donelson's son was born around 1720. He spent much time with his mother and her family because his father was at sea. John Donelson, II, was around 15 when his parents died and he went to live with his grandfather, Sam Davis. During those years with his grandfather, John completed an excellent education. His spelling, writing, grammar, and vocabulary, all indicate that he was well educated for that period in the colonies. (One major difficulty the Presbyterian churches experienced in the colonies was the requirement that all ministers attend seminary and get a degree. As the colonies expanded westward, not enough Presbyterian ministers were available to meet the demand.)

We don't know what happened to John Donelson, II, in the intervening years, but, by the 1760s he had a well-established foundry business in Danville, Virginia. John was sufficiently prominent to be elected to the House of Burgesses and to be invited to participate in the Committees of Correspondence. His revolutionary activities must have had something to do with the serious financial difficulties that forced him to sell the foundry. Some of John Donelson's Committee of Correspondence letters have been recovered, and these include remarkable communications with George Washington, Thomas Jefferson, John Adams, and others.

Meanwhile, he began to survey in the West. Many educated men gravitated toward surveying because the thirst for new lands was insatiable. Sometime during the 1760s, he negotiated a treaty with the Indians to open up territory to white settlers. The negotiation took place on the Long Island of the Holston River (now Kingsport, Tennessee), a traditional meeting place for Indian peace negotiations. No record exists that John Donelson moved to East Tennessee or participated in the Watauga settlements. During the 1760s and 1770s, he did survey in Tennessee. Logs in the family report him in the Tennessee hill country, camping by himself, not knowing what was over the next hill. What amazing courage to explore by yourself! He was noted for his ability to deal with Indians, probably speaking some of their language and participating in negotiations, particularly with the Cherokee.

By 1779, he conceived a plan with James Robertson to build a new settlement on the Cumberland River at the salt lick. Robertson was to take the men overland to the site and build a fort. Donelson would lead the women and children and his large family with several adult males down the river in flat boats. The plan: to start from the Long Island of the Holston River, go down the Holston to the Tennessee River, down the Tennessee, and meet the Robertson party at Muscle Shoals. If Robertson was not there, the alternative was to go on down the Tennessee, up the Ohio River, and up the Cumberland River to the site of Nashville.

For an inexplicable reason, the Donelson party left on Christmas Eve during one of the coldest winters on record. It took them 30 days to get from the Long Island of the Holston to the conjunction of the Tennessee and Holston rivers on flat boats with no locomotion. The boats required poling to move along the rivers. Despite Indian attacks, they arrived in Muscle Shoals and found a note from the Robertson party advising them to continue by water. The note cited the many Indians in the area and rough terrain as reasons to proceed on down the river. They traveled with reasonable speed and progress until arrival at the mouth of the Tennessee and Ohio. They then traveled up the Ohio for some 12 miles and then up the Cumberland to Nashville. This was incredibly hard poling. The trip down the Tennessee and up the Ohio and Cumberland rivers was reported in a journal, now in the Tennessee State Library and Archives; it records a perilous and difficult journey.

Fifteen boats left the Long Island of the Holston. On one boat someone got smallpox and that boat had to fall back. Indians probably attacked, and the group was never heard from again. In addition, one other person died. During one of the Indian attacks, the polers had to get the boats off rocks to escape. They threw things overboard to lighten the boat including, unintentionally, a newborn baby in a box, the customary cradle of the frontier. Remarkably, the remaining 14 boats reached Nashville.

Rachel Donelson (Jackson) and Sam Donelson, (her brother and my great-great-grandfather) as young teenagers were among the principal polers and probably among the sturdiest in the group. The last stage of the journey, up the Cumberland River, was much slower than anticipated. Many were near starvation and with possible scurvy. They lived on cornmeal and beef jerky. Some Indians taught them to eat dandelion greens or poke salad, which saved many lives. When they arrived in Nashville on April 20, 1780, the Revolutionary War was not over. (Nashville was the first major town in Tennessee before Knoxville, Chattanooga, and most of the cities in East Tennessee except Jamestown, which became the capital of the Watauga settlements and the State of Franklin.)

The Robertson party had built a fort and greeted the Donelson party with great enthusiasm. Donelson settled out in Clover Bottom, which promptly flooded. Donelson then moved down the Cumberland River into Kentucky and, a year or so later, moved back and established a farm in the area now known as Donelson in Davidson County.

Donelson also did surveying for the United States. On his way back alone from Washington in 1785, having collected the money due him, he was probably at that time at least 65 years old. Two young men came through Nashville and reported passing him on the trail. There were many Indians in the area who might have attacked him. When he didn't appear in Nashville in the subsequent days, the family went up the trail and found him dead and the money gone.

John had 11 children, and his oldest child, known as Captain John, had 12. This large family permeated the whole settlement. Within a few years, everybody in the area had some kinship or connection with the Donelsons. The most famous was Andrew Jackson who married Rachel Donelson, who had been married to Lewis Robards. The two believed Robards had obtained a divorce, but, in fact, he had not completed divorce proceedings. This failure resulted in political abuse and agony, especially for Rachel. She went from a lively, attractive young woman to an extremely devout Christian who suffered from the merciless discussion of her possibly bigamous marriage. Rachel and Andrew even went to the trouble of remarrying after Robards' divorce became final.

When Andrew Jackson arrived on the scene, the Donelson family was certainly not only the most prolific in the territory, but the largest landholders. Some descendants were quite successful. When Andrew Jackson married Rachel, he married his own political organization. Many of his closest advisers—John Coffee, John C. McLemore, John Caffrey, and Samuel Hayes—were brothers-in-law.

Andrew Jackson negotiated a treaty with the Chickasaws, opening west Tennessee. Then he, James Winchester, and John Overton, bought the Rice tract, including most of downtown Memphis, along the river. McLemore, who bought Andrew Jackson's interest in Memphis, was the only one of the original owners of the Rice tract who ever lived in Memphis. He moved here, and his family has been here ever since. McLemore Avenue is named for the family. Andrew Jackson, whose negotiation of the Indian treaty that enabled the purchase of the Rice tract, got first choice; he chose the South Bluff because of the existing town of Fort Pickering on high ground, which he thought would be the most valuable property. General James Winchester got second choice and picked the north end where the Wolf River came in, because he expected that area would be the port. John Overton got what was left over, and as the town grew, his descendants became the wealthiest people in the community.

John Donelson's son, Sam Donelson, the closest brother to Rachel, was my great-great-grandfather. Sam fell in love with Polly Smith, the daughter of General Daniel Smith, one of the first U.S. senators from Tennessee and general of the state militia. Smith also had been secretary of the First Constitutional Convention of Tennessee and drawn the line between Tennessee and Kentucky. He is reputed to have selected the name for the state of Tennessee and was the principal draftsman of the original Tennessee Constitution. His home, Rock Castle, north of Nashville, still stands and is owned by the state. When I was commissioner of Finance and Administration for the state, I was privileged to be the official host at the re-opening of Rock Castle after the state purchased it. It was a lovely evening, only candlelight in the 1785 home giving a real sense of how it must have looked and felt in its glory days.

Polly Smith was only 16 and General Smith was not pleased with her getting married. He had planned to send her to school in Philadelphia. The couple, with the assistance of Andrew Jackson, a great romantic, eloped. At Rock Castle, you can see the window from which Polly climbed down the ladder held by Jackson, who assisted them across the river to get married. Polly and Sam had three sons, Andrew Jackson Donelson, Daniel Smith Donelson, and John Samuel Donelson.

Daniel Smith was born in Virginia. His parents sent him to Charlottesville to live with a doctor who educated young men. Like all successful men on the edge of the frontier, the doctor speculated in western land. He sent Daniel down to Abingdon, Virginia, to manage his land in that area. Daniel rapidly became a leading citizen and was elected to the County Court and chosen to represent Virginia in drawing the line between Virginia (now Kentucky) and North Carolina (now Tennessee). He was the only experienced surveyor on the politically selected Boundary Commission and the actual surveying work fell mostly on him. In his surveying travels he learned of Fort Nashborough and decided to visit. He left the surveying party to investigate Fort Nashborough (now Nashville) and decided to move there after the line was finished. He was promptly elected to the county court although his term in Virginia had not expired.

When General Smith was on his deathbed he wrote a letter to his grandson Andrew Jackson Donelson, then a cadet at West Point. The letter (in fact, the last letter he wrote) read: "I have been wanting to write to you but I have felt so poorly that I put it off. But in your last letter you seemed so desirous of hearing from me I am going to make the effort. I hope you will always conduct yourself according to the highest moral precepts which can best be found in the New Testament which you have read in its original language (Greek). I think Chesterfield's letters would be of some benefit to you. But as to fluxions (calculus) and other forms of higher mathematics, I don't think you need bother with them further." He goes on to write about family matters. He died the next day.

Two things interest me about this letter. It indicates closeness and regular correspondence between grandfather and grandson. But I notice especially the reference to reading the New Testament in Greek. Here is a young man born in 1799, raised on the frontier in Nashville, and he reads Greek well. Yes, education has changed.

During Smith's initial visit to Fort Nashborough, legend has it the remaining surveying party knew little about surveying, and as they attempted to draw the line across the Tennessee, they made a mistake of many miles (now that bump in the Tennessee-Kentucky boundary line). When Smith returned and saw they had gone so far, he said, "It's too much trouble to go back and correct it." So it remains today.

Andrew Jackson Donelson was my great-grandfather. His father, Sam, died around 1803. Legend has it that he was killed by Indians when returning from a neighboring town where he had tried a case. Andrew Jackson Donelson went to live with Rachel and Andrew Jackson, and they raised him like a son. Jackson sent him to West Point in 1816 or 1817 and he graduated second in his class.

An amusing story on me: I always visualized my great-grandfather growing up in the Hermitage as it is now. I have been active in the Hermitage and serve on the National Advisory Board. When the Ladies Hermitage Association restored the original Hermitage (a log cabin) located behind the present home, the archaeologist showed us the restoration and said "The Jacksons lived here from 1802 until 1821." I turned to Jan, my wife, and said, "I just realized for the first time that Andrew Jackson Donelson grew up in this log cabin, then a two-story cabin—not the big house first built in 1821."

Originally, the Hermitage property was held in the name of trustees appointed by the state. My grandfather, my father, and my brother served as trustees until the property was actually deeded to the Ladies Hermitage Association. I have been going to the Hermitage all my life. I remember playing in the carriage (now beautifully restored). There were rat holes in the upholstery and it was almost destroyed. When I was commissioner of Finance and Administration, a Ladies Hermitage Association regent and others approached me about an appropriation from the state to build a visitors' center. The state had never given money to the operation and maintenance of the home. I agreed to get the legislature to appropriate $1.5 million, if the association would raise the funds to match it.

The ladies said, "We could never do that." I replied, "You won't even have to go outside your husbands to raise that much." I was right. I acted as chair, with Doctor Byrd, of the subsequent campaign. After I left the commissioner's office, I became chair of the National Advisory Board. Several years ago the association created a new award for "a person who had rendered outstanding service to the Hermitage" and named it the Lewis R. Donelson Award. I was touched and humbled because so many have done so much more than I. It was a signal honor.

One story about my great-grandfather and his West Point experiences has come down in the family. During Andrew Jackson Donelson's third year, a new drill instructor who was extremely severe had picked out a somewhat effeminate plebe to torment. He ordered an unreasonable punishment of lashes to the young cadet. A group of whom Donelson was one got up a petition to protest this treatment and presented it to the superintendent who was old Army. The superintendent promptly expelled them all for questioning the authority of a superior officer. Andrew Jackson Donelson apparently was able to get to Andrew Jackson to provide support while the group attempted to get themselves reinstated.

Unfortunately, I do not have the letter from Andrew Jackson Donelson to Andrew Jackson about their predicament. I do realize that it was not long after the Battle of New Orleans when Andrew Jackson was *the* hero of the country. Always moved by an injustice, Jackson responded with a strong letter of support. Apparently, Jackson's letter to the superintendent was sufficiently convincing that the cadets were reinstated and the drillmaster moved to another assignment. Interestingly, when Andrew Jackson Donelson's oldest son, Andrew Jackson Donelson, Jr., attended West Point, he was also second in his class.

When Andrew Jackson Donelson returned from West Point, Andrew Jackson sent him to Transylvania Law School up in Kentucky, the only law school west of the Alleghenies. He attended for two years, read law, and was admitted to the bar in 1821. He practiced sporadically thereafter, but his primary responsibility was as an aide to his uncle. He went with him to Florida when General Jackson was governor there. He was involved in the 1824 and 1828 presidential campaigns. When Rachel died following Jackson's election to the presidency, he and his wife, Emily, went to live in the White House where she served as first lady. Emily died in 1836 shortly before Donelson returned from the White House at the end of Jackson's term. A touching story: Each day she had herself propped up in the bed at Tulip Grove, the family home that sits near the Hermitage at the end of Rachel's Lane and looks straight down toward the main road. She would look down that lane for sight of her husband. Unfortunately, she died the day before he made it home from Washington.

In the next years, Andrew Jackson Donelson became known as Major Donelson and continued to serve as Jackson's political emissary and aide. He had a small law practice and began to try to farm his Tulip Grove properties. In 1841 he remarried. His second wife, Elizabeth Martin, is my great-grandmother. She had originally been married to Meriwether Lewis Randolph, Thomas Jefferson's grandson.

Jackson had appointed Randolph secretary (principal aide) to the territorial governor of Arkansas. Elizabeth and Meriweather met in Washington, married in the White House, and moved to Arkansas. They had a young son, Lewis Randolph. Meriwether contracted malaria and died. Elizabeth then returned to Tennessee. Elizabeth Martin Randolph was the niece of Emily Donelson. I have among my possessions a letter written by Emily Donelson to her niece on the occasion of her marriage to Meriwether Lewis Randolph, advising her about the responsibilities, the joys, and the sorrows of marriage—a touching letter, in the light of Elizabeth's becoming Emily's successor as Andrew Jackson Donelson's second wife.

My name is Lewis Randolph Donelson, III. My grandfather was named for his deceased older brother, my great-grandmother's son by Meriwether Lewis Randolph. The legend is that Elizabeth called out for her first husband during childbirth, and the major suggested the child be named Lewis Randolph. In any event, Elizabeth and Andrew Jackson Donelson had a long marriage and eight children.

President Benjamin Harrison's administration was the shortest on record. He made a long, rambling inaugural speech in the rain and got pneumonia from which he never recovered. Vice President John Tyler succeeded him. Harrison was a Whig but Tyler was of uncertain party connection, probably more of a Democrat. In any event, Tyler appointed Andrew Jackson Donelson as chargé d'affaires to the Republic of Texas to negotiate the annexation of Texas. Before leaving for Texas, Donelson acted as the principal floor leader for James K. Polk at the 1844 Democrat Convention, securing his nomination as the first dark horse candidate. Polk was referred to as "Little Hickory," as he was Andrew Jackson's protégé. Speaker of the U.S. House, he had run unsuccessfully for governor. In the first round in the nominations, he was not nominated. With a hot contest among three candidates, it was unlikely that any one of the three could achieve a majority. Donelson, helped by Andrew Jackson, maneuvered a situation where one of the three agreed to withdraw and, after Polk was nominated, to endorse Polk. This maneuver helped Polk secure the nomination and, to everybody's surprise, he won the presidency.

The annexation of Texas, strongly promoted by Sam Houston, was a difficult process. Opposition in the U.S. Congress arose because Texas would be admitted as a slave state, destroying the balance between the anti-slavery and the pro-slavery forces. Other opposition was fomented by the British who offered military and financial support to the young, struggling republic. The British sought to block the further growth of the United States. The government of Mexico also wanted Texas to remain independent, believing that the small republic (of Texas) would be easier to deal with than the United States. The Texas Congress approved of the annexation and sent a draft of a treaty to the U.S. Congress, which had rejected it. This congressional action irritated Sam Houston and his support began to waiver. The major actually proved his worth primarily by bringing Sam Houston back on track and by pushing through a revised proposal which he then took back to Congress, and it was approved. An amazing amount of intrigue went on, because, when the treaty actually came to a vote, the Texas Convention ratified the treaty unanimously, as did Congress, overwhelmingly. All the behind-the-scenes activity went on in the Texas legislature and with the president of the Republic of Texas, who enjoyed the job and hated to see himself reduced to the status of a state governor.

The treaty permitted Texas, at any time, to divide itself into five states. Imagine what this would do to change the consistency of the United States Senate—eight new senators would be added. Of course, all eight of them would not be Republicans but, assuming that six would be, the majority balance in the Senate would be changed by four.

Unfortunately, the details kept the major in Texas for several months after the ratification. He was not there when Andrew Jackson died, although his wife Elizabeth was. I grew up with a lithograph of the deathbed scene that showed Andrew Jackson Donelson present. He did not return to Nashville for several months; going first to Washington to report to President Polk. On that occasion, he discussed with the president what other job in the administration he would take. It had been reported that he was to be offered the secretary of War job, but he did not get that offer. There was no indication that, before Jackson's death, Jackson supported him for that job. Finally, he was offered, and accepted, the job of ambassador to Prussia. This job was particularly attractive because it carried a generous living allowance. He picked up the whole family and moved them to Berlin.

His oldest daughter, Mary, by his first wife Emily was the first baby born in the White House. She was about 17 when the family moved to Europe. In later life, she wrote two short published accounts of life in the White House as a child, one titled "Christmas in the White House."

Mary learned French, the language of courts all over Europe, and she learned the German language while living in Germany. Her father sent her to Italy one winter to learn Spanish and Italian, which she did, remarkable for a 17-year-old girl in 1848. After her husband was killed early in the Civil War, she got a job as a translator in the State Department.

When Grant became president, under the prevailing spoils system, she was fired because she was a Democrat. I have a letter she wrote to President Grant: "My name is Mary Donelson Wilcox and my father was Andrew Jackson Donelson who was your classmate at West Point. I had a job at the State Department as a translator and I needed the job badly because my husband was killed in the war and I have two small daughters. I was fired because I was a Democrat and I am a Democrat but I was hoping that you might order me to be restored to my job because of your friendship with my father." Back came a letter from Grant in his own handwriting saying, "I remember your father. He was my classmate. I am ordering you to be restored to your job and you are to hold it until you die." In 1899, my father went to Washington to visit his aunt, who still had that job with the State Department. She took my father out to an international exposition that was going on; she spoke French to the French, German to the Germans, Italian to the Italians, and Spanish to the Spanish. My father was totally bowled over and went back to school and changed his major to Romance languages.

Back to the major: After he returned to the states, he became involved again in politics and served briefly as editor at the *Washington Globe*, the Democrat party voice. Because he was strongly pro-Union and against secession, he had a hard time getting along with the Democrats and became unpopular in Nashville. He viewed anyone who advocated secession as a traitor to the country.

In an interesting twist of my history, the major and Senator A.O.P. Nicholson (my great-great-grandfather on my mother's side) organized the Nashville convention of 1850, an attempt to develop a common Southern position on the slavery issue. The convention ended in deadlock. Family history has it that they toured the South debating the issue of secession; of course, he and Nicholson had no disagreement on slavery. Another story describes a debate in Nashville between the major and General Pike. He called the general a traitor for advocating secession; whereupon the general beat him to the ground with his cane to the applause of the crowd.

It must have been a difficult time for the major because he probably wrote the speech in which Jackson challenged Calhoun with the toast, "Our federal Union: It must be preserved!" At that time the major wrote most of Jackson's speeches. He believed secession was wrong but also foolhardy because of the growing size and wealth of the North over the South.

He left the Democratic party and became involved with the American Party, known as the "Know Nothing" party. At the 1856 convention, he was nominated for vice president to run with Millard Fillmore, a Whig, who became president after the death of Zachary Taylor. They were soundly defeated in the election; Buchanan won easily. The major, a slaveholder and a supporter of slavery, but against secession, was, you might say, on the wrong side of both issues. The most important issue to the South: secession; to the North, slavery. He became extremely bitter.

I have a letter he wrote to his son toward the end of the election stating, "I can forgive Andrew Jackson, Jr., for coming out against me because he's a fool but I'll never forgive my brother Daniel." Andrew Jackson, Jr., like his younger brother had been raised at the Hermitage. The major was 10 years older than Andrew Jackson, Jr., but Daniel Smith Donelson was his full-fledged blood brother. Both of them came out against him. After the election he left Nashville immediately, moved to Memphis, and concentrated on operating his plantation in Mississippi, with minimal success. Like most planters, he was always in debt up to his ears. A biography of the major, *Old Hickory's Nephew*, discusses in detail his financial struggles.

My grandfather, who was born in 1856 in Nashville, was named Lewis Randolph for his deceased older brother Lewis Randolph, Elizabeth Martin's son by her first husband. Naming children after their deceased siblings was a strong custom. The major and Elizabeth had six sons and two daughters; both died in infancy. My grandfather was the fifth son. The major had two sons by his first wife, and two daughters. Elizabeth's older sons—William Alexander, Martin, Danny, and Vinay—never accomplished much. Andrew J. Donelson, Jr. (Emily's son), a career Army officer and West Point graduate, died of natural causes before the Civil War. Two of the major's sons, John Samuel and Daniel Smith, died in the Civil War. Martin died young leaving two sons, Glen and Martin. William Alexander lived at Tulip Grove until his last years on the sufferance of the person who foreclosed on the property, selling off the major's valuables. These included a sword Andrew Jackson left him, given to Jackson by the people for his victory in the Battle of New Orleans, a silver service from the king of Prussia, and a copy of the U.S. Constitution with Thomas Jefferson's handwritten notes prepared for the Virginia House of Burgesses. I'm sure many other interesting documents and valuable belongings were also among the legacy. Vinay lived on in Nashville and had one son, Vinay, Jr.

TWO

MY NICHOLSON LEGACY

On my mother's side, her mother was a Nicholson. My grandmother's grandfather, A.O.P. Nicholson, a resident of Columbia, Tennessee, served twice as United States senator. He was in the Senate when Tennessee seceded from the Union. In family reports Nicholson traveled the state speaking for the Democrat ticket in presidential years. According to one account, the average length of his speech was four hours. Apparently, he would go to the county seat, get up on the square, and take on all comers. Just like a rock concert, people would come and go and listen as long as they wanted and then wander away. Nicholson's fellow Tennessee senator during his last term was Andrew Johnson, later the provisional governor of Tennessee during the Union occupation, then vice president, and then president.

Nicholson was also connected with the Heiskell family. During one stage of its history, Baker Donelson was known as "Heiskell Donelson." When the Federal troops took Columbia, Senator Nicholson was taken prisoner to serve as a hostage for the community. He was in a federal prison camp when he met Joe Heiskell, a young Confederate lieutenant and a Tennessee lawyer. They became friends during their captivity.

According to Longstreet Heiskell, "My grandfather Joe told me he got to know Senator Nicholson well and asked him, "What are you going to do when the war's over?" His response: 'Well, I'm a good friend of Andrew Johnson. We served in the Senate together. I'm going to go back to Tennessee and get a pardon. And then, I'm going to be able to run for office and I'm going to run for the Supreme Court. I believe I'll be elected and I think I'll be made chief justice.'" (Johnny Rebs were required to obtain a pardon and sign a loyalty oath to become eligible to run for office.) Joe Heiskell said, "Well, Senator, how about making me attorney general?" And that's what happened. Tennessee is the only state in which the Supreme Court chooses the Attorney General.

Another family story further highlights the problem Rebels faced. I have correspondence one of my grandmother's uncles carried on with his sister. In the last letter the sister wrote, "Papa says the war is over and to tell you to sign the loyalty oath and come home. We need you." Apparently he was a die-hard Confederate and was refusing to sign the oath.

Nicholson served as a member of the Constitutional Convention of 1870 and chairman of the Revenue Committee; he was already chief justice when he served as a delegate to the Nashville convention. He was a very influential delegate because of his judicial position. As chairman of the Revenue Committee he drafted that portion of the new constitution. When asked about the revenue provision, he is reported to have said, "We have authorized all forms of taxation now known." (Of course, the the federal government had an income tax at that time.) When Tennessee passed an income tax in about 1930, it was held unconstitutional in Evans v. McCabe. The constitution specifically authorized the taxation of the income from stocks and bonds that were not taxed ad valorem, that is, by a property tax on their value. The court held that because they authorized an income tax on stocks and bonds not taxed ad valorem, by inference this prohibited any other income tax although the records of the convention indicated that the language was intended to prohibit the double taxation of stock and bonds. Chief Justice Nicholson would have been shocked by their tortured interpretation of his language. Nicholson, who was on the court for about eight years, wrote, I believe, a majority of the opinions for the whole court during his tenure. He died in 1878 after a long and distinguished career.

His son (my great-grandfather) was called "Maury" Nicholson after the county where the family lived. A Confederate officer, after the war, he went to the University of Tennessee as a professor of Natural Science, which was agriculture. He served in that capacity from approximately 1865 until almost 1900. He is credited as the father of the agriculture school. Recognizing the importance of cattle to the area, he brought the first jersey cow to East Tennessee.

THREE

MY GRANDPARENTS

My maternal grandmother grew up in Knoxville with her father, the professor. She met my grandfather, J.W. Campbell, as a student at the University of Tennessee. He graduated from UT in 1881. I have a swagger stick given to him in 1881 for his service in the military. He ultimately settled in Memphis, and for a number of years, worked as an agent with Equitable Life Insurance Company where Colonel Lake was manager of the office. J.W. Campbell established the first industrial-type policy in Memphis, which was sold in the African American community for a weekly premium of 25 to 50 cents. He later branched out into real estate development.

Around 1915, he suffered a serious stroke and I never knew him when he was fully himself. I remember him, however, as pleasant and loving. He and Grandmother Campbell lived with my family from my earliest memory until I was a sophomore in college. Then they agreed to join the Andrew Freedman Home in the Bronx in New York, a forerunner of the modern-day retirement-nursing homes. My grandfather died several years after the move.

When I was in law school, I often went to New York to see Nama, my grandmother who in her eighties was very active. We would go to dinner and to Radio City. Then, I would walk her over to the subway. She would go down by herself, ride out to her station and walk three blocks to her home without a problem. Those were memorable times, usually just the two of us. She was always young at heart.

My Grandmother Campbell was an important influence on my life, almost a second mother. I learned to love chocolate from her. I was about three or four when she took me out to the fair, where she was in charge of handiwork at the women's building. We went to lunch together, and—a true chocoholic, she ordered chocolate pie. I asked for a piece. She never denied me anything, and that began my love of chocolate. Active and outgoing, she had lots of friends. My brother and I didn't realize how lucky we were to have her, constantly supporting and praising us. She lived until I was practicing law.

I heard many family stories from her. A delightful one was about her grandfather, Senator and Justice Nicholson. One afternoon at his home in Columbia she made a daisy chain which she wrapped around her grandfather's stovepipe hat. He customarily rose early in the dark and caught the train to Nashville. That morning he got up early and donned his hat without noticing the daisy chain. He walked to the station, boarded, and rode to Nashville. Then he walked up the hill to the court. He was a distinguished man with a long white beard, and no one had the courage to mention the daisy chain until he arrived at the court and took off his hat. My grandmother didn't remember any punishment, because Chief Justice Nicholson was amused.

When I graduated from law school I won several cash prizes and used the money to buy my first car (1941). Nama and I drove home together from Washington, probably my last extended time with her. When we passed through Knoxville, she said, "You know, Lewie, when your Grandfather Campbell graduated from UT in 1881, he planted the class tree. Let's drive on the Hill and see if we can find it." We did. She found it easily and we both cried at that poignant moment. How wonderful she was.

My Grandfather Donelson claimed he came to Memphis with two bits and no job after graduation from high school. In 1881, he founded a merchandise food brokerage business that my father and then my brother ran for many years. About 1900, he bought an interest in a flour mill known as Yates & Donelson. Yates put up most of the money; my grandfather ran the mill successfully. In approximately 1920, he sold the mill for a substantial price. He also helped found the Grain Exchange. I have a picture of an organizational meeting with him sitting in the front. He served as a director of the First National Bank of Memphis, the forerunner of the present First Tennessee Bank. He died in 1926 when I was eight years old. I didn't get to know him well, but I remember him. We had dinner over at their home frequently.

My grandmother, his widow, lived for many years. She was from Nashville and family legend describes how she came to Memphis to take care of my grandfather when he contracted yellow fever. After he recovered, they married. My grandmother's father, W.J. McAlister, was a lawyer and a judge in Nashville and served as chancellor in Davidson County. His brother was also a lawyer and a judge. One of them—I'm not sure which—served on the Supreme Court of Tennessee. My grandmother was the youngest of nine children. Her mother died at the time of her birth, and she was raised by older sisters. A beautiful young woman, apparently she was called "Lady," although her name was Louisa DeSalles McAlister. One nephew, Hill McAlister, was a prominent politician in Tennessee in the 1920s and 1930s and served as governor of Tennessee in the mid-1930s. For many years thereafter, he was a bankruptcy referee.

FOUR

MY PARENTS

My father dreamed of becoming a doctor and he would have been an excellent one. He also thought about being a professor. At home every night, he was involved with our education and inspired a love of learning. He also taught us to work at our studies and to enjoy learning and to realize the importance of education. He frequently quoted from Alexander Pope's "Essay on Criticism:" "A little learning is a dangerous thing. Drink deep, or taste not the Pierian spring." He graduated from Memphis University School in 1899 and went on to the University of Virginia. In 1902, when his father bought the Yates & Donelson Flour Mill, he insisted my father return to run the brokerage business. My father did so reluctantly, and eventually hired someone to run the business. In 1904, he went back to the University of Virginia to finish his degree. He then came back home and was in the food brokerage business all of his life. He did reasonably well, but never thought he was particularly suited for the business. This produced a coolness between my grandfather and my father, and therefore, I didn't know my grandfather as well as I might have. My father loved French and studied it most of his adult life. When he was 80 he went to Paris for a month. He and my mother stayed in a little pension with a French-speaking friend; he got to speak French every day. I don't know how my mother stood it.

He had a photographic memory—which I don't have—and could quote line after line of poetry: Wordsworth, Keats, Omar Khayyam, *Paradise Lost* and *The Iliad* and *The Odyssey*. He grew up in the days of the Klondike gold rush and he could quote Robert W. Service at great length including, *The Shooting of Dan McGrew, The Cremation of Sam McGee*, and others. He certainly inspired in me a desire to learn and an understanding that learning required work and concentration.

The first story about my father involves Nash Buckingham, a well-known hunter and fisherman, author of many books about hunting and fishing, and founder of the Grand National Field Trials at Grand Junction, Tennessee. He and my father were friends and hunting and fishing buddies. After my father died, I ran into Nash on the street and he said, "Lewie, I have something for you. I'll bring it to you." But he never did. When he died his son-in-law called and said, "We found this envelope among Nash's things which says, 'Deliver to Lewis Donelson.' Can I bring it over?" He did. We both eagerly opened the envelope and it contained a medal. The inscription read: "Memphis University School 1899—Lewis R. Donelson, Jr., First in Class." The son-in-law was puzzled. "How in the world did Nash get this?" I replied, "I can tell you exactly. He won it in a poker game." I knew they had some big poker games at the Chickasaw Club, then a downtown club. It is too bad Nash didn't give it to me himself because I am sure that there was a story about that hand. My father considered himself an excellent poker player and played often in the years before he married.

Another Nash Buckingham story shows what a son of the South Nash was. Daddy described a hunt with Nash. "We always had excellent bird dogs. We rode on horseback and had a black man with us on a mule. When the dogs made a point, he would get off the mule and hold the reins of the horses. When we got ready to shoot, the dogs flushed the covey and we did our shooting. The black man would pick up the birds. We got back on our horses and moved on to the next point."

Daddy had a tragic hunting accident when I was about 12. He took an inexperienced guest hunter on a duck hunt on the St. Francis River, which had flooded. As they paddled through the woods, the guest lost his paddle, hit a tree, and reached to catch it, overturning the boat. Both had on waders. The guest sank immediately, never to surface. Daddy kicked off his waders and waded three or four hours in the winter water to be rescued. He never hunted again.

My mother was born in 1889 and made her debut in Memphis. When my mother and father married in 1910, my father was 28 years old and my mother was 21. I was not born until 1917. It wasn't until the last few months of my mother's life that she told me that she had had three miscarriages before my birth, and they thought that they would never have any children. When I came, I seemed like a gift from God. Fortunately for me, they had another son 21 months later, my brother Bill.

My mother, one of the wisest people I have ever known, understood people and was sensitive to their feelings. She taught me to think about how someone would react to something I said or did. My father was brilliant, scholarly, but my mother had common sense. She treated everyone with loving concern and, as a result, had a multitude of friends. We had a wonderful relationship and she never ordered me to do anything. She proposed, and we discussed. One day, when I was a young boy, she was talking to someone about me and said, "Lewie is so plausible."

Both my parents were great examples and guided me with unconditional love. They treated me as an equal, not as a child. From them I learned what I consider my greatest lesson about raising children: listen to them with respect, and respond seriously to their feelings, their questions, and their dreams.

FIVE

A GOLDEN CHILDHOOD

My earliest memories are of my Grandmother Campbell's house at 1076 Peabody. Because of my grandfather's stroke and the resulting financial restrictions, she had taken in as boarders the sons of friends who moved to Memphis to make their careers. Two of them, Marion Evans and Tom Airey Evans, became lawyers. Marion Evans founded the Evans Petree law firm.

In 1900, my father had been sent by his parents in the Teddy Roosevelt style to spend the summer in Colorado to improve his health. Daddy went by train to Colorado Springs to meet the men with whom he was to spend the summer. They rode five days on horseback to a place called Hidden Lake, where they planned to catch and break wild horses. He recalled that he caught a few wild horses, but didn't break any. They lived on summer venison, trout, cornmeal, and an occasional gathered vegetable. We have these astonishing pictures of these cowboys with handlebar mustaches, goatskin chaps, pistols on their hips—a glimpse of a then fading Wild West. This trip sparked an already strong interest in fly-fishing for my father; he thought the absolute ideal fishing was in the trout streams in the Rocky Mountains.

One summer, my mother and father went to Colorado for a couple of months where Daddy fished the trout streams. I stayed with my grandmother that summer. Tom Evans, whom everybody called

"Airey," was one paying guest. One night, she served ham. My grand-mother operated on the principle that I could do anything I wanted to do. So, I wanted ham and I asked her for some. Airey spoke up to me and said, "You know, little boys like you shouldn't be eatin' ham. It's bad for you. You'll be seeing pink tigers all night." He laid it on probably with even more detail. I dreamed of those pink tigers that night. Some back steps were under construction at the house, and the tigers chased me up and down those steps all night long. It was a vivid, vivid dream.

The house at 1076 Peabody was on the northeast corner of Peabody and Somerville, a gravel road. While we were living there, I peered out the window and saw a man lying there on that gravel road. His car windshield had shattered and there was blood and glass all over everywhere. I also remember an "extra" the newspaper issued, the death of either Wilson or Harding.

The saddest memory of my grandmother's house is about Buster, a shaggy male dog. I was standing out in the front yard when Buster ran out in the street, was run over by a car, and killed. An older boy from up the street came down and picked Buster up out of the street, carried him in, and called my grandmother. He was so kind to me. Goldie Hudson was a hunchback with a terrific personality, so caring and kind. I always thought the world of him because he was so understand-ing to a little boy of three during that first major tragedy in his life.

When they put in Linden Circle, my Daddy proclaimed that, "I'm not going to try to raise any children on a thoroughfare like Linden Circle, so we're going to move." We moved first to an apartment out on Barksdale opposite the police station (off Union Avenue), the first substation of the Memphis police force. We didn't stay there long.

Another strong memory: The boy next door (whose name is lost in time) and I were wandering around in a field behind the duplex (the future site of Hutchison School and now the police station) when he walked into a hornet's nest. I was behind him. He got most of the stings but I got plenty myself. Both of us were put to bed. He almost died and was ill for over a week.

A GREAT NEIGHBORHOOD—GROWING UP

In 1923, we moved to 1677 Autumn between Evergreen and Dickinson in the Evergreen neighborhood, and lived there until I was a sophomore in college. Autumn Avenue is in the shadow of Overton Park, about three blocks away. In those days, people walked and rode bicycles. Before air conditioning, with the windows open at night, we could hear the the roar of the lions in the zoo. The wooded section of the park was virgin forest; we roamed it often and knew it thoroughly. When my children were little I took them walking in those woods, a true introduction to the real outdoors.

The Overton Park Golf Course—which is only a nine-hole course, almost a pitch 'n putt—was free. You could go out there—of course, you waited your turn in line for a long time on some occasions, but you could play for nothin'. When they started charging two bits a round, we thought it was unreasonable. I began golf when I was about seven years old, mostly self-taught. Finally, when I was about 12, my father gave me a couple of lessons on hitting the wood clubs— as we used to call them—the driver, the brassie and the spoon. My best score for the nine-hole course was a 32 when I was in prep school. My first was well over 60, as I remember.

It was a typical neighborhood with lots of children. On our block between Dickinson and Evergreen, there were about 25 children, and in the neighborhood that extended down on to Dickinson, particularly over onto Galloway and to Overton Park Avenue, there must have been close to 50.

We had our own sandlot football and baseball games with no adult supervision. It is amazing what children miss today. We learned when we played games to work things out ourselves. If you got into an argument and everybody walked off, the game would be over and everybody would be the loser. We accepted some realities in dealing with whether it was a ball, or a strike, or whether we were inbounds, out-of-bounds, and all the arguments that can arise. We played softball right in front of our house. There was a vacant lot across the street, and on top of a slight rise, if the ball hit there it was a sure home run. One of my close friends was Ray Phillips, called "Son" because he was the only boy in a family of five. Next door to us were Ann and Cary Eckert.

When I was born my parents had lived next door to the Eckerts on Harbert. Then we moved next to them on Autumn, and Mr. and Mrs. Eckert lived there until they both died. Their daughters were lovely girls, more like sisters to us than romantic interests. Another neighborhood friend was Kalford Ratcliff, who moved there when I was about 11 or 12. He said when he first moved into the house, on the northwest corner of Overton Park and Evergreen, he went out into the backyard and saw this young kid standing on the top of the garage and the fool jumped off. That was me. Kalford and I became friends and later fraternity brothers in college at Southwestern. He was a year ahead of me. When I went to Washington to law school he came up there to finish because his stepfather had died and the family could no longer afford to send him to Vanderbilt. We roomed together and boarded together in Washington for two years until he met a wonderful girl from Mississippi and got married. He came back briefly to Memphis to practice law. After his time in the service, he moved to Laurel, Mississippi, and practiced down there for the rest of his life.

Another special neighborhood friend, Buddy Miller, lived on Autumn, east of Evergreen. Buddy at his death was my oldest friend except for my brother. I met Buddy before I started school while throwing rocks at each other across Evergreen where the streetcar ran. We were friends in high school and fraternity brothers in college. I became attorney for him, his company, and his family, and represented the company until it was sold. Buddy married and had six little girls. He never named me the godfather, because he said he was waiting to have a boy. Mrs. Miller used to tell me that it was my job to look after Buddy and the six little girls. In some ways, I was like a father to Buddy. He was one of the group I played bridge with starting in high school, through college, and after law school.

Through Buddy I met Hubert Turley, a classmate at Snowden. Hubert and I also became close friends during those high school and college years. I was the nondrinker, and every time anyone got into a scrape I was called to help out. One night Hubert and I went to a dance. He had quite a few drinks. The next morning he was supposed to play in the prep-school golf tournament. We went to the Chickasaw Club for his match. He teed off and made a bogie on the first hole. I thought, by jiminy, he's going to do well, but after that the wheels came off. He lost the next 10 holes in succession.

Buddy was a wild automobile driver. Once we tried out his father's new Oldsmobile by heading up Highway 51 North toward Millington, going really fast. Buddy started up a hill and came up on a slow-moving truck. He swung out to pass the truck and faced a car coming over the hill. We went right between those two cars. He touched one of them, and it was like a rifle shot—a pop. If he had been an inch the wrong way we all would have been killed. In later years Buddy's family lived out in Germantown. Everyone in the family, Mr. Miller, Mrs. Miller, his sister, Ann Clark, and Buddy all had a wreck in that turn at White Station down at the bottom of the hill.

My brother also had some trouble with that turn. We lived on Park Avenue just east of Haney. Once, we turned on to Poplar at the top of the hill where the White Spot was. Bill related hitting about 70 when he hit that turn and a wagon came slowly out of the feed store and gas station. He turned onto the gravel area and spun around several times but did not stop. I told him that by the time he hit Goodlett the feed store owner had called our father on the phone.

Bill was an amazing brother, always supportive, never jealous. We became extremely close. Growing up, we fought all the time. Our fighting in public places was legendary. Daddy loved to recount a story about a fight with a group of boys; I was getting the worst of it until Bill pitched in to help me.

One great experience of my early years was a trip with our mother to California, I believe in 1925. I was seven years old and Bill turned six out there. We left in early June headed to California on the train.

It went through Kansas City, and then to Denver and Salt Lake City into Los Angeles. I don't know how my mother stood us, two boys on a train that long, a passenger berth for seven days and nights. We slept in our berths. We ate in the dining car. We did have a brief lay-over in Denver and got a look at the city. We spent the night in Salt Lake City with friends of my father's. This included a tour of the Great Salt Lake and an evening with a Mormon family who told us about the great trek out to Utah. I wrote a letter to my father about the greatest man I have ever heard of: Brigham Young. He had something like 28 wives and 85 children. My father got a huge kick out of that.

We went to California to visit my mother's cousins. My mother's great-aunt had gone out to Southern California with her husband in 1875. They had three sons and three daughters; most lived on ranches in the Glendora area. Hugh Gordon, the patriarch, had practiced law in Los Angeles. One son, Hugh Gordon, was also a lawyer in Los Angeles. One daughter married Marshall Stimson, who was another L.A. lawyer. We stayed primarily on the ranches. In July we had a cottage on the beach in Santa Monica. Under construction down the beach was the home William Randolph Hearst built for his mistress, Marion Davies. Mother and Auntie, my mother's aunt, talked about the scandal. The house was a huge mansion on the beach.

I didn't learn to swim that summer but I came close. It is hard to learn to swim in the ocean. Except for our getting badly sunburned, Bill and I enjoyed being on the beach every day in that ocean. With this much extended family, there were many children of our age. Families gathered weekly, and everybody performed. That was never done in my family, and I was fascinated by these performances. Somebody would sing, somebody would play the piano, somebody would tell stories. It showed you what families did. They had such resources to entertain themselves and to enjoy life, because then radio was just getting started. One family had a big tank, a reservoir for irrigation. We all swam in that tank. I think I made a lot more progress toward learning how to swim in that tank than I did in the ocean.

Out there, we stayed with a family called the McKenzies who lived in a big house. Hector McKenzie, a Canadian/Scotsman, came to California. The McKenzie property included a cemetery. They swapped this property with Basil Gordon, who had a larger agricultural plot with orange trees. Basil Gordon went on to convert that cemetery into a huge business with five or six cemeteries around Glendora and Pomona, and Azusa. I understand the family continues in the cemetery business today. The McKenzies had one daughter, my age, called Posey. She subsequently married a man named Grubbs, a Naval Academy graduate. When he left the Navy he dropped the Grubbs name, which he hated, and became a McKenzie. Years later, one of Posey's son's was at Choate School with my son. That glorious summer apparently was marred by how much my brother and I fought. When he and I went back to California in 1937, everyone recalled our fighting. Pointing to a tree, they would note that Billy and Lewie had a fight beside that big tree. Or, this is where Billy and Lewie had that fight on the interurban train. Or, this is the movie theater where they had a fight in the lobby while their mother and Auntie were in the restroom. Nevertheless, we had a great time. On the Fourth of July, I ate so much watermelon I didn't eat watermelon for years and still don't enjoy it. Charles Gordon had a home in the foothills at the base of the mountains. And you could hear the mountain lions roaring at night outside at his house. This was long before air conditioning and windows were kept open. Of all the members of the family, we kept contact with Gordon Stimson. He came to Memphis and was dutiful about keeping in touch. After he died, I began to be close with Dinie, whose husband was Gordon Webb, one of the Webb School families. He worked for the University of Wisconsin-Madison. She came to Memphis and explored Nicholson family history and stayed with us. We went three times, in the summer, to visit them in Madison.

In our college days, the California families wanted my brother and me to move out there. Two lawyers in the California branch meant opportunities, but I decided not to do that. My brother thought much more seriously about a move and talked about becoming a CPA. That whole family was crazy about Bill. I wish he had gone because I think he would have had a more successful career. Because of his strong sense of loyalty to our father and out of father's desire for Bill to go into the business, he stayed in Memphis. We did not come home from that glorious summer until after Labor Day. At that point, we attended Pentecost which didn't start until the middle of September.

SIX

THE BEST SCHOOL EVER—
PENTECOST

I could not enter grammar school until I was six. Because of my October birthday, I had to wait until the mid-term semester in February 1924. Snowden Elementary was a neighborhood school. All my friends went there. At the end of first semester, the school put me up into the second grade and, at the end of the next semester, the teachers wanted to put me up into the third grade. My father was opposed to this plan.

He went to see the principal, Professor Newt, who lived on the other side of Evergreen on Autumn. Daddy recalled the conversation with the professor: "I am concerned about my son. You moved him up. He's going to be small and he's going to get so far ahead of himself, it will create social difficulties for him." Professor Newt replied, "But he has a wonderful mind. If you don't put him up, he won't be challenged. He'll get bored and get out of the habit of studying." My father answered, "I don't think I'm going to let him do that. What would you do if he were your son?" The principal of Snowden School said, "If he was my son, I'd send him to Pentecost." Daddy had never heard of Pentecost, but he investigated and, sure enough, he thought it was a great idea.

He sent me to Pentecost, a tremendous influence on my young life. Pentecost was as fine a school as you could find anywhere. Miss

Althea Pentecost, a remarkable educator ahead of her time, taught math and ran the school. Ms. Bea Garrison joined her, and the school became Pentecost Garrison. Ms. Bea was the geography and spelling teacher and a good one, but Ms. Pentecost was the moving force at the school.

I then went to Central High School, then to Choate School and Southwestern (now Rhodes College), Georgetown Law School, all excellent. Pentecost ranked right alongside them in the quality of education provided, which was simply superb. In the middle of the 1920s Ms. Pentecost taught us what they now call "new math," working on the relationship of numbers, the duodecimal system, learning to think in terms of how numbers relate to each other and how you could multiply long figures by thinking in terms of 12x10 and then, you just add a zero (0), and when you do 12x12, you add two more 12s. That sort of thing was so helpful in my later life.

Pentecost also gave us speed-reading classes. Your eye is trained to go right down the middle of the page, taking in all that the eye can comprehend. Ms. Pentecost used to say that if you are not reading at your maximum speed, your mind is wandering, and you are not taking it in as clearly as you should; you are certainly not reading as fast as you could, and the mind still works at its normal pace, therefore, you are thinking about something else.

In later life, I had it explained more explicitly. Everyone thinks at the rate of at least 500 words per minute and, most of us, even faster. If you are reading less than that, your mind is thinking about something else which destroys the concentration. In any event, it taught me a valuable lesson and made schooling so much easier because I could read so rapidly. Pentecost made us concentrate on English grammar and spelling. I got a sound foundation. Diagramming sentences started in about the fourth grade. We started Latin in the seventh grade, and I had had two years of Latin before I ever went to Central High School.

The rule at Pentecost was that if you did not have your lesson, you stayed after school until you got it. If you did not get it that afternoon, you came back on Saturday or the following afternoon to catch up. No one ever got behind and everyone did their lessons, or attempted to, every day. My friend and law partner, Leo Bearman, also went to Pentecost, then to Central, then to Yale, then to Harvard. He says, "Pentecost was clearly the best school I ever attended." There were some drawbacks. Ms. Pentecost had little interest in sports, and there were few opportunities for such activities.

One secret of its great effectiveness: small classes, never more than 12 in our class, most years, 10. This meant personal attention. You knew you would be called on every day. The emphasis was on academic excellence. The rest was left to the parents. I remember most of our outstanding teachers still. Ms. Bea taught the lower grades, spelling and geography; Mrs. Nash, English; Ms. Pentecost, mathematics; Miss Walton, Latin; and a succession of French teachers. One standard requirement in geography was to learn all the states and their capitals. We wrote themes in the sixth, seventh, and eighth grades. To be able to go into the 11th grade (fifth form) at Choate, having skipped the ninth grade and coasted through the 10th at Central, finishing second in my class at Choate, is a true testament to my preparation at Pentecost.

After I became a lawyer, I tried to persuade Ms. Pentecost to establish a tax-free corporation to operate the school, but she never agreed. Miss Hutchison sold her school to Dr. Atkinson, and after his death, it became a tax-free corporation and flourishes today. At the time, I was mystified, but from my perspective now I believe she didn't believe that any successor would maintain her standards. When she died, the school closed and Presbyterian Day School was formed, taking over most of the faculty.

When she died I had the occasion to go into her bedroom. There were three pictures of students, and I was one. It makes me proud to think that I stood that high in her estimation.

When I was at Pentecost, this incident exemplifies the relationship that I had with my parents. I hated to carry cold lunches to school. In particular, tomatoes in sandwiches made the bread soggy. I complained I wanted a hot lunch. My mother went to see Ms. Pentecost and said, "Why don't you have a lunchroom over here?" Ms. Pentecost said, "I am not only running this school, but I am teaching mathematics and my hands are full. I just can't take on anything else." But she said, "I will tell you what I will do. I will fix up the garage and equip it with a stove, a sink and all the necessities of running a lunchroom if you will run it." The entire time that my brother and I were at Pentecost, my mother ran the lunchroom. My mother knew all the boys and all the boys knew our wonderful mother. It gave her a special closeness with Bill and me, to the school and to others in the school, because of this additional connection. My mother used the money she made from the lunchroom to send us to camp.

SEVEN

MANY HAPPY SUMMERS—
CAMP CHICKASAW

Mother told me that her mother was controlling, watched everything she did, and tried to influence her life. Because Mother resented her, she was determined that we would be our own people, not completely dependent upon our parents to tell us what to do or think. In 1926, she sent me, at age eight, to camp for two months. Bill was also going at age seven, but he got whooping cough. I was a few days late because I was quarantined.

Camp Chickasaw in North Carolina was owned by George Morris, then publisher of *The Commercial Appeal.* His wife stayed at the camp full time every summer. The camp, with 15 cabins, ran for two months. Each cabin held eight boys, for a total of about 120 boys. The youngest, my age, were called "mites." There were also the "midgets," "juniors," and the "seniors."

This camp was early in the history of camping in the South and wasn't what I would call super organized. We had tennis courts, a gym, a baseball diamond, canoes, and a lake for swimming. I was in the cabin of George Morris, Jr., our counselor, son of the camp's owner. On my side of the cabin were George Livermore, my closest friend who remained so throughout grammar school, and Bradley Bond, who was also a very close friend. George lived on the northeast corner of Carr and Melrose, and Bradley, on the northwest corner of McLean and Central. Don Scruggs, the other member of the cabin, was slightly younger than the rest of us.

Camp Chickasaw didn't have planned activities for the morning or afternoon. They allowed us to do whatever you wanted to do, except for swimming. We got up every morning and skinny-dipped before breakfast. We spent an hour swimming before both lunch and supper. Otherwise, you could play tennis, basketball, baseball, or canoe; you could also work at shop and crafts. It made camp so much more enjoyable and more of a growing experience, because you decided what you would do. You learned to begin to make decisions for yourself and were not supervised or watched over like a hawk. There was more gentle supervision and encouragement to go out and do things, based on what you liked to do.

Bill and I were together in camp for five summers. The Depression prevented our going in 1931, but we went to scout camp, in Hardy, Arkansas, for two weeks. I went back to Chickasaw in 1932. I believe the camp was open only about 10 years. The last summer the camp was open was 1932. Mr. Morris sold it and it became a girl's camp known as Deerwood.

The camp was in a lovely location on the side of a small mountain above a floodplain in front of the French Broad River, up against a mountain on the other side, with the big bend of the French Broad River circling the camp. The cabin sat upon the foothills of the mountain and the tennis and basketball courts, baseball diamonds, track and football field were down in the open area. It was always amazing to me that the water of the French Broad flowed not into the Atlantic but the Mississippi River.

To swim in the lake, you had to be able to swim 100 yards, which for eight-year-old-boys was a good challenge. I passed my swimming test. I also passed my lifesaving test there. The food was good; however, we were young and healthy boys who probably would have liked anything served us. Most of the campers were from Memphis, some from the North Mississippi Delta, a few from Nashville, and other places.

Most cabins had two counselors, one a junior type counselor. I got to know some wonderful people during the camp summers. Herbert Jordan, of the Jordan Lumber Company family, was one, a delightful guy. One of the counselors was George Grider, a superb swimmer who taught us lifesaving. George was one of those people who couldn't float because of his body weight. He just sank to the bottom. When he got hold of you, you too sank to the bottom and had to fight to get out.

I began to play tennis. Some counselors were excellent tennis instructors. As a matter of fact, George Morris was a tennis player and helped us enormously with our game. Two brothers from Asheville, the Rogers brothers, George and Ken, were also fine players. Over the years I improved my game and was a good player by my last year at Camp Chickasaw.

One summer the French Broad River flooded and we canoed around the trees and the cornfield in the low area. Despite the flood, we had the usual canoe trip down the river. The current was so strong we made it to Asheville in one day, instead of staying over at the Long Shoals, as we normally did. That was one of the highlights of the trip at the end of the camp, the last week. Usually we took this trip to Asheville from Brevard, and at Long Shoals we camped for the night at the foot of Biltmore Castle, as we called it in those days. The house was semi-occupied most of the fall and spring, sometimes in the winter. During the summer, the house up there, unlit except for moonlight, was an inspiration for ghost stories, and we heard some scary ones. One night, when we camped at Long Shoals, it rained "cats and dogs." We tried to put together some kind of protection with our ponchos and turned over the canoe to make a shelter to shield us from the rain, but not very successfully.

My most miserable night was directly opposite the camp. A good-sized mountain on the south side of the French Broad had an open meadow at the top called "See-off." You would climb up there and look down and see the camp and other sites. All of us in our cabin planned to go up and spend the night. George Morris was to come up at suppertime and bring supper and spend the night. It began to rain before we got up there, and it rained hard. We struggled to keep ourselves dry, digging ditches you are supposed to build around your ponchos and all that sort of stuff. But this was a hard mountain rain and we were all soaked. We waited and waited, and George Morris didn't arrive. He thought we would be smart enough to come home. We weren't. We spent this miserable night by the fire, huddled under the ponchos trying to keep dry and warm. The next morning we picked some blackberries. A farmer gave each one of us a cup of milk, the best tasting stuff I ever drank. The rain ended, and at dawn we left. We were at camp well before time for breakfast, waiting impatiently to get into the mess hall. It was a miserable night and a reminder of the difficulty of sleeping in the open.

I was always an adequate athlete and became a competitive tennis player in my teens, but was never outstanding at any sport. We gathered in the gym every night after supper, a movie was fairly rare. Sometimes we knew to expect a grudge match. If two boys got to fighting they were separated and invited to put on the gloves and go into a ring and fight it out. I never had a grudge fight of that sort but when a larger boy picked on my brother, I intervened. Instead of my brother and this boy fighting, I agreed to fight for my brother. So, I did participate in that one grudge fight because I was mad. I held my own in that encounter.

By the end of six years, we thought we owned the camp. We knew more than most counselors about the camp. In that final year, they made a special rule that the four of us, George, Bradley, Don Scruggs, and myself, could take a canoe down on the annual canoe trip without a counselor. George Morris, Jr., our counselor, provided special adventures, because he had a car. In the 1920s and early 1930s not everyone had cars, especially the counselors at Camp Chickasaw. Once he took us to see Bobby Jones play an exhibition at the Highlands Country Club. Jones was then at the height of his career. We also made trips to Mt. Pisgah and other enjoyable places.

We went on hikes, mostly to a falls. Our favorite was Looking Glass

Falls, back in the woods off the road, a picture-book falls, with a heavy, even flow and a big pond at the bottom. We went there to swim. One time a big limb had fallen off a tree into the middle of the pond. We spent hours trying to chop up that limb and get it out of there. Our efforts didn't do much good. The next time we went back, it was gone.

Years later when my son was attending Duke, we rode by on the Blue Ridge Parkway and I saw a sign that said "Looking Glass Falls." The next time we came by we went down to see it. Sadly, the road came within 20 feet of the falls, and you can imagine there was trash everywhere. Nevertheless, we got out and my children went sliding on the rocks above the falls and then swimming in the falls.

Camp Chickasaw also broadened my acquaintances. Only a very few friends from camp are still alive. Dan Canale became a lifelong friend, as did D.O. Andrews. George Livermore, my closest friend, cemented our relationship in summer camp. George and I played tennis together almost every day. We got to be such good friends, we didn't want each other to lose. One would serve five times, then the other, and we never kept score. In my memory George finished first in the class and I was second. George's memory was the reverse. In any event, it was a rare, wonderful friendship because we were devoted to each other and wanted the other to do well. George, extremely smart, went on to St. Paul's, then to Princeton, to Harvard Medical School and then the Mayo Clinic. From the time he left Pentecost in the eighth grade, he was gone from Memphis close to 20 years. Our friendship waned during that time. Although when he returned to Memphis we saw each other frequently, but the intimacy of the relationship never resumed.

In 1933, his mother lent him her car and we drove to Chicago to see the World's Fair. We stayed with some relatives of George's in Evanston. Two innocents abroad, we had not seen much of the world. We were approached at the fair by these young girls who looked to be younger than we were, and they would say, "I will sell you my body for two bits." This was the bottom of the Depression. At first George and I didn't realize what they were offering, but when we finally did we were horrified. We were two spoiled boys growing up in loving families and in private schools. On the way to Chicago we had a blow-out and had fix the tire. And I mean to tell you, we were two boys who had never learned how to change a tire. We got it off, and the spare on, but it took us a long time. We had so much fun together.

Bradley Bond's mother insisted on his being a musician. He played the saxophone and got a scholarship to LSU to play in the band. He told me you don't know what it is to be in good condition until you have to march 100 yards down the football field blowing the saxophone. Bradley joined one of the big bands and traveled the country. He told me that it was one of the worst types of life imaginable, different hotels, up all night, sleeping most of the day, drinking and womanizing. He finally gave that life up and went back to Lafayette, Louisiana, to work for a relative in the automotive parts business. Bradley didn't like that. He got involved in and became head of the musicians union for Louisiana. He told me that he was going to succeed Jimmy Petrillo, national head of the musicians union. Unfortunately, Bradley died before Petrillo.

Willard Dixon was another lifelong close friend. Also a lawyer, we played a lot of golf together in our later years. I teased Willard, because he was bright, but lazy. When he had a legal problem, he called and asked me the answer. I told him he practiced law "by ear." When Willard went on the bench, he was gracious to me and I picked up most of his remaining clients. John Overton and Billy McKee also remained friends. Billy died fairly young. John had the unfortunate experience of being struck twice by lightning on the golf course. The second time he contacted Parkinson's and never recovered. He suffered the terrible handicaps of Parkinson's for many years.

John's family, one of the wealthiest and most prominent in Memphis, owned most of the property downtown. John came to school in a red Packard with a chauffeur. His weekly allowance was $5, which is comparable to $50 today. When I ran into him after my first year in college, in front of the old Cossitt Library, I asked, "John, when are you going back to school?" He said, "I am not going." I said, "What do you mean?" He said, "We can't afford for me to go. I have gotten a job in the library making $50 a month." The Overtons' property was heavily mortgaged, and they lost everything during the Depression. John's father, William Overton, a nice man, couldn't grasp what had happened, because he had always been wealthy. Money rolled in via rents. All he did was collect the money. He was unable to cope with the problems. When I was going to Rhodes, we had moved out on Park Avenue, and my father would drive us into school. Occasionally, we would see Mr. Overton (Daddy would call him Billy) standing on the corner and would offer him a ride to town. Their oldest son, William Overton, Jr., also called Billy, was driving out Union one night, exceeding the speed limit, possibly intoxicated, when he ran into a car and killed a young preacher, his wife, and two children. It was a tremendous scandal and a terrible embarrassment to the family. Billy Overton moved away and I never saw him again. John went on and made a success of his career becoming a top executive of the American Snuff Company.

Those camp summers instilled in me a love of the Smoky Mountains. I have often said that if I retired I would go to the mountains, not the seaside. The mountain air was so clear and pure, the weather never hot, almost always perfect. In the summertime, we didn't have much rain but lots of showers, mountain showers, that didn't last more than 30 minutes or an hour.

In those days, children were allowed to grow up and were not supervised in every activity, the way camps and even home lives are now. You belong to some team for this or that; activities are regimented and organized, supervised by adults and governed by coaches. In my mind, this approach impedes growing up if children don't make their own decisions or interact with other children without adults present. I look back on those days at Camp Chickasaw fondly. Bradley said one day as we were walking along, "You know these are probably the happiest days of our lives. And the great thing about it is we know it." That camp and the friends I made there greatly enriched my childhood.

EIGHT

CHOATE—A NEW WORLD

I went from the eighth grade at Pentecost into the tenth grade at Central. At Central that first year I took Caesar. When called on the third or fourth day, I did what I would have done at Pentecost—I read the rest of the lessons. Somebody in the back of the room said in this sotto voce, "If he's reading from a pony, he ought to read slower." Everyone laughed, including the teacher. I forgot about homework, because I did not want to be embarrassed by an outstanding performance. My Daddy complained about my not studying. He said, "Don't worry. When your report card comes out, you'll be grounded." But, when the report card came out, it was straight A's. Then he said, "Wait until next year because you won't be there."

My parents planned on sending me to McCallie School, but Ms. Pentecost, who had had such a major influence on me and who cared deeply for her students, admired the Choate school, where she got me a half-scholarship. In 1932 my parents must have struggled because a half-scholarship still required $900 tuition, plus all my expenses, including my train travel back and forth. Unfortunately, in the fall of 1932, a gall bladder operation delayed my entry until after Christmas. I was at Choate only for a year and a half. I returned to Central in the fall of 1932 and to Choate in January 1933. I graduated in June of 1934. I was in Pentecost, Chickasaw, and Choate during most of the Depression, insulated to a certain extent from its impact. At Choate, where current events were discussed in depth, I was aware of the Depression's tremendous disruption of the normal life of our country.

In June 1932 my father and I went to New York to see a doctor who was supposed to help me to grow. Going into the tenth grade, I was not much over 4' 10" and weighed 85 pounds. Whether the doctor helped or not, I did begin to grow and took shots for several years. Such a wonderful visit in New York, where I met my cousins Farris and Mary Clayton Russell. Farris, a stockbroker on Wall Street, was my mother's cousin. Mary, the sister of John D. Martin, who would play such an important part in my legal career, was a cousin of my father. Our cousins took us to their home on Long Island. We played golf at one of the fancy courses. I did not play as well as I wanted to and got mad. Daddy, in an effort to calm me down, in front of Mr. Russell said to me, "Who are you to think you can hit two good shots in a row?" I remember that to this day and when I get two good shots in a row, I say to myself, "See Daddy, I can do it sometimes." We saw a lot of sights in New York.

When I headed for New York and on to Wallingford, Connecticut, I went up on the train. I spent the night at the Barbizon Plaza Hotel where Daddy and I had stayed in June. I took a cab from the Pennsylvania Station. When I got to the hotel the cab driver attempted to charge an outrageous fare. I had enough savvy and maturity to ask the doorman what the fare should be. The doorman negotiated for me, and I paid a much smaller taxi fare. That night I went to dinner with my cousins, who introduced me to Bill Dearborn, a Choate student. His mother was from Nashville, and his father was a doctor in New York. I went to my first hockey game. The only person I knew at Choate other than the newly-met Bill Dearborn, was Walter Armstrong, who was a year ahead of me at Pentecost. Walter, unfortunately, an introvert at that time, wasn't much help, but I did make my way. I had an early scare when I lost a check for the tuition. After unpacking I couldn't find the check but a search of the wastebasket located the envelope, much to my great relief.

Everybody called me "Memphis" because of my broad Southern accent. My roommate, Jim Filor, was a third former, and I was a fifth former. He and his family were so friendly and kind. They invited me down to New York for a weekend. At spring break I spent several days with Jim in New York and went up to their home on the Hudson River. Their lovely apartment was on Fifth Avenue. I remember my first experience with a Franklin car (water cooled). The chauffeur, in a separated front seat, talked with his passengers via a little speaker. A real taste of how the other half lives.

The home up on the Hudson at Haverstraw was magnificent: three floors with a top story devoted to quarters for the servants. This was 1933. The grounds with a swimming pool, tennis court, a little pitch and putt four- or five-hole golf course overlooked the Hudson River down over the little town of Haverstraw, which nestled along the river; an amazing introduction to the truly rich. I asked Jim about his family's wealth. He told me, "My father was with a brokerage firm in New York, and in March of 1929 he had a serious heart attack. When he recovered the doctor said, 'I don't want you to be playing the market at all. It's too much stress on you.' He said, 'I want you to sell everything you have and convert it into cash.' So in October of 1929 when the stock market crashed, all we had was cash. We suddenly became quite wealthy."

My experience at Choate was exhilarating. I did well academically, and my Pentecost preparation was more than adequate. I finished second in my class to Bill Dearborn, with Walter, third. Three boys with Tennessee roots were one, two, and three in that class at Choate. Bill, who became a lawyer as Walter and I did, practiced for many years in Nashville.

The first winter I took hockey to learn how to ice-skate. It was a misnomer to call it hockey because in my group we only learned to ice-skate. In the spring I played tennis and did fairly well. I never could get on the ladder high enough to be on the team, but I played a lot of tennis. I lived in the Long House that first half year.

The second year I met Jim Shattuck from Neenah, Wisconsin. His father was treasurer of Kimberly-Clark, the Kleenex people, and we roomed together in the Atwater house. The system at Choate was that the sixth-formers, seniors, had responsibilities. One was to keep a semblance of order in the corridors. Another was to be sure everybody was in study hall. Jim and I had the large room nearest the front door, and that way we could check people going in and out. A master, as we called them, lived in the house with his family as well.

In my second year Jack Kennedy lived on the second floor in a room by himself. When I was first at Choate, a rumor went around that before the federal gift tax law went into effect in 1932 Joe Kennedy had given each one of his nine children $1 million. Joe Jr. was an outstanding leader, president of the sixth form, and captain of the football team. I didn't get to know Jack well. He was quiet and often sick. I was not aware of that or I had forgotten it. But I did know that he wasn't doing well in school because he had to be in many study halls. When you were in the top two groups by grades you didn't go to any study halls, and in the third group you could skip night study hall and afternoon study hall. As the grades went down, the required study halls you could skip declined.

Choate, a superb school, had excellent teachers, masters as they were called. All of the masters lived on the campus, usually in a house, a dormitory, with the boys. Even more traditional dormitories had a master, sometimes with a wife, who lived on the corridor. This attention provided a special atmosphere.

Every semester Dr. George St. John, the headmaster, wrote a personal letter to the parents of each of the 500 or so students commenting upon their progress. A tremendous undertaking, but it showed how well in touch with each student Choate was. Students sat at a table with a master at every meal. The boys waited on the table. A rotation meant an opportunity to get know other masters and other boys. One day each term the headmaster would announce "holiday today." It would usually be a beautiful fall, winter, or spring day. The enormous campus was 400 acres with woodland trails and a dairy farm, providing the opportunity to roam around everywhere. The magnificent physical plant included an unbelievable Winter Exercise Building with indoor tennis and squash courts, basketball court, bowling alley and a baseball cage the size of a full infield. Outside facilities provided track, hockey, football and baseball fields along with a chapel, academic buildings, and dining hall—a dream campus.

Our math instructors were especially superior. I took the short course in calculus. We also had excellent English masters, several heavily into Thomas Hardy. We read most of Hardy's tragic novels. We also studied Shakespeare, and my first A+ assignment was an article about what it was like to attend a performance at the Globe Theater. I pretended to be a reporter attending opening night, describing who was present and commenting upon the play.

Because I was late coming in and because of my gall bladder operation, I was prevented from participating in football, the most popular sport. I might have gotten a wider acquaintance if I had. I did make a number of reasonably close friends. In addition to Jim Filor and Jim Shattuck, I developed a friendship with Francis Silk, who had also come in the fifth form, and I formed a special bond with Neil Levinson, with whom I had several classes. Neil had been there for the full six years.

Choate opened up a new world to me. The Current Events Club brought in a knowledgeable and prominent speaker every month to talk about the world situation. Hitler was the red-hot topic. I wrote my Daddy and said, "Daddy, up here everybody is talking about this guy named Hitler in Germany." I was a student of current events and national affairs before I went to Choate, but this experience showed how much more in touch with world events people in the Northeast were than those in the South. I began to take the *New York Herald Tribune* and read it. My knowledge of current events expanded tremendously in that year and a half. The Filor family continued to welcome me, and I made other visits to their home up on the Hudson.

We went back and forth to Memphis on the train. My second year at Choate there were four of us, Walter Armstrong mentioned earlier, Harry Anderson, John D. Canale, and me. Walter's lawyer father became president of the American Bar. Anderson was the son of the federal judge and of the Anderson Lumber Company family, now Anderson-Tully. John D. Canale's family owned D. Canale and later the Budweiser franchise for Memphis. Our trips back and forth on the train were fascinating, and we got to be good friends. Coming home we would leave Choate about two p.m. right after lunch, get to New York about five. We always went somewhere, sometimes to Radio City. We went to nightclubs where we were let in to hear a particular band and required to leave by nine, and not drink. I heard Jimmy and Tommy Dorsey and Guy Lombardo and Glen Gray, one of my favorites.

Walter, a bookworm, would leave us and go directly to the bookstores. There were no credit cards. Every time, he would return out of money, and we lent him the money to eat during the trip home. We left New York about midnight and were on the train all day the next day and the following morning, and didn't get to Memphis until about 9:30 or 10. John D. Canale would get mad that Walter spent his money and then borrowed to eat. After that happened on several trips John D. said, "I want you all to promise me not to lend Walter any money." So we told Walter, "Save yourself enough money to get home on because we won't lend you any." Walter arrived at the train as usual without a nickel, and we didn't give him any money all that next day. By about 7:30 p.m. he was starving. Harry and I took pity on him and to John D.'s disgust, lent him 50 cents to buy himself a sandwich.

We traveled on the New York Central Railroad to Pittsburgh, switched off to the B&O down to Cincinnati and the L&N to Memphis. Cincinnati sported a handsome new terminal, the most modern and newest railroad station in the country, a beautiful place at the time.

What a broadening experience to meet people from all over the country, some whose families were rich, with a different perspective from mine, and to live in a culture much more oriented toward the world, particularly toward Europe, than we were in Memphis. Choate insulated me from the Depression because the subject never came up. Except for my visits with classmates' families, there was never an inkling of parents' wealth or position. Most who knew me visualized my family on a plantation in a big white house with columns and lots of servants. The whole atmosphere was permeated with Eastern aristocratic elitism, people who knew each other and went to Harvard, Yale, Princeton, and some to Columbia. They assumed as a natural course they would be the people running the United States. It wasn't conceit, but a state of mind.

The entire experience opened up new vistas. I realized that I could compete, academically. When I graduated I planned to go to the University of Virginia, where I had been accepted, following in my father's footsteps. As I mentioned, every decision that was made, including my going to camp at eight, was discussed. They told me the reason for a decision and convinced me that it was the right thing. I don't know that I ever really bucked their decisions, but I felt I could. They talked to me about Choate at great length. I was never truly conscious of their sacrifices, but I was aware of how much the opportunity meant to me.

Anyway, my father sat me down and talked to me and said my uncle had become ill, no longer able to work, and he was going to have to support him, because in 1934 there was no real safety net. He asked if I wouldn't mind going to Southwestern for a year at least, and I agreed, happy to help.

NINE

SOUTHWESTERN (RHODES COLLEGE)

W hen I graduated from Choate I was the youngest and smallest person in the class. I was also the youngest person in
the class at Southwestern at Memphis, also probably the smallest person. I joined a fraternity, Sigma Alpha Epsilon. Most students joined
a fraternity or sorority. My father had been a member of SAE, and
SAE was the largest and perhaps the leading fraternity on campus, so
I joined. It was a good decision, although the first two years I was a
little socially handicapped because I was so much younger than most
of the students. I made new friends in the fraternity and renewed
others; among these were Woody Butler, Waddy West, Shep Tate, and
Kalford Ratcliff, a neighborhood friend before college. Hubert Turley
had been a close friend in my high school days. I had known Tom
White through Camp Chickasaw. My new friends became lifelong
friends: Bob Montgomery from Clarksdale, Frank Campbell from For-
rest City, H.R. Holcomb from Tupelo, Raford Herbert from Lexington,
MS, David Gibson, Jim Merrin, Jameson Jones and his brother, Tom
Jones from Corinth, Ward Archer from Kansas City, Dan Carruthers,
Billy Craddock, Bobby Elder, all from Memphis.

Southwestern in 1934 was unique. As Dr. Sam Monk, who later
became close a friend, explained, because of the Depression, families

that would have normally sent their children to Ivy League schools couldn't afford the expense and sent them to Southwestern. Accordingly, we had, particularly among men, a talented and focused student body. In the fraternity, eight men or more were on the honor roll, no easy academic feat, because Southwestern was a tough school.

The size of the student body was about 450 with tuition at $500 a year. Dr. Diehl, the president, had this unbelievable ability to hire and hold tremendously able people. I was most familiar with Dr. Monk, who taught English. Dr. Theodore Johnson, also an English teacher, was dean. Dr. Cooper and Dr. Davis taught history. Dr. Mac-Queen, Dr. Hartley, and Dr. Pond taught mathematics. Dr. MacQueen was a superb mathematics teacher. I was in his class in what we used to call the "long course" in calculus. We had Dr. Shewmaker, Dr. Hayden, and Dr. Kelso in the Bible department. You took freshman Bible from Dr. Shewmaker and took senior Bible, as we called it, from Dr. Kelso, and then philosophy or ethics from Dr. Kelso, emerging with a strong background in Bible and theology. Dr. Shewmaker had a delightful sense of humor. On one pop quiz on the Old Testament a question was, "Where did the witch of Endor live?" Only two of us got it right.

When Dr. Monk arrived in Memphis, he knew no one other than Mr. and Mrs. James Collier, good friends of my parents who then met Dr. Monk. During sophomore English, a review of English literature (they let me skip freshman English), Dr. Monk said, "This is an example of Aristotelian theory of tragedy. Does anyone know what that is?" I put up my hand and said, "Simply explained, the true tragedy is of a good man brought to his downfall by a good trait he had to excess." Dr. Monk asked me to approach his desk after class, and he said, "I've been teaching this class for about 10 years now, and no one's ever answered that question before. How did you learn that?" I told him about Choate. We became friends. Student assistants could get paid for grading papers for the professors. I graded papers for Dr. Monk, and that brought us closer. One day Dr. Johnson, the dean, called me in and said, "Lewie, they tell me you can read Dr. Monk's handwriting." And I said, "I do pretty well with it." He continued,

"He's put an exam on the board, and the whole English department has gone in there, and nobody can read his writing. Would you come over here and read it to the students?" I did.

I told Dr. Monk later, "I'm not sure that I gave them the exam that you gave them, but I gave them an exam." He got a great laugh out of it. A sidelight: My brother also had terrible handwriting. One day he got a paper back with a "B" on it. He complained to Dr. Monk, and Dr. Monk said, "I wrote you a note on your last paper, saying that if your handwriting wasn't any better that I was going to take off a grade." My brother said, "Oh, is that what that note said?" Dr. Monk laughed and said, "Give me the paper." He marked it back up to an "A."

Dr. Monk and I developed a wonderful friendship. He married a wonderful woman shortly before the war. Tragically, they were swimming down in the Gulf one day, and she got caught in the undertow and drowned, and he never got over it. Shortly thereafter, he went into the Army Air Corps and served as an intelligence officer.

When he came back to Memphis I talked to him about it, and he said, "Lewie, I just don't believe I can live here with the memories of Wanda," his wife. "So," he said, "I'm going to take a professorship somewhere else." He taught for many years in Minnesota and became head of the English department up there. We remained good friends, although we didn't keep in close contact. When I was Minneapolis on business, lunching in a fancy downtown club, our host asked, "Do you know anyone in Minneapolis?" I replied "Only one person," and added, "he is coming in the door right now." We had a delightful visit, one of the last times I saw him.

Dr. Amacker was another favorite professor. When I first started in political science, Dr. Siefkin taught my first course, but he moved on to become professor and later president of another small college. Dr. Amacker, a good political science professor, not as entertaining as Siefkin, not as full of stories but soundly based, had been at the Paris Peace Conference, assisting in the preparation of the Treaty of Versailles. He loved to talk about it.

Dr. Diehl introduced a system of reading courses modeled on those at Oxford. A professor would assign you about eight to 10 hours of reading on your subject each week. You would meet with the professor for discussion for about two hours. You learned an awful lot and got to know the professor very well. I took a reading course on the English novel from Sam Monk, an exhilarating experience. He gave me Fielding's *Tom Jones*. I met Sam on Friday. He said, "How far did you get?" I said, "I finished it." My version was 1,500 pages. He asked, "How long did it take you?" I replied, "I started about 8:30 last night and finished about four this morning. He couldn't believe it and began asking me detailed questions like, "Who did Tom meet in such and such town." I answered every question. Of course I had just finished the book. I don't know if I would have done as well a couple of weeks later.

The reading course system allowed you to read for Honors or for Distinction. The Honors course required you to take nothing but your chosen subject in your last years, and I didn't want to do that. I wanted a wider variety of courses. So I read for Distinction, which required a double reading course in your subject and a long thesis-like paper. I believe I called my paper, which was on politics at the current time, "Liberty and Authority." Amacker had me write about fascist Germany, fascist Italy, communist Russia, and democratic United States, England, and France. In the 1930s communism was well regarded by many, and there were many ardent socialists. At that time many thought FDR's New Deal program was socialistic, and I guess it was. My topic involved most of the major political philosophers, among others, John Locke, John Stuart Mill, Hobbes, and Berkeley. I analyzed the difference between a democratic government and a fascist or communist one, which seemed always to involve a strong, authoritarian leader. We were unaware of the tremendous atrocities and killings under the communists and Stalin, but glimpses of what was happening in Germany emerged by 1937 and 1938. Dr. Amacker wanted me to concentrate on how a democracy could achieve the goals such as Franklin Roosevelt's efforts to provide a better safety net without an authoritarian form of government. I did well and graduated with Distinction.

During my senior year I took a course in creative writing. I began writing at Pentecost. From the fifth grade on we wrote themes frequently. This continued at Choate. I had written a world of themes, even more at Southwestern, but I had never done any creative writing, and I found myself cramped without much imagination. My mother told me that when she wanted to read me a story as a very young boy, I would say, "Is it true?" And she would say, "No, it's just a story." As a child I would reply, "Then I don't want to hear it." I couldn't dream up ideas. I was great at spewing out what I knew, with some reasoning behind it, but the idea of creating something new and original was extremely difficult. I managed a "C" in the course, but it was particularly instructive to see those people who had that talent for creative writing. The class did open me up somewhat, and I began to write more freely. My only "A" paper was a memory from my childhood, a story that I told earlier, about eating ham and dreaming of pink tigers. In that class, I did learn why creative writers want to experience every possible situation. It gives the writing that realistic touch that makes the event come alive.

During my last two years I was active in campus politics. I was elected chairman of the Publications Board that loosely supervised *The Sou'wester*, the college newspaper, and the annual. Southwestern's venerable honor system provided an honor council that could expel a student, but in complete privacy with no names. Ward Archer, my good friend and fraternity brother and a bright student, edited the newspaper. He felt the names of those who had been expelled should be published. As president of the Publications Board, I thought that was a bad idea. We went before Dr. Diehl to discuss the situation. Dr. Diehl sided with me, and Ward acquiesced in our position. Then he wrote an article about it for *The Commercial Appeal* and left school. He was not expelled. He left on his own. I became editor of *The Sou'wester* for the balance of the year. I also held several offices in the fraternity. Although we did not have class standings, we had an honor society that subsequently became Phi Beta Kappa. I am confident that I finished first in my class academically.

My brother and I were interested in accounting, and we wanted Southwestern to offer an accounting course. I went to see Dr. Diehl myself, and he agreed with me, and he said, "Next year we will offer an accounting course." Dr. Ross Jenkins, an economics professor assigned the class, later admitted, "I knew very little about it. I remember how your brother and you pressed me. Most weeks, I was one week ahead of you, but some weeks I was a week or so behind you. I learned later that I gave you almost three years of accounting in that one year, because I didn't know how much I was supposed to give, and y'all were pushing me to go further and faster every week." Dr. Jenkins went on to a career as a CPA. It was the only class that my brother and I ever had together, and he told me in recent years he made a better grade than I did, a great source of pride to him. I learned so much accounting in that course that when I took legal accounting in law school the professor asked if I was a CPA. He couldn't believe it when I told him I had only had one year of accounting.

In our last year, or maybe our last two years, a discussion group met at our church on Sunday afternoons; it was primarily my fraternity brothers, H.R. Holcomb, who later earned a doctor of theology from Harvard, Frank Campbell, Bob Montgomery, Waddy West, Woody Butler, Ward Archer, and Henry Mobley, not a fraternity brother, but a good friend. Mobley became an even better one through these mind-stretching discussions which helped us search for our values.

Memphis during the thirties was dominated by the Crump political machine. Mr. Crump served one term as a congressman in 1932 and 1933 and didn't like it. My father and I ran into him on the train going to New York. An utterly charming man, he invited us to dinner and let me participate in the conversation. I wrote my mother to say that I had met "the most charming man I had ever met, Mr. Ed Crump." An example of his power from 75 years ago: The newspaper noted the Crump candidates were all elected, getting 96 percent of the vote. They didn't make any speeches. They didn't have any political rallies. They didn't run any ads. They didn't spend any money.

By that time, Mr. Crump, interested in the betterment of Memphis, brought many new industries to the city. Firestone was the first, then International Harvester, Dupont, Kimberly-Clark, and many others.

Toward the end of the thirties, Mr. Crump became involved in state-wide politics. With his ability to deliver huge Memphis majorities, he became a tremendous power, selecting a gubernatorial candidate, who would almost always win.

In the mid-thirties, my cousin Hill McAlister, my paternal grandmother's nephew, served as governor. The Crump machine backed Gordon Browning in his first race for governor, then Crump and Browning fell out and Crump didn't back him the next time. Browning was defeated. During that period Memphis won numerous awards for being the cleanest city in the country. Ms. Fowler, the head of the City Beautiful Commission, brought crape myrtles to Memphis. It was also known as the quietest city. An ordinance against horn honking exists even today. Memphis is certainly one of the quietest cities. If you think about any other big city, the amount of honking and noise that you hear, there is a dramatic difference.

During the 1937 flood Mr. Crump's son, John, was killed in a plane crash taking pictures of the flood over in Arkansas, and this changed Mr. Crump. He had planned for John to succeed him. Crump chose a new public commissioner known as "Holy Joe" Boyle and things changed dramatically. All the brothels were closed, all the gambling tables shut down, all the bootleggers put out of business. The city became a model of propriety.

A friend of mine who lived down in Mississippi described how, when the prostitutes were all forced out of Memphis, they worked their way to New Orleans by going from little Mississippi town to little Mississippi town. He said, "When they hit my hometown it was like something we had never seen before." It was an interesting side effect of Mr. Crump's change of heart.

In any event, for the rest of his life, Crump ran an upright, straight government with lots of interest in developing the economic strength of the community. Memphis was different from many Southern cities because black people always voted. The *Press-Scimitar* used to run articles about how the Crump machine would load up black voters on the back of a truck. The driver would be sitting there with a huge wad of poll tax receipts, and the vehicle would pull up in front of a polling place, and everybody would get out with a poll tax receipt and go in and vote. Then they'd move on to the next precinct, and he'd hand out a new bunch of poll tax receipts, and they'd vote again.

Mr. Crump had an unspoken agreement with the business community: "You stay out of my business, and I'll stay out of your business." He created a Memphis tradition, hard to break, where businessmen do not get involved in politics. There were some exceptions. Edmund Orgill from Orgill Brothers did run and serve as mayor, but for the most part business leaders kept their hands off politics. Orgill's term was after Crump's death, and the impact of that Crump influence on Memphis and on Memphis politics has been severe and, in my view, adverse.

Another demographic change occurred in the years immediately before World War II. Farms in the South began to mechanize, and field hands, some tenants, and particularly sharecroppers, began to move to the city. This migration added to the city population those who were virtually uneducated and poorly prepared to work in city jobs. These refugees from the land were used to a system where the plantation owner, who might and probably did mistreat them and take advantage of them, was a last resort for support. Those people who came to Memphis with ambition and some means moved on to Chicago, to Detroit, to Cleveland for better jobs. The migrants left in Memphis, and their descendants, four generations now, had the least social and emotional resources. The only program that Memphis had, in those years, to look after those at the bottom of the economic scale was John Gaston Hospital, which provided free medical care.

At Southwestern, my social skills grew as I matured. I dated, but without a serious relationship with any girl. In Memphis those first two years I could associate with friends who were still in high school, socialize with them, and that made it much more comfortable. My last two years, my friends came to Southwestern, and I dated some girls I had known in high school.

An example of the excellence of students at Southwestern is that Dr. Amacker offered a class on constitutional law. I can name most of the 10 in the class: Gerald Burrow, Shep Tate, Herb Bingham, Ward Archer, H.R. Holcomb, Frank Campbell, Henry Mobley, Norman Shapiro, and me. After the exam, Dr. Amarker said, "This year I'm going to do something that I've never done before in my whole teaching career. I have given everyone an 'A.'" It was a tribute to the quality of the student body.

In my junior year I came home with a report card with all "A"s. I showed it to my father, and he said, "That's pretty good, son." And I said, "Pretty good, Daddy? It's perfect." He teased me about that for the rest of his life.

When I think back, those were wonderful years with marvelous student and faculty friends. I maintained ties with several faculty members: Dr. Hon, the economics professor from whom I had taken several courses; I handled Dr. Kelso's personal affairs and represented his estate. I did the same for Larry Kinney, who came to Southwestern shortly thereafter and was one of the most beloved professors at the college. The Kinney program, where students work in the community to help the less fortunate, is named for him. Recently Rhodes was chosen as the most community minded college in the U.S. I maintained my friendship with Dr. Diehl and became good friends with Dr. Peyton Rhodes, from whom I did not take a course, because he taught physics. I also have a good relationship with Dr. Daughrill and Dr. Troutt. I served on the board for about 10 years, resigning when elected to the City Council. I am pleased to be back on the emeriti board and am looking forward to participating with relish.

The sum total of my education experience up to law school was to learn to love learning. I had gotten a superb education. I had acquired those basic skills so crucial to learning, a love of reading, an ability to read rapidly, the power of concentration, the ability to communicate well, orally and in writing, and an insatiable desire to learn more. Those of us blessed with a good education and preparation for success in life owe back to the community for the opportunities given to us. I feel that God puts us here to try to make the world a better place, and those of us with special opportunities and special talents owe more than anyone else. This philosophy has been a motivating factor in my life. Dr. Diehl often told us, "The good is ever the enemy of the best," and you'll never be great if you're satisfied with being good. A change in family fortune forced me to go to Southwestern, but Southwestern was exactly the right place for me. It gave me everything I needed and more, and it's had a tremendous influence on my life and still does. One of my proudest moments was receiving an honorary doctorate (L.L.D.) from Rhodes.

_____

TEN

LAW SCHOOL—BORN
TO BE A LAWYER

A group of us, including my brother, Sam Carter, Buddy Miller, and Ferd Heckle, planned a trip to Washington and New York for the summer of 1937. As with our trip out West the summer before, our mother loaned us her car. We drove first to New York. Part of the plan was to see our grandmother Campbell at the retirement home on Grand Concourse Boulevard, in the Bronx. We had great fun in New York doing all the tourist spots because Bill and I were the only ones who had been there before. We went to the Statue of Liberty, Battery Park, Rockefeller Center, Radio City Music Hall, and a play.

We also drove up to Choate with our grandmother, who saw the school for the first time. Buddy, Sam, and Fred were impressed with the beautiful campus and magnificent facilities. My Choate friend, Frances Silk, who had just graduated from the Naval Academy, went with us. He had a career in the Navy and ultimately became a captain, probably retiring as an admiral. School was out, but we did see a few friends there. One highlight of the trip was hearing Glen Gray's orchestra at the Glen Island Casino. There was a cover charge. We ordered a bottle of wine and ended up smuggling the bottle out of the casino, because none of us was much of a drinker.

We made the usual tour of Washington, the Washington Monument, the Lincoln Memorial, the Capitol, and the Senate, where Senator

McKellar's office got us an opportunity to sit in the Senate gallery. Then we went down to Mount Vernon and they left me there. I caught the bus back to Alexandria to live with my first cousin, Carolyn Mc-Kellar Dunn, in a row house on Duke Street, a charming place, for the summer. Carolyn's husband, Irwin, was an official with the Department of Agriculture.

Judge John Donelson Martin, my father's cousin and roommate at the University of Virginia, influenced my decision to become a lawyer. I planned to go to Harvard Law School, but again that same uncle called upon my father for support. He had married and, to everyone's surprise, had produced a child. We held a family conference and I agreed to go to law school where I could support myself. The logical place was Washington, because of our family connection with Senator McKellar. His brother had been married to my aunt. The senator promised to get me a federal job. I began to work seriously on getting a job while staying with my cousin Carolyn and her husband. As members of the Belle Haven Country Club, they obtained a summer membership for me. I played a lot of golf and met some delightful people. When I arrived I hadn't made a decision about whether to go to Georgetown or George Washington.

My Southwestern friend, Raford Herbert, in law school at Georgetown, convinced me that Georgetown was a better law school. I believe he was correct. I walked down to Georgetown law school in July, said I want to go to law school, and was taken in to see the dean. There was no dean of admissions. I handed him my transcript. He looked it over and asked me two or three questions. Then he said, "The first semester's tuition would be $80," $8 per semester hour. We felt outraged when tuition was increased to $10 per semester hour. Senator McKellar got me a job with the Federal Housing Administration as a messenger, paying $90 a month, considered a good job at that time. I finished out that lovely summer. My golf game probably was as good as it would be for many, many years, if ever again.

My childhood and college friend, also a fraternity brother, Kalford (Rudy) Ratcliff, told me he was coming to Washington for law school and he would be doing the same thing, working and going to school at night. He had just finished a year at Vandy. Georgetown refused to accept those Vanderbilt credits. Instead he went to Columbia Law School, now a part of American University. We roomed at a house on Cathedral Avenue, $50 a month for the two of us and arranged to take our meals around the corner from our room on Woodley Road where Raford lived.

I remember talking to myself about my law school studies. Although always a good student, I never was driven to do my absolute best. I told myself this was my lifetime calling and to give it everything I had. In law school I briefed every assigned case in each course, and at the end of the course and before the exam, I outlined the course with citations. My work schedule those first two years was up at 7:30 a.m.; work by 8:30; off at 4:30 p.m.; law school at 5:00; finished at 7:00; home after dinner, start studying at 8:30. I studied till 3:00 a.m., sometimes later. We worked on Saturday; that really was the schedule for six days a week. It was grueling, and I worked as hard as I could.

At first, I was a messenger, then an accounting clerk. What we did was to check the accuracy of amortization schedules. I called myself an adding machine jockey. I could really make one of those electric 10-key machines hum. My first year, I did extremely well in all my courses except for legal bibliography. This involved looking up the law—law cases, articles, and textbook material, an important, but easy course. During the exam Raford came in and stood in the doorway because he had already finished his exam. I hurried to finish. The questions became increasingly difficult, but most required the processes outlined earlier to be repeated, and additional steps added. Instead of writing the process each time, I referred to the process in the previous question and added the new steps. The professor, offended by my derogation of the importance of the course, counted off those references. I got a 78 on the course. I am sure I made no errors. This was my only grade below 88 while I was in law school. Unfortunately, it caused me to finish, I think 12th in my class, instead of first.

Georgetown was a large law school with a freshman class of 400, mostly night school students. It is still the largest law school in the country with 600 freshmen. We took 10 hours a semester, or 20 hours a year credit, and during the summer, I think four hours of credit.

We were taught, for the most part, using the case method. Professor Yeager, who taught contracts, called on us to analyze each assigned case. It was not unusual for a student to read the case and decide the wrong party won. It produced sarcastic comments from the professor and laughter from the class. There were plaintiffs and defendants, complainants, or petitioners and respondents and appellants and appellees. Some judges threw the terms around freely. If you didn't follow closely, you could get mixed up as to who was who. To one student who constantly raised his hand and asked questions, Dr. Yeager said, "Mr. Arnett, I believe you have the greatest collection of erroneous information I have ever encountered."

Dr. Keigwin, who taught common law pleading, was very old. The Rules of Civil Procedure had recently been adopted, but common law pleadings were in effect in many states. Keigwin was a real expert on the subject. Because Keigwin was old and set in his ways, he started in every class with the alphabetical roll. The same students were called every day—Adams, Brown. I don't think he got to me more than twice during the whole year. Keigwin was one professor who never let you sit down until you admitted something you didn't know about the case. First, he asked when the case was decided. Many cases were in the 16th and 17th centuries. Then he wanted to know the name of the judge who wrote the opinion. Once, a student answered all his questions. Finally Keigwin asked, "What important event happened in that year?" The student admitted that he didn't know. Keigwin commented, "My, you must have had an arid youth. That was the year that the English won the Battle of Blenheim and Lord Churchill was made Duke of Marlborough."

One professor did not use the strict case method. We read cases and discussed them but he lectured and asked questions to the class about what we had learned from the cases. His name was Francis Xavier Nash, a Jesuit, a good lecturer and an enjoyable professor. Georgetown had an excellent faculty. Professor Stanton taught real property law. The saying was that his course in second-year real property was the one that separated the men from the boys. That's the course that covered remainder and reverter interests, vested and unvested remainders, and springing uses. I am sure that Professor Stanton flunked more than half the class. This was wartime; from our class of 400, 99 graduated.

Georgetown was a Jesuit school. But in typical Jesuit fashion it didn't appear to be Catholic. The dean, I would say, was Catholic, as were most faculty, but there was not a priest except for the chancellor. Otherwise, you would not notice anything particularly Catholic about the law school. One day, in the second year when I arrived at school, a sign on the board said, "No classes today—the Feast of the Immaculate Conception." I believe the only day we had off before was Good Friday. Everybody was utterly puzzled about what was going on and somebody said, "The archbishop was here today and he discovered we were not observing these Catholic holidays. So, this was in response to the archbishop's complaints."

A sidelight of my first two law school years: my betting activities. That first Saturday as a messenger, a couple of people wanted to bet on the Georgia Tech-Notre Dame football game. Notre Dame was in a down period, and I believe Georgia Tech was the favorite. I was so cautious because I was betting $5 and only making $90 a month. I got 14 points. Georgia Tech won the game. The word got around that I bet; I began to take more and more bets. I learned that P.T. Barnum was right: "There's a sucker born every minute." Most people wanted to bet even when they didn't know anything about football. I did extremely well. I hit a couple of early football pools, one time for $400. Then I hit for $1,000 but my "dealer" skipped, and I never got it. Taught me a lesson and I never played them again. I bet mostly on football and some World Series baseball games. I don't think I bet on any basketball at all, but I walked around all the time as gamblers do with all this cash in my pocket. One day, while with a law school friend, I pulled out this wad of money. He said, "Where in the world did you get all that money? Don't you have a bank account?" I replied, "No, I just deal with cash and pay with cash." He said, "Come with me and we're going to put that money in the bank."

At the end of the second year, June 1940, the winds of war blew strongly. The draft had started I was anxious to finish school before the war started, not realizing that I would be classified as 4-F, because of my gall bladder operation at 14. I decided to quit working and go to school full time. I finished first in the class in my second year. I went to the dean and worked out an arrangement to take 20 hours per semester and finish in three years, graduating in June of 1941. The dean consented.

Back then you could take the Tennessee bar after two years of law school and two years of college. I had been to Memphis to take the bar, and learned in September that I had passed. During the summer I told my father of my plan. He asked, "How can you afford that?" I explained I had saved some money. He responded, "Saved some money on $90 a month?" "Well, Daddy, I had a raise to $120." He said, "All right, $120 a month." Finally I admitted to my success with gambling. "First thing I have to do is to apologize to your brother," he said. "What do you mean by that?" I asked. And he said, "He always complains about his insufficient allowance and I tell him Lewie gets by on his allowance. I didn't know you had supplemented your allowance with gambling." (In college I won regularly on bridge, golf, some tennis, and a lot of pool from a pool table at the fraternity house where there were plenty of suckers.). Daddy told me, "When I came down from college to run Donelson & Poston, the food brokerage business, my father came and checked the books. This was before income tax. He said, 'You haven't drawn any money all year.' I responded, 'I have been living at home and getting most of my meals there.' He replied, 'That's not true. You have been out almost every night playing the social circuit.' I admitted to winning money in poker games at the Chickasaw Club. My father said to me, 'I hired you to run this business, not to play poker at the Chickasaw Club.'"

Later, I told Judge Martin this story and the judge said, "I remember the year well. I supported him." Daddy commented that Judge Martin was the world's worst poker player. He had to see every pot. He never folded.

Georgetown day law school was much smaller, with fewer than 100 students. By the third year that had been reduced by half with only about 50 of us. I made some good friends. I hung around at school when I wasn't in class and continued to study hard. I made outstanding grades, made the Law Review in my second year and Recent Decisions editor my third year. I assigned staff members to prepare a brief comment. Then I reviewed and edited them before publication.

After the first two years, my roommate Rudy Ratcliff got married. Red Water invited me to stay with him at his mother's and aunt's apartment on Connecticut Avenue with free rent. I began taking all my meals out. I realized Red's difficulty with law school came from his inability to study continuously for more than five or 10 minutes. I said, "Red, you'll never get it if you can't concentrate. You get up, you get a Coke, or you get a cigarette, or you get something to eat, and so forth. I am going to teach you how to concentrate." I checked my watch and said, "Red, you look at the book, whether you read it or not, for 20 minutes without looking up and saying a word. Concentrate on that." By the end of that year he was able to go over an hour totally concentrating. He said that was absolutely the only thing that got him through law school. He did graduate and pass the West Virginia bar and went down there to practice. West Virginia was his home state. Red remained a good friend the rest of his life. He didn't take to the practice of law; he should have gone into the construction business, which his father had done, and used his personal skills and his law knowledge to help him. A track star in prep school and college, he was wonderful with men—he was a man's man. He married, but it didn't work out, and was divorced. He returned to Washington and worked at a government agency doing mostly title work, a dull but safe job. He died fairly young. Red would get a few beers in him and he would call me in the middle of the night and talk to "good ole Lewie," rambling for 30 minutes or more every time he called.

I enjoyed my experience in day school. I teased my Catholic friends by always having a hamburger or hot dog for Friday lunch, while they ate fish. Probably my closest friend was Barrett McDonnell, maybe a very distant cousin. The Donelson name may come from the Donell strain of the clan Donald. Barrett was in the class behind me, but we kept up. One day not long after his graduation from law school, he called and said, "Lewie, I am going to go into an order, a closed order. I won't be able to talk to anyone, including my family, for a whole year." I didn't hear from him for a year, but then he called and said, "It was not for me, I'm going to practice law." After I lost touch with him, I learned he spent most of his career helping Catholic Charities and other organizations.

Another very good friend was Ed Stocker from Little Rock, who practiced there for many years. I also became friends with Milton Nixon. We were a team for the moot court competition. Clubs sponsored the moot court teams, and Milton and I won the right to represent our club in the final debate. Our judge in the finals was Supreme Court Justice Wiley Rutledge. Judge Rutledge told me he selected me as the best advocate because of the way I answered questions involving a case: Overnite Transportation Company versus Bisell, a wage-and-hour case. I was not familiar with the case; the judge outlined its ruling for me, and I applied the facts as we argued. My primary opponent responded to a question from the justice saying, "Your honor, I'm coming to that in a minute," and Justice Rutledge said afterward, "Don't ever do that. When the court asks you a question, answer it then. Because that's when the judge wants to hear your answer."

My grades in my last years were outstanding. My classmates teased me that when I signed my name on the paper the professor automatically gave me a 95; my average grades were over 95. The next highest average was below 90. My academic success showed two things: (1) I worked hard and gave my studies everything I had; and (2) I had a natural flare for law. I had always been a good student, a rapid reader with a quick mind. All of these worked together to produce good grades, not always a sign of who knows the most.

I had a great law school career. I was first in my class and winner
of the moot court competition, the only person to this day to do that.
I am proud that Georgetown has gone to greater heights since I was
there. It is certainly one of the very top law schools in the country, and
uses its presence in Washington to a substantial advantage.

The law school was highly supportive, giving me lots of opportunities. Impressive because I was a Presbyterian among a sea of Catholics.
One job was to assist in writing a brief for an alumnus who had a case
in the Court of Appeals. I learned about actual law practice with this
case involving a workmen's compensation claim. Perhaps the most
memorable job was an opportunity to serve as assistant counsel to
the Truman Committee, which was investigating war contracts. I was
interviewed by the to-be-famous Clark Clifford, who later became
"Mr. Fix-it" in Washington. He turned me off completely, telling me
this was going to be a stepping-stone to big things, and how much
money we could make, and how we would get in with the powers that
be, and learn how people handled things in government. He certainly
carried out his plans. I did get to see then-Senator Harry Truman, exactly as he appeared on television: straightforward and no put-on. I
had already made up my mind not to work for Clark Clifford, and
I am glad of that decision.

ELEVEN

MY YEAR AS A BUREAUCRAT

I worked for a year with the Civil Aeronautics Board in Washington, D.C., encouraged by advice from Judge Martin, my godfather-in-the-law who thought it would be good training to be a government bureaucrat so that I would learn how bureaucrats think. The Civil Aeronautics Board regulated the air transportation industry, granting routes, fixing rates, overseeing safety, including the inspection of planes. It was a regulatory agency with tremendous power. Welch Pogue was the general counsel, and I worked there from June of 1941 until April of 1942.

I was in Washington when Pearl Harbor was bombed. Shortly thereafter the general counsel called me in and said, "The White House called and the president wants to know if he could seize all of the commercial airliners. I want you to develop a memo on that. I know you will get this done promptly." You can imagine my reaction: I thought this might be one of my wartime contributions. I spent night and day for the next week getting the memorandum ready. I came to the conclusion, based on cases decided following the Civil War related to Lincoln's actions, that under the "war power," the president could seize all the commercial airplanes with appropriate compensation. One morning a guard who had been on the night shift said to me, "What are you doing here; I thought you worked at night?" I replied, "I have been working both." He looked at me and laughed.

Finally, I took my memorandum to Welch Pogue. He wanted some revisions, and I rushed to make them. He told me to take it over to the Air Corps (then a part of the Army) to offices on the mall in one of the World War I temporary buildings and deliver it to a certain colonel for approval before it went to the White House. I rushed over and arrived about 4:00 p.m., so I went through security. When I told the guard the name of the colonel, he said, "You can go up there if you want to but he won't see you. He goes home at 4:30 sharp every day and he is putting on his coat now." I replied, "This is a memorandum for the White House and they are waiting for it." He said, "Suit yourself and go on up." Sure enough, I went up and the colonel, peacetime Army, was putting on his coat and said, "I am sorry, you will have to come back in the morning." I told him how I had been working on it night and day and the White House had been calling about when they were going to get it. He said again, "I am sorry, you will have to come back in the morning," which I did.

The next morning he skimmed over it hurriedly and approved it; I rushed it over to the White House. The aide at the White House who received the memorandum was the movie star Robert Montgomery. We had a delightful chat. He complained about his cushy White House job because he wanted active duty. Shortly after that he was ordered to duty on a combat ship and served with distinction.

The president never did seize any airliners, although the government leased or purchased a number of commercial airplanes. The president always had that legal threat to assure that he got full co-operation.

The most interesting case I had at the CAB was a dispute between the Matson Steamship Line and Pan American Airways. When Pan American began its original flights to the Pacific, it used flying boats and secured landing rights from Matson Steamship Line in the important harbors. Part of that agreement provided that when traffic between the mainland and the Hawaiian islands was sufficient to support flights to Hawaii and back, Pan American would establish a joint venture with Matson to own and operate an airline for those flights similar to the structure Pan Am had established in South America with

Grace Steamship Line, known as Panagra. Traffic was now sufficient to justify a separate airline to Hawaii, but Pan American had refused to honor its contract on the grounds that it violated public policy. Matson was so powerful in the islands as to constitute an antitrust violation by providing a monopoly for Matson that owned the airline operating between the islands. Matson also owned most regularly scheduled boat trips between the islands as well as the main steamship lines from the west coast to Hawaii and over the Pacific.

Pan American produced significant proof that six families owned virtually everything on the island, including the Matson interests, the Dole pineapple interests, and the Waterhouse family interests. It showed interconnections among the six families, the overlapping boards of directors, and the control of the major banks on the island. Clearly these wealthy families dominated the economy of the islands. My legal position was that Pan American be required to live up to its agreement because ownership of this separate airline would not greatly enhance the power and position of the families and that Pan American's operation of other Pacific flights diminished the impact of that combination.

Juan Trippe, chairman of Pan Am, dominated the commercial aviation industry and the board responded to his power; it did not require him to live up to the agreement. This provided an insight into the nature of bureaucracies that tend to become cozy with the people they regulate. Matson Steamship line was not in the aviation business and was relatively unknown to the CAB, but Juan Trippe was the fair-haired boy of the era, and what he wanted, he got. The board even refused to require anything in penalties from Trippe, who boldly violated an agreement supposedly signed in good faith.

I also learned about bureaucracies' insatiable reach for more authority. In one of my last cases, an action came before the board against an airline for failure to notify a passenger of a flight cancellation that caused him to miss an appointment with considerable economic loss. The general counsel asked me to write an opinion. I recommended that we not take the matter as it was inappropriate for the Civil Aeronautics Board. I thought the courts far better equipped to determine such disputes, which were heavily dependent upon factual determinations. The CAB took it. As I expected, they were inundated with claims against airlines. After a year or so the board reversed itself and sent such cases back to the courts.

At the beginning of the war, the population of the District of Columbia exploded. You could never get into a movie theater or restaurant without waiting in line. You couldn't sit down on a bus. Everything was overcrowded. You could feel the tension and excitement build as the country was swept up into war.

Red finished law school and headed off to West Virginia and I had to move again. My college friend Frank Campbell invited me to join him in his apartment after his brother finished law school and returned to Mississippi. Miles Watkins was from Birmingham and in the Navy. Mallory Buford ultimately made a career in Washington in government, but then, he talked about the girls of Washington and how they looked like peasants stepping over cotton rows, showing the planter contempt for the field worker. He married a Washington government worker and spent his whole life in the city. Watkins was a real Southern charmer, a ladies' man whom Frank and I watched in awe. He always had some girl on his string and seemed to be having sex with most of them. Frank and I were two innocents watching wide-eyed at his exploits.

On December 7, 1941, we lived on Q Street, right off Dupont Circle. I have told the story of Pearl Harbor many times. When I told it to my friend Kaye Pallen, she said I ought to write it down. I sent Frank a copy and he said it wasn't that way at all. Here is the reconciled version. We had lunch at our favorite restaurant on Dupont Circle where Buddy Watkins liked to go because of the voluptuous hostess. Upon returning to our apartment, we turned on the Redskins football game. Almost immediately there began to be announcements on the loudspeaker, "Admiral-so-and-so, report to your office immediately." There must have been at least 25 calls for admirals and generals. We were all puzzled. Then came the shocker: "The Japs have attacked Pearl Harbor." You can imagine the football game was forgotten. All the talk was of war.

The Japanese Embassy was nearby and we agreed to go over to see what was happening. When we arrived they were scurrying around burning papers and, as we watched, their envoys in their swallowtail coats returned from the State Department in a big limo. Remember, they were actually in Secretary of State Cordell Hull's office when he heard about the attacks. Legend has it that he gave them a good Tennessee cussing.

Some of the crowd began to shout insults and prepare to throw stones. But Frank and I, budding lawyers, said, "Don't do that. There are some Americans in Tokyo doing the same thing. Think about them." It calmed the crowd, which dispersed after all the Japanese retreated into the embassy.

We returned to our apartment and you can imagine the radio reports, "Jap sub sighted off the California coast; a German sub in Chesapeake Bay." Wild stuff.

That evening we rode around D.C. No one had thought of blackouts yet. But it was chilling to see anti-aircraft guns on the White House and the Capitol and troops appearing everywhere. Wartime Washington had begun with a jolt. The thought of real war and possible attacks on U.S. soil were very sobering. It was a memorable day. It was, as FDR said, "A day which will live in infamy."

As I remember it, Frank volunteered the next day, but he said it was actually a week later. Buddy Watkins had been called up. So we had to give up the apartment—it was too expensive for us, Mal and me. I basically looked for a room for a few weeks. A colleague offered me a place. When I got there, he had a mattress on the floor, a lamp sitting on the floor, and one single card table and chair. I lived there for several months before I returned to Memphis. I had been called up by the draft board. I recall going to Georgetown Hospital for a physical; there was a long line—I had a shot, and remember that three or four men fainted when given theirs. It is amazing how frightened people can get over a simple hypodermic needle. So ended my stay in Washington.

TWELVE

MY YEAR AS A LAW CLERK

When I received my Draft Board notice in early 1942, I decided to leave the CAB and return to Memphis. I was sent to Fort Oglethorpe, Georgia, for physicals. At that point they were calling up all 4-Fs and some 18-year-olds. Ours was a motley group, a mixture of mentally deficient, physically handicapped, and the very young. The train ride to Chattanooga on the Southern Railway was uneventful until lunch at Corinth. Towns along the route had volunteered to provide lunch for the draftees. The time between that lunch and our ultimate meal at Fort Oglethorpe after a bus ride from Chattanooga was very long, from about 10:00 a.m. to 9:00 p.m. A mix-up meant almost no food for us. At our assigned quarters, a sergeant gave instructions on how to make up the bed, warning if we failed to do it properly we would be subject to severe punishment. Some poor fellows were so frightened of messing up, they slept under their beds. I helped two or three make their beds. The next morning we went in for physicals; when I came to the end of the line, the doctor said, "I understand you've had a gallbladder operation, a cholecystectomy when you were fourteen, absolute grounds for 4-F classification. I don't know exactly why they sent you down here. You'll be an invalid all your life." Here I am, a healthy 94 years old.

The sergeant took me aside and said, "We're going to send back with you the people who have also been turned down. Most are marginal. Promise me you will look after them on the train and stay at the station until everyone is picked up." I had immediate questions from each: "Why was I turned down?" I looked at the card and on the back it was marked, "Mentally deficient." I was at a loss for words, but when I had time to think I said, "It says you were generally deficient." That seemed to satisfy them. I did manage to get them all back to Memphis and stayed at the station until everybody had been picked up.

Most of my friends were in the service by that time, but a few were still in town for various reasons. Winston Braun, Hurbert Turley, and Sam Carter were in medical school. Charlie Freeburg was 4-F like I was. Memphis was in the throes of rationing and other wartime conditions. My job as Judge Martin's law clerk required us to be in Cincinnati for three weeks every other month. I began with a shorter session in Cincinnati in June, and then we did not return until September.

In 1942, Memphis was prosperous. Cotton prices were reasonably high. Farmers were spending. Citizens bragged about Memphis being chosen as the quietest and the cleanest city in the country for several successive years under the benevolent dictatorship of Boss Crump. Mr. Crump was at the zenith of his power. The old Memphis, a wide-open river town, featured secret gaming tables in most of the hotels and some nightclubs. Brothels operated in many places downtown with lots of bootleg whiskey. As a curious teenager then, I found myself in some of those places, just looking, of course. A good friend had a great run at the dice table in The Peabody, winning over $500. All this was gone when I returned to Memphis. The city had been cleaned up under the reign of "Holy Joe" Boyle, the police commissioner who shut down the brothels and the gaming tables in the hotels and night-clubs and mostly enforced prohibition. Mr. Crump reportedly got religion after the tragic death of his son, his heir. Mr. Crump had begun to bring industry to Memphis. It's hard to remember exactly when, but the Firestone plant was going strong during the war as was the Fisher Body Plant, a product of the 1920s. The Millington Naval Base was a hub, with sailors everywhere. The Army Depot grew rapidly. The Ferry Command had a base at the airport. Their poker games were legendary: no limit, high stakes games with lots of dollars changing hands. I actually went out to watch one night.

The Peabody remained the center of social life with its outdoor roof garden and dance floor, the scene of many big social events. There was no air conditioning. The ballroom was the center of social activities in the winter. The original Peabody on the northwest corner of Main and Monroe, built during the 1860s, was torn down in the mid-twenties, and replaced by the modern, grand Peabody on Union. During the war The Peabody was less than 20 years old. My great-grandfather died of a heart attack in the lobby of the old Peabody in 1871. The Cotton Carnival, somewhat toned down during the war, was still the big social event of the year. Secret societies sponsored constant parties. Each year, a king and queen, then always from families associated with cotton, reigned over the festivities. The private clubs sponsored princesses, duchesses, ladies-in-waiting, and surrounding small towns sent their ladies-in-waiting. The court was a large group. I was never in the court, but belonged briefly to a secret society, attendeding several parties a year. At the University Club Tea Dance, an afternoon event, we wore white dinner jackets for summer formal occasions. At a white dinner jacket evening, I double dated with a good friend who had several drinks. We went to Fortune's at intermission and he got into an argument and took a swing at a well-known tough guy. Fortunately, my friend missed, fell down, and rolled under the car. When we pulled him out, his jacket was a mess. Later I asked, "What did you tell your mother about that jacket?" He said, "I explained some drunk started a fight."

I lived at home as did most unmarried young men. In the summer of 1942, my brother went to Alabama to prepare himself to join the weather service in the Army Air Corps. Bill was the talk of the campus because he took advanced calculus, physics, and thermodynamics. He roomed with Hugo Black, Jr., the son of the Supreme Court justice. Bill then went into the service and on to weather school.

As mentioned, I clerked for Judge Martin on the Sixth Circuit U.S. Court of Appeals, a formative experience. John Donelson Martin was my father's second cousin and college roommate. When my father and Judge Martin went to the University of Virginia, their third room-mate was Martin Donelson, my father's first cousin.

I learned about briefing and oral arguments. I read every brief filed in every case Judge Martin considered. I also reviewed most briefs in matters where Judge Martin was not part of the panel. I heard all the oral arguments in his cases. Listening to the judge in conferences after argument, I realized that appellate briefs were not judicial decisions or law journal articles, but opportunities to present your side of the case in written form and to persuade the court and sell your position. They had to present the facts and applicable law and be soundly reasoned from the facts in the record. In short, I came to believe briefs should be argumentative, partisan, and persuasive. Most were not; some were too analytical; some too simple in laying out the facts and leaving the court to sort out the issue and decide the case. It was great preparation for law practice.

My relationship with Judge Martin began because of the strong friendship between my father and the judge, who lived with my grandparents while going to MUS, and then roomed with my father at the University of Virginia. I learned stories about my grandfather and my father from Judge Martin.

The first matter he handed me was an opinion by another judge on the panel involving a federal cabaret tax. The judge upheld the validity of the tax. I read the opinion and felt the tax unconstitutional because it extended beyond the federal government's tax power. It only applied to nightclubs that sold alcohol and had entertainment, and it was difficult to see how the federal government's authority in the Interstate Commerce Clause reached these businesses.

This was long before Justice Douglas' theory extended federal legislative powers by holding that if it could be shown by an inference on an inference that the matter affected interstate commerce, that was sufficient. When my memorandum disagreed with the other judge's opinion, Judge Martin agreed with me, and submitted a revised opinion; the third judge agreed with us. Judge Martin said that I had reversed the court on my very first case.

We had wide-ranging philosophical discussions. In one of the first, he told of when he and my father were in college, my father argued that most men under sufficient pressure are dishonest, and he argued that most are essentially honest. Now that my father had been in business many years and he on the bench, their positions had reversed. My father believed men essentially honest, and Judge Martin believed under sufficient pressure, especially under pressure of a substantial reversal of the standing and financial security of his family, he would steal.

After over 60 years of law practice, I come down the middle. Most people are honest, but under pressure some do break. I had a client who sold a coal lease. The purchaser agreed to an open-ended annual percentage royalty. The tax law was cloudy as to whether such open-ended royalty promises should be characterized as capital gain or ordinary income, a major difference. I suggested a 12-year limit because case law supported that. The purchaser said, "If the law is clarified, I will give you an open-ended royalty payment"—completely nonbinding. Years later, the client called and told me the purchaser was about to resell the lease and asked if the law was clarified. The law had changed: Open-ended royalty agreements were entitled to capital gain treatment. He called his purchaser back and told him. Then he said, "Send me a new agreement concerning this and I'll sign it before I sell." We did it and he signed. I asked how much money that would mean to my client. He said, "At least $2 million." That man was as good as his word.

The judge used to tease me about having a circumstantial memory. I remembered the case citation and would refer to the case as 166 Tenn. 203. He said, "Lewie, you don't want to clutter up your mind with all that circumstantial memory. You want to remember important principles, develop a philosophical memory." Not long after our discussion my grandmother called to make a change in her will that the judge had drawn up. On the way to his old office, he told me he had owned the safe with the wills since he began practicing law 30 years ago. None of the lawyers were there; the office manager was at lunch.

He walked over to the safe, sat down, began to fiddle around and fiddle around and fiddle around, and, finally, he reluctantly admitted he couldn't remember the combination. I said, "Judge, that philosophical memory isn't worth a damn when it comes to opening that safe." He enjoyed a joke on himself and thought that was one of the funniest things that had ever happened. He told all the judges about my teasing his philosophical memory that couldn't open safes.

We had a big patent case involving RCA and radio aerials. Neither of us knew how radios worked. All we could do was turn them on and off. If something went wrong with them, we were helpless. We couldn't even tune them well. He suggested perhaps experts in those areas should decide the cases. I was a brash young man, and I knew the basic principle of whether something was patentable, whether it advanced the state of the art. I said, "Having people like us decide these cases might be worthwhile because scientists see any little improvement as an advancement, but somebody like yourself or me would have to see some big change to feel it really advanced the state of the art." He said, "Maybe that's what we can contribute. It would certainly have to be a big change for us to understand it." Judge Martin's theory won the day and now there is a court for patent appeals.

The judge had been Mr. E.H. Crump's personal attorney. Judge Martin undoubtedly was responsible for my receiving an inquiry later from the Crump organization about going to the legislature. Martin also represented the Union Planters Bank when Clarence Saunders attempted to corner the market in Piggly Wiggly stock. Saunders created the first self-service grocery store, a tremendous change from the store with a counter where you told the clerk what you wanted and he went behind the counter and got it for you, a slow and labor-intensive process. The new system not only saved clerks, but also allowed the customer to see all the merchandise available. Impulse buying began in earnest. The concept was instantly successful, and stores spread over the country. The company went public with numerous stockholders.

In the early 1920s, Clarence and his original investors found New York Stock Exchange control irksome. They hatched a plan to regain control and began to buy up the stock to "corner" the market. Union Planters was the stakeholder in the matter, holding all of the stock of the consortium Clarence had put together.

Clarence did corner the market. The short sellers did not have enough stock to cover their sales position when it came time to deliver their stock. It should have been a stunning coup, with all of Clarence's investors realizing a huge profit. But Clarence was an outsider and these short sellers, all market insiders, persuaded the exchange to allow them an extra two weeks to collect enough stock to meet the outstanding sell orders. Unfortunately for Clarence, after two weeks of paying exorbitant prices for the stock, they not only delivered enough to cover their position, but more than Clarence could pay for. The corner was broken, and Clarence Saunders went broke.

During his heyday, Clarence, a flamboyant character, bought what is now Chickasaw Gardens, and built the Pink Palace home. He never lived there because of his bankruptcy.

I made my first trip to Cincinnati with Judge Martin in June of 1942. We rode up on the train. My father's good friend was a vice president of Kroger, and I contacted him. He and his wife had a daughter in her twenties who invited me to parties during my frequent trips to the city. The first Sunday they invited me to dinner at the country club, and then the daughter and I toured Cincinnati in her father's Cadillac. The clerk of the court rode by as I drove out of the country club grounds in a Cadillac with a blond at my side. It gave me a reputation as playboy, totally unreal, but I enjoyed Cincinnati, primarily because of this family's gracious hospitality.

It was a strange time, because with so many in the service, only a few young men remained. Some worked in the court, and I got to know some of the other judge's law clerks, who were older men in those days. Each of the judges had only one law clerk. The judge talked frequently about other cases during his career. When he talked about his losses, he would say, "You always had the right to retire to the tavern and curse the court." What a privilege to sit at the feet of a talented lawyer with broad experience, a priceless opportunity to learn.

Judge Martin advocated fewer opinions from the Court of Appeals and pushed for per curium orders, particularly when appeals were denied and the lower courts sustained. Instead of more or less reciting what the lower court had decided, he felt it wasted a judge's time to write such redundant opinions. As the caseload increased for the Court of Appeals, he argued this would be one major way to speed up the process. He won; many cases are decided per curium today. Writing memos for the judge on his cases was another learning experience, as I heard his reactions to my reasoning and conclusions.

The judge did not put on airs. He was down-to-earth, with a courteous and friendly courtroom demeanor. I learned from him about dealing with other lawyers and with clients. He always told me if he called my office and my secretary asked, "Who is calling, please?" he would know that I had gotten too big for my britches. I have not lived up to that, but when I am in the office alone or even with company, I answer my own phone. To this day, major clients say, "I can't believe I got straight to you." It makes a good impression.

To work with the man who got me interested in the practice of law, who was not only interested in me as a person and as a kinsman, capped my preparation to practice. I realized a lawyer was first and foremost an advocate, not a priest of the mysterious cult of "the Law." Lawyer and client were essentially equal. The lawyer provided specialized knowledge, but the client knew the most about his legal problem. Experience taught me to listen to the client who might not know the legal principle involved in the issue, but knew the facts and all their nuances. Many lawyers talk down to their clients as though they are too dumb to understand the esoteric culture of "the Law." This is not only bad client relations, but also inhibits the search for the best legal position. That year had a major impact on my law career.

THIRTEEN

A GREAT BEGINNING

After my clerkship, I went to the firm of Canada, Russell, and Turner, one of the largest firms in the city with about 12 lawyers. Some partners and associates were in the service; I was assigned all of the unimportant cases (known as the junk). The firm represented Union Planters Bank, Plough, Memphis Natural Gas Company, five railroad companies, and many others.

Colonel J.W. Canada, the senior partner, was in his mid-70s and near retirement. My mother and his wife were friends. The colonel, a dynamic, charismatic man with a mustache, about average size, was articulate and persuasive. He took a shine to me, and I worked closely with him that year. He let me try a couple of moderately important cases, although he sat with me and helped. After we won the first one he said, "I told you that when I threw that cub at them it would discombobulate them completely because they would be wonderin' what I was plannin'." He was an aviation pioneer, first chairman of the Memphis Airport Commission, with his home across from the airport.

My most important case with Colonel Canada involved our successful defense of a suit against the Union Planters Bank to force it to pay a certified check on which the maker, the bank's good customer, had requested we stop payment. He bragged about it without explaining that the check maker made the check payable to himself, had it certified to himself, and then endorsed it over to the holder. After much research, I found old Massachusetts cases that held that the certification ran only to the payee, which in this case was the payer as well. Then, there was little Tennessee law on commercial issues. We established the principle that the named payee had the right to stop payment on the check if he wanted to, even though he was also the payor and that the certification ran only to the payee, although there was a holder in due course. I was lucky to have that year's experience with Colonel Canada, who built such a successful law practice. From him I learned law was a profession, but you also could make a good living.

Canada, Russell, and Turner defended the Frisco Railroad in a switching accident case, in which I assisted Cooper Turner. The new railroad liability act, I believe the Jones Act, put the burden of proof on the railroad to prove that it was not negligent, a heavy burden. In a mysterious accident in the Yale Yards of Frisco Railroad, a car ran over and killed a switchman. In switching, recognized practices were followed by switch engineers and switchmen. This involved a certain order of the switching of the cars and certain whistles to indicate changes from one track to another. We struggled to show the railroad had followed every rule and procedure and the negligence was by the switchman. The federal statute shifted the burden, and although no one knew exactly what happened, the burden of proof was on us. We not only lost the case, the jury turned in a $30,000 verdict. When we returned to the office, Colonel Canada called us in and chewed us out. We had disgraced the firm; no one had ever gotten a $30,000 verdict against the firm in its history. We were going to lose all of our railroad business because we couldn't handle these cases and so on, and so on, and so on.

After the colonel calmed down, he said, "I know we'll take it upon appeal and see what we can do, but there is one thing that irks me. That darn Garland Draper handled that case and he used to be a claim agent for the railroad, and now he's assistant U.S. district attorney. He is trying cases before the same jury panels that he appears before as assistant U.S. district attorney. Lewie, I want you to file a motion for a new trial on the grounds that the assistant U.S. district attorney should not be permitted to practice in the court where he was also appearing as government counsel."

This was a very common practice in those days, because virtually all of the assistant U.S. DAs were part-time. I couldn't find any law whatsoever to support this position, but I tried to prepare some kind of an argument. There was a moral argument and a justice argument that could be made. I took it in to the colonel and he tuned it up higher and made it an angry motion.

Cooper Turner, the partner who tried the case, didn't want to have anything to do with the motion. I took it over to Judge Marion Boyd, the sole judge in the Western District of Tennessee, and gave it my best, most persuasive argument, crying for justice on behalf of my poor old railroad. When I got through, Judge Boyd said, "Mr. Donelson, that's an interesting argument, but there is absolutely no law to support it, no basis for such a theory. Assistant U.S. district attorneys have been practicing before this court for many years, and we don't bar them from practicing before this court in other capacities." He denied the motion. I went back to report that to Colonel Canada, and he was not too happy.

Apparently, a reporter sitting in the courtroom was intrigued by my argument and thought it unjust for assistant U.S. DAs to appear in dual capacity before the same jury panels. He wrote a stinging article criticizing the judge and criticizing the practice, and he called Mr. Crump, who bought the argument, as well. Mr. Crump said, "I agree with you, young man, and I'll never support the appointment of another assistant U.S. DA who doesn't commit not to represent private clients before the district court as long as he is an assistant U.S. district attorney." It was at least 20 years before Garland Draper spoke to me. Garland had to resign as assistant U.S. district attorney to keep his lucrative practice of suing railroads in the Federal District Court.

Canada, Russell, and Turner paid me $150 dollars a month, and I kept any fees from clients I brought in myself. They told me a beginning lawyer had never been paid before. With so few young lawyers around, I had done well. Shortly before the colonel's death in the spring of 1944, I turned down an offer to become a junior partner with two former colleagues in the general counsel's office of the Civil Aeronautics Board in their new Washington firm with the Air Transport Association as their base client. My salary was to be $600 a month with a small share of the profits. When I told the colonel about the offer, as an inducement to stay, he gave me a $100 per month raise.

At the colonel's death, Mrs. Canada asked me to be a pallbearer, along with Vance Alexander, chairman of Union Planters Bank; Abe Plough, founder of Plough, Inc.; the president of Memphis Natural Gas Co.; and the president of Union Station Company. In retrospect, it was an unfortunate honor. After the funeral, Ed Russell called me to his office and said they were unaware Colonel Canada had given me a raise. He wanted to eliminate the $100 raise and have me pay the firm a third of the fees I collected from my own clients. I decided on the spot to quit. I had picked up some regular clients, Charles Freeburg, a homebuilder, and David Gibson, who had a soft drink bottling company. I recently probated the will of Freeburg, a client for over 60 years.

That certified check case that we won for the Union Planters Bank gave me an early moment of satisfaction. I had been out on my own for several months when Ed Russell called and said the certified check case was up on appeal. They needed me to argue the case before the Court of Appeals and would, of course, pay me for my time. I had the pleasure of telling Ed Russell I was awfully busy, but thought I could manage to squeeze it in. We won the case in the Tennessee Court of Appeals for the Western Division.

One other case at Canada, Russell & Turner is too good to overlook. Western Union, the national telegraph company, has almost faded from the scene in the last 50-odd years, but it was big in the mid-1940s. The colonel called me in. The manager of the Western Union office, Mr. Whitsitt, wanted us to represent a delivery boy charged with attempted rape. The young man delivering a telegram to a rooming house in South Memphis had unwisely gone into an adjoining room to hand the telegram to a woman in a nightgown. The kid was 17, and, at that time, there was a hiatus in the state law. Juvenile Court took care of people up to age 16, and Criminal Court took people at 18; 17-year-olds went to Probate Court.

The probate judge, Sam Bates, was a family friend, a hunting and fishing buddy of Stewart Poston, my father's lifelong business partner. The prosecuting attorney put the husband on first, who said he was coming into the building when he saw the young African-American teenager coming out of his room, and when he entered his room his wife was in the bed in a nightgown. He was incensed, raced back and got in his car and proceeded to chase down the delivery boy who was on his bicycle, run him down with his car, and hold him until the police came to arrest him. When I questioned him if he had seen anything, he said all he saw was the boy coming out of his room. The wife went on the stand and testified the young man came into the room to hand her the telegram and she was afraid he was going to attack her.

On cross-examination, I asked, "Did you ask him to come into the room?" She said, "Yes, he was knocking on the door across the hall, and he said he wanted to find the lady who lived there and I said, 'Give me the telegram because I know that she'll be back in a few minutes.' So he came into the room and he handed me the telegram." I said, "Well, did he touch you?" She said, "Oh, no." I said, "Did he attempt to get in the bed with you?" She said, "Oh, no." I said, "Well what made you think that he might attack you?" She said, "Well, he made an indecent proposal."

I put the poor kid on the stand, and he was terrified. This was Memphis in 1943. His story was much like the wife's except that he said he knocked on the door, and the woman called him and said, "What are you doing?" When he told her, she said, "Come give it to me."

The kid stated that he wasn't supposed to do that but "she had insisted." He said after some hesitation he walked into her room and "was surprised she was in the bed." He testified she said, "Come over and give me the telegram," and he gave her the telegram and left.

I questioned him, "Did you make any indecent proposal?" and he denied that he had.

When it was over, the judge dismissed the charges, because he thought it was a misunderstanding. He instructed, "Now I want the lawyers to approach the bench" (with a twinkle in his eye), and I knew he was up to something. He said, "I could not announce this in open court, but I wanted the lawyers to know that the basis of my ruling is: If everybody who has asked for some and didn't get it was in jail, we wouldn't have room enough for all of them." That was the one criminal case of my career.

I became involved in the American Bar Association when a lawyer from Oklahoma City named Jimmy Fellers, chairman of the Junior Bar Conference of the American Bar, visited me about setting up a Junior Bar in Tennessee in early 1945. He proclaimed me chairman of the Junior Bar for Tennessee, and we began to set it up. I attended my first American Bar Association meeting in Cleveland during the summer of 1945. My experience in the Junior Bar was challenging and useful. Elected to the council the following year, I remained very active until I reached 36, the maximum age limit. I made many fabulous friends, three lifelong friends: Jimmy Fellers and his wife, Randy; Carlos Morris from Houston, Texas, Chairman of Stewart Title Company, and his wife, Doris, all of whom have died; and Randolph Thrower and his wife, Margaret. Margaret has died. Randolph is now senior partner with Sutherland Asbill in Atlanta. I believe he is the only man to have been both commissioner of Internal Revenue and chairman of the Tax Section of the American Bar. We have continued the close relationship with Randolph Throwers, although I discontinued my active participation in the American Bar many years ago.

From 1945 to 1953, I listened to lawyers, young and old, about how firms operated, kept time records, and billed on an hourly basis. We discussed methods of compensation within law firms and the structure of compensation system to retain lawyers. As a member of the Junior

Bar, I chaired a major committee, the Public Information Committee, and served on the Public Relations Committee of the Senior Bar. I got to know George Morris, one of the deans of the bar and chairman of that committee; Bill Sutherland, senior partner at Sutherland Asbill in Atlanta; Dana Latham, senior partner of Latham & Watkins and later president of the American Bar; and a number of others. Through these leaders of the ABA I got a feel for the power and force of the whole American Bar.

I continued my activity in the Bar Association until 1979, the year I became the commissioner of Finance and Administration for Governor Lamar Alexander. My bar activities were a rewarding experience. After the Junior Bar, I became active in the Tax Section. I participated regularly, attending most meetings, and kept abreast of the latest developments in tax law. I chaired two different Tax Section committees. You benefited from the involvement to the amount you invested in it.

My stay with Canada, Russell, and Turner was fateful far beyond what I learned from working with Colonel Canada; I met my future wife, who was Colonel Canada's secretary. Janice Ost was five years younger than I, a lifelong Memphian, but I had never known her before joining Canada. We became good friends long before our first date. Our first date was not a real date at all. I invited her along to deliver Christmas baskets to the tenants in some duplexes Charlie Freeburg and I owned in Orange Mound. Charlie and I were longtime friends through Idlewild Church. He wanted to be a homebuilder. He found land; we formed a partnership. I did the books, some of the legal work, title, FHA loans, etc. These duplexes were our first venture.

Charlie then joined up with Mark Hammond in a real estate firm. Mark, with a great eye for real estate, found land cheap that had real potential. The three of us bought another tract of land and sold part of it to Wallace Johnson, the biggest homebuilder of his day, holding back enough for Charlie to build more houses. Then we bought a third tract on Shotwell. Charlie moved up, building nicer houses. We sold them for $4,000 and made a nice profit. Years later, they sold for $40,000.

I met Charlie one day and he handed me $400 in cash, a down payment on one house. I returned to the office; it was late so I didn't take it to the bank. The next morning I couldn't find the cash. I searched everywhere—at home, our trash, the office trash. It was nowhere to be found. Charlie was nice about it, but I was embarrassed. About a year later I opened a file and found the $400 in cash. I had been working on a file, put the money on the top of the open file, put other papers on top and closed the file. It was a happy find, and Charlie was grateful.

Mark was drafted. He told me to keep buying and selling land tracts. "Don't let Charlie build houses on them. That's no way to make money," he said. It was Charlie's initiative, and he built. We did sell one tract of 12 lots on Highland Park. Then we bid on the Golightly tract, a dairy farm on the northwest corner of Highland and Poplar. Unfortunately, Hall Jones outbid us. In 1945, when Charlie's brother, Nelson Freeburg, came home, they went in together and my partnership with Charlie ended. When I married, I had over $10,000 in the bank, a tidy sum in those days. Charlie and Nelson became successful homebuilders and good clients.

LEWIE DONELSON
A PHOTO ALBUM

Full of potential

My brother, Billy, and me with our mother, Katharine Loring Campbell Donelson

The Donelson boys

Andrew Jackson, seventh president of the United States,
and husband of my ancestor, Rachel Donelson Jackson

The young equestrian

A golden childhood

(Top) Four generations of Donelsons: My father, Lewis R. Donelson, Jr.; me holding a picture of my grandfather, Lewis R. Donelson, Sr.; and my son, Lewis R. Donelson, IV. (Below left:) The all-star. (Below right): My cousin and "father-in-the-law," Judge John Donelson Martin.

Class picture at Choate. (Below): Graduation day from Southwestern (now Rhodes College) in 1938 and 49 years later, with an honorary degree from my alma mater, 1987.

Accepting the Rhodes Distinguished Service Medal, Commencement 2001, alongside Rhodes Board of Trustees Chair Spence Wilson

Lewis
Donelson
has

courageability*

*the courage to say it
the ability to do it

for
councilman
at-large

POSITION 4

Running for a Memphis City
Council seat in the 1960s

Breaking ground for
the Rivermont Club.
(Below): On the
campaign trail

With my wife, Jan

Mr. and Mrs. Donelson, February 3, 1945. (Below): Our children, Lewis, IV, Janice, and Loring

With President George H.W. Bush and staff aboard Air Force One
(Below): At the 1964 Republican National Convention with Charlie Howell,
my deputy while I was state commissioner of Finance and Administration

The Tennessee GOP: Lamar Alexander, Howard Baker, me, and Fred
Thompson. (Below): Trustees of the Paul Barret, Jr., Trust: John Douglas,
Graves Leggett, and me holding personal library cards at the announcement
of Paul's gift of the Paul Barret, Jr., Library to Rhodes College, April 30, 2001.

90th birthday party at the firm

FOURTEEN

MARRIAGE TO JANICE OST

My romance with Janice gradually evolved from friendship to love. Then in the summer Jan decided to go back to Northwestern in Chicago. I went up to see her and told her I loved her and wanted to marry her, and she agreed. She wanted to finish college, but I wanted to get married. We agreed to marry in February 1945. Jan said that if she'd known me better, she would have made me wait. My response was, "Then you would have been married to someone else, because I was ready to get married." In any event, it was the best thing that ever happened to me. We were married for 65 years, and despite our ups and downs, when she died, we loved each other more than ever.

When Jan went away to school, I started to visit with her mother Sunday afternoons, and she and I became close friends before I became a member of the family. Jan's family was always loving to me, as my family was to Jan. We used to tease and say that if we got divorced, that I would go home to her parents and she would go home to mine. Our wedding day was February 3, 1945.

My brother got leave to come home and to serve as my best man. Buddy Miller, Hubert Turley, and Winston Braun, my closest friends, were away in the service. Hubert had gotten into the Army as a doctor and was away in training and could not participate in the wedding, although when he married a month later I was able to be in his wedding.

Sometime in the spring of 1944, Hubert and I were sitting on the porch at the University Club, refreshing ourselves after a tennis match. This good-looking girl walks by and spoke to me. Hubert said, "Who is that?" I replied, "Hubert, she's not your type; much too nice for you," an indirect comment on his current taste in girls. He said, "No, I'm really serious." So I became matchmaker. Less than a year later, he and Aggie married. Hubert and I played tennis and golf together; double-dated a lot. He is a wonderful person, able, and down-to-earth.

One of my best Hubert stories goes back to the mid-1930s. In the summer my brother and I worked in Shelby Warehouse, which was operated by our father. Our job was to unload boxcars. In a Memphis summer this was extremely hot work. Hubert begged me about coming down to work with me. One day we had four carloads of dried beans in 100-pound sacks to unload. I called Hubert. He arrived about 1 p.m. on a scorching day; the heat in the boxcar was almost unbearable. We opened the first car door, and to my dismay, it had been loaded up to the doors. Usually, they left room to pull in a float on which we would load the bags then pull the float into the warehouse (of course unair-conditioned), and stack the beans about head high. Hubert, very macho, said he'd clear the door. When he finished, water was running in his shoes. I had practiced handling the big heavy gunnysacks, and I was merciless, working him without stopping. When we finished about five, Hubert went to get his pay, 80 cents—four hours at 20 cents an hour. He looked at it with disgust and said, "My father has been telling me I didn't know the value of a dollar. Well now I do." He never came back.

I learned a great deal from my wife. I was amused when George W. Bush was asked the question what he had learned from his wife. He said, "To listen," and I found the same thing. I have been influenced more by her than she has by me. She taught me not to take myself too seriously and to let my sense of humor, which was not bad, show. In making public speeches, she improved my effectiveness by introducing humor into those occasions and taking a self-deprecating attitude. When we married I was very serious-minded. A picture of me in the Southwestern newspaper office showed me standing in the door concentrating thoroughly. The caption read, "Quiet, I'm thinking." That was the impression people had of me then, and they were correct.

As I mentioned, most of my closest friends were away in the service. Dr. Sam Carter, also 4-F after tuberculosis during his residency, was one of my groomsmen. We remained close until he died, although he had lived in Harlingen, Texas, for many years. Though I grew away from Hubert and Winston, Buddy and I remained close until his death. Our friendship was the longest of my life, over 75 years. He was loyal always. I became close to his parents after we were grown. They looked on me as Buddy's older brother, and both charged me with taking care of him and his six daughters. It was a charge I took seriously. As a result, I represented the Miller family for over 50 years until both Buddy and his wife Sis died.

Charlie Freeburg, another groomsman, and I remained good friends until his recent death. Another friend from Southwestern, David Gibson, a college fraternity brother, died many years ago. Harold Falls was the other groomsman. We grew apart, but have remained friends, although he has now died. All of Jan's bridesmaids have either died or moved out of town, but she still remained close to two of them, Jackie Goodrich Gleaves and Louisa McLean Stephens.

We went to New York and Washington for our honeymoon, traveling by train. Two funny stories: Jan went to the restroom on our Pullman and came back to borrow some money to tip the attendant. She came on the honeymoon with 25 cents. Later, she went again and didn't return for a long time. Finally, I went to look for her. She was waiting outside the door, not of the restroom, but of a drawing room. She didn't see well without her glasses. Next morning, the occupant of the drawing room, a dapper-looking man who worked for one of my clients, came out. Jan thought with horror about her reaction if he had opened the door. We went to New York primarily to see my grandmother Campbell (Nama to me) who was too ill with cancer to come to the wedding.

We stayed at the Barbizon Plaza, where my father and I stayed on my first trip to New York. I knew New York well, having visited many times during my Choate and law school years. I delighted in introducing Jan to New York. She saw her first Broadway play, "The Moon is Blue;" we went to Radio City and saw the Rockettes. We dined overlooking the skating rink in Rockefeller Center. We went to the usual tourist sights, Battery Park, the Statue of Liberty, the Empire State Building, Fifth Avenue, Central Park, the subways. A perfect and wonderful time, except for one night: We planned a big evening, dining, dancing, and a floorshow at the St. Regis, one of New York's finest hotels. In those days, as an aftermath of my gallbladder operation, I took hydrochloric acid in diluted form after meals. I probably neglected it, and got terribly sick—nausea, etc., and we had to hurry back to the hotel. Jan, of course, wanted to be helpful and comforting, but all I wanted was to be left alone. After a while, she understood.

The first morning in New York, Jan was decked out in her going-away suit with a hat and a dainty veil to show to my grandmother. We stepped out of the hotel into a snowstorm. I was eager for Jan to ride the subway and didn't want to pay for a cab ride to the Bronx. By the time we arrived at the Freedman home, the veil was wet. Nama's friend, Mrs. Crutcher, who had told her about the home and persuaded her to buy in, wanted to be helpful. She got an iron and proceeded to try to iron the veil dry. Unfortunately, Mrs. Crutcher didn't see very well, and tore it to pieces. We had rushed out with only a continental breakfast, and we made a meal off of Nama's very expensive dark Belgian chocolates. Jan was embarrassed when she realized how expensive they were. I knew that Nama wanted me to have whatever my heart desired. While she was frail, she was alert and still herself in spirit. She and Jan had a common bond, Christian Science, and they were immediately simpatico. We had several long visits during our stay in New York. It was a wonderful farewell, for we both knew we would not see each other again. She died in December, right before Christmas. She had a great spirit, forever young, a delightful person and a major part of my growing up.

Then we went on to Washington. I wanted Jan to see the sights of the Capitol and the law school. We stayed at the Wardman Park Hotel off Connecticut Avenue on Woodley Road. I had lived across the street, and boarded around the corner in a house that faced the Stimson property. Henry Stimson, a cabinet member in F.D. Roosevelt's administration, had a magnificent piece of land with a historic house.

Two outstanding restaurants in Washington in those days were Harvey's, which adjoined the Mayflower Hotel, and the Occidental, which adjoined the Willard Hotel. We went to Harvey's for lunch. Jan, an adventurous eater, loved to try new things. She saw turtle soup on the menu, and ordered it. It was priced at about a dollar. It turned out that the special of the day was Diamondback Terrapin Stew. When the waiter brought in a large tureen on a trolley and began to dish up the stew, she discovered her mistake—price: $7.50, a most expensive lunch for those days. But she enjoyed her new gourmet dining experience.

One evening we went out with my closest cousin, Marianne McKellar, and her husband, Bill Highburger. Marianne, the youngest daughter of my father's sister and thus my first cousin, spent weeks at our house. Her mother was divorced. She was between me and my brother, Bill, in age, almost the sister we never had. Her husband was the art and layout director for *U.S. News & World Report*. As we walked along behind them toward dinner, they held hands. Janice was touched and asked, "How long have they been married?" I replied, "Seven years." Jan said, "I fully expect to be married to you all my life, but seven years, that's a long time."

When we returned from our honeymoon, we had not arranged for any place to live because we expected to start immediately building our first home. My mother heard a fraternity house on the Southwestern campus was available for rent, because the chapter was inactive during the war. It had been occupied by an Army officer who was teaching a training course. Mother was a little dismayed at the possibility we might live with her and found us this place to live. We spent the first nine months of our married life in the fraternity house.

A typical fraternity house, it had a huge chapter room downstairs, a small kitchen in the back, with a bath downstairs. Upstairs, we used the chapter room for our bedroom. It was pretty Spartan, but as honeymooners we did not mind.

Immediately upon our return, Gilbert Wilson, who had been the chapter adviser for the SAE chapter of which I had been a member, asked me to take over the job, which was convenient for me. This began my career of nonpaying tasks for what I considered worthwhile causes. I enjoyed it thoroughly and served as chapter adviser for about 10 years. I got to know several generations of SAEs. This broadened my acquaintances into a younger generation. One of those was Paul Barret, Jr., who many years later became my client, and I handled his estate.

I remember one minor domestic tragedy of early married life. On our first Sunday back from our honeymoon, Jan decided to fix a special Sunday breakfast. She made biscuits from scratch and scrambled eggs and bacon and, of course, milk and orange juice, and she was going to serve it to me in bed. I had never cared for breakfast in bed, but I couldn't refuse such a loving gesture. In the entrance to the chapter room, a small strip of steel, apparently there to reduce the draft, was loose. Jan, with everything on a tray, tripped over this bit of steel, and the whole thing went splashing down. I rushed down and she was crying. I tried to console her, picking up the scrambled eggs off the floor and putting them back on the plate, gathering up the biscuits and bacon. We had our first great crisis on the first Sunday morning at home. I probably ate it all off the floor, introducing Jan to how men aren't that concerned about cleanliness.

FIFTEEN

IDLEWILD

When I attended Southwestern, it was predominantly Presbyterian, moreso than it is today, and encouraged discussions of religion and religious issues. That atmosphere pervaded the campus. One vivid memory is a discussion group about predestination. We argued about exactly how it worked. Jameson Jones, whom we all called Hinky, said, "I don't know if I can tell you exactly how it works, but I can tell you one thing. I am going back to my room now to study and on my desk is a Hershey Bar. I don't have to eat that Hershey Bar but God knows I will." One of the most powerful descriptions of predestination I ever heard.

Choate was an Episcopal school with chapel every day. We had guest preachers most Sundays and, being in the New York area, some powerful preachers taught including the headmaster, Dr. George St. John, an Episcopal priest. When I was in law school we attended the New York Avenue Presbyterian Church with Peter Marshall as the senior minister, certainly one of, if not the best, preacher I ever heard. He held you spellbound.

In one sermon, he talked about a wealthy man who gave a Christmas party but none of his friends could come. He sent his chauffeur to invite street people to the Christmas celebration. Initially the invitation was met with disbelief, but the chauffeur persuaded about 20 to come. It was a Christmas dinner with presents and Christmas carols. By the end of the evening everyone was calling each other by their first names. Dr. Marshall presented a vivid picture of the occasion. You could sense the moment. He ended the story by telling how they got together and sang "Silent Night" at the end. Then he stopped; silence hung in the air. Everyone was waiting. It felt as if no one were breathing. He concluded, "Of course, this really didn't happen, but think how often it should happen."

Another story of Dr. Marshall's I remember vividly is based upon the story of Alvin C. York and the men he inspired. Alvin York got the Congressional Medal of Honor and most of the other men got medals and awards. He traced the lives of those people subsequent to the event: Sergeant York had a reasonably successful life; many of the others were failures. One lived in a shack made out of old license plates, another on the street, an alcoholic. All were in dire circumstances. Peter Marshall went on to say that sometimes if you have inspiring leadership, you can have great courage in a great crisis, but when you are by yourself and face the challenges of everyday life, it is much harder to show real courage. He ended by saying that is what we are supposed to get from Jesus, inspiration that is with us every day.

Peter Marshall, a remarkable man, was an important part of my faith. Even in those days, when I worked 48 hours a week, going to law school 10 hours a week, studying probably another 30 to 40 hours a week, I still felt moved to get up and attend church on New York Avenue to hear Peter Marshall.

When I taught junior high classes, I told them stories about Dr. Marshall, who died during this period. The young Sunday school kids asked the hard question, "Why would God let a man like Peter Marshall die so young?" I struggled with the usual answer: "Our minds are too small to understand God's ways." Several years later, Peter Marshall's wife wrote a book about him. There was a movie and other nationwide recognition, and I pointed out to the young girl and the other students in the Pioneer Department how God's plan worked. Marshall's untimely death called attention to his great service. He probably had more influence for good after his death than before. God does work in mysterious ways.

A strong Presbyterian tradition abides in our family. My great-great-grandfather, my great-grandmother's father, James Glasgow Martin, was a Presbyterian minister, the fifth in succession of Presbyterian ministers carrying that same name. As I previously mentioned, my great- great- great-grandfather's mother, Catherine, was a daughter of Sam Davis, the first Presbyterian minister at the first Presbyterian Church in the colonies. My father was raised as a member of Second Presbyterian Church and his father and mother were active in that church. I recall that on the cornerstone of the old Second Presbyterian Church at Hernando and Pontotoc, Lewis R. Donelson is listed as treasurer of the church. My grandfather also was a longtime elder. My father became attracted by Dr. Crow, a minister at Idlewild. Daddy heard him preach, met him, and decided to move his membership there, sometime around 1919 or '20. I was two or three years old. I was baptized at Idlewild and joined as a church member in my youth. The earliest church building I remember was on the corner of McLean and Union, the southwest corner. I recall sitting restlessly in the pews there.

My father was on the committee that called Dr. Young to the church about 1932. Dr. Young also had a big influence on me. I have many strong memories of him, particularly passages of Scripture from his sermons, for example, putting on the "armor of God." I attended Sunday school and church regularly and became soundly grounded in the Bible. This was greatly enhanced when I took two courses in the Bible at Southwestern and courses in philosophy and in ethics from Dr. Kelso. I was active among young people of the church and a speaker at one early youth Sunday. At Southwestern, with a strong group of ministerial students, we all discussed religion, the problems of life, and our personal philosophies.

My brother and I vividly remembered the groundbreaking ceremony for the new church on Union, between Evergreen and Auburndale, but not the dedication of the church building. We probably were banned from the dedication because we behaved so badly at the groundbreaking. I did learn in later years that our father was the chairman of the committee that handled the dedication services. He probably didn't feel he could handle two lively little boys with all his other responsibilities.

I have more memories of Sunday school, particularly Ms. Goodwin who taught me in the 12th grade, and Hunter Lane who taught when I was in college. Perhaps our church experiences will highlight the relationship I had with my parents. I remember listening to my father talk about one of the ministers, Stanley Frazier. Frazier wasn't doing well in the ministry and considered leaving to return to life as a layman, and he did so. After the conversation, my father answered my questions about why this was happening. I was probably 13 years old and my questioning was not unusual.

When I returned to Memphis after law school, I immediately began to teach Sunday school in the Pioneer Department for junior high ages. I was a teacher, then superintendent of that department. One day I talked about Paul's letter to the Romans and how Paul discusses the problem of what happened to those people who had never heard about Christ. How would they be saved if they didn't know Christ, and I told them Paul's answer was that they would be judged on what was in their hearts. I had a call from Dr. Young, because one student had talked about what I said to his parents, who had complained about me to Dr. Young. They held strictly to the statement of Jesus, "I am the Way." We had a delightful discussion, and, with great grace and skill, he basically said that he agreed with me about what Paul said in the letter.

On another occasion, we talked about how I never had what I would call an experience of being saved, a moment when I realized I was saved. I grew up in the church, I learned my catechism, I had become a member of the church, and I was baptized as an infant. I always had been a believer. There wasn't any time to which I could point that marked the moment of my conversion. I didn't experience a new life. Dr. Young and I talked about this at some length. He was patient and very concerned. He said he had the same experience. He never had the incident where he felt like he became a new person. He understood the meaning that when you join the church you do become a new person in the sense that you recognize and accept your responsibilities, your duties, and your changed attitude toward life.

I may have acquired my habit of using big words from Dr. Young. One of my friends said, "Lewie never uses a one-syllable word when a three-syllable word would do." Dr. Young, a son of a coal miner way up in the hills of West Virginia, had the most magnificent vocabulary. He was a big man with a booming voice. My brother claimed that when the church doors were open in the summer, you could stand across Union Avenue in Seessels' parking lot and hear every word Dr. Young said.

Dr. Young, chairman of the Southern Churches' Commission on Church Union, worked for several years to develop a plan for church union. His heart was broken when it failed to pass the required majority of the Presbyteries of the Southern Church. Elected moderator of the Presbyterian Church U.S. (Southern branch), he was certainly one of its leaders. He built Idlewild from a small church to a huge congregation with at least 4,000 members. On many Easter and Christmas services we had to put chairs in the aisles to handle the crowd. I grew up in awe of him; as I got older and got to know him as a person, I found him a delightful man with a tremendous presence.

My Sunday school teaching in the Pioneer Division, which included evening meetings, was a very fruitful period. Pioneers were extremely difficult to work with. Sometimes you were so disappointed, but there were tremendous rewards when you felt like you really reached a young mind. Those occasions made up for all the disappointments and the struggles to reach them. Many of the active members of the church today went through the Pioneer Department and were my students. That's always a heartwarming feeling.

After 10 years, I moved on to teach adults, with several different assignments. I ended up taking over as a teacher for the LeMaster class, which started in 1941, with my father as the first teacher. He taught the class almost until his death in 1966. I now have taught the LeMaster class for over 15 years. So, together, Daddy and I had taught the LeMaster class for 40 years. Some of the original members are still in the class. They laugh when my son comes and teaches for me. My father and I, my son and I, do not look very much alike, but we have all the same gestures and mannerisms. It is just hysterical. The class members are particularly touched and pleased by these recognizable similarities, passed from generation to generation.

The LeMaster class is a joy to me. We are truly Christian brothers and sisters who love each other, look after each other, and care for each other. As the years move on, the class shrinks, but we should be able to continue a few more years.

As a young man, I was elected to the diaconate and served a full term as a deacon, headed up the Every Member Canvass, and then at age 33, was elected to the session. I had the rare privilege of serving on the session with my father; it was unusual for father and son to serve together. (Back then, you were elected for life. Terms were created after I came on the session. I was governed by that and more than willing to be so.) My father was a wonderful churchman and a voice of wisdom who provided great leadership for the session. One of my best memories is of the sit-ins at churches in the early sixties. When the demonstrators came to Idlewild, they were seated naturally, a magnificent unplanned response. As far as I know Idlewild was the only white church in Memphis to seat these visitors when they arrived unannounced. Other churches followed, but this showed the leadership at Idlewild, part of our ministry, and our tradition. All of us are God's children.

After that Sunday, Idlewild held a meeting of elders and deacons, past and present, which filled up the T.K. Young Room, to discuss our response to the sit-ins. There were various suggestions on seating the participants in a special section, or in the balcony, or in the rear. My father, a wonderful man, taught me to be open-minded about race, but he was raised by parents who believed in segregation. My grandmother, a lovely lady, used to quote from the Bible that the blacks were the children of Ham and destined to be servants.

After the discussion went on and on, my father got up and said, "I move that our policy be to seat them like everyone else." The motion passed overwhelmingly. It was a proud moment for me and a great privilege to be there. I served on the session a number of times, and then was elected as one of the trustees.

In the middle of the Depression, Idlewild struggled with the budget, particularly with debt. The original plan was to construct the church building for $500,000, but it cost more. The church borrowed $125,000 from First National Bank of Memphis to complete the building, and paying those two debts was a tremendous burden. One legendary story: The church got several months behind in payments. The bankers in St. Louis who held the initial mortgage made threatening noises about bringing the payments up-to-date. James D. Collier, Sr., treasurer and a pillar of the church, who watched expenses like a hawk, prepared a brochure explaining the church would bring the interest up-to-date, spread out the payments on the principal, and keep them current. A committee from the church went to St. Louis to discuss the plan with the bank. Another church elder and a trustee, Al Pritchard, was a successful plumbing contractor and a wonderful, but somewhat salty, man. Also among the group was Longstreet Heiskell, an elder also acting as church attorney, and Mr. Buxton. The bank brushed aside Collier's carefully prepared brochure and insisted the mortgage be brought up-to-date immediately. Finally, Mr. Pritchard, who was called Uncle Al, said, "Do you gentlemen have a preacher?" The banker replied, "Oh, no, what are you talking about? We are a bank." Mr. Pritchard lowered the boom and said, "Well, you've got a church." Mr. Heiskell told me that changed the whole tone of the conversation and the church leaders were able to work out an agreement with the bankers and get the church back on solid financial footing.

As I noted earlier, the original note came from the time when the church was under construction and struggling to meet the costs. The church borrowed the additional $125,000 from First National Bank of Memphis, which held the second mortgage on the property. The trustees signed the note individually. I know from Mr. Heiskell, whose father was one of the trustees who signed the note, that the bank held up the closing of Judge Heiskell's estate for a number of years because of this. A foreclosure of the first mortgage would have wiped out the second mortgage and left the trustees financially responsible for their share of the First National note. Thus, the Idlewild trustees, who were individually and personally responsible for the church debt, became a very influential body with unusual power and influence. It was unique among Presbyterian churches. I can remember Dr. Jones and all the subsequent ministers saying, "Why do the trustees at Idlewild Church have so much power?" I explained to them the fact they had been the signors on the note and what they said carried great weight. The debt has long since been paid off and the true power of the trustees has disappeared. But tradition has given them a heavy voice in major decisions in regard to church property and church priority.

Dr. Young grew the church dramatically and soon the financial troubles were behind it. When I was at Southwestern, I spoke at the Youth Program, my first appearance in the pulpit. My parents sat in the third row on the west side of the sanctuary where I still sit unless it is pre-empted by a large baptismal group. I have many personal memories of Dr. Young which I've mentioned earlier. As an example of how young and brash I was in those years, once when I headed the Every Member Canvass, I went through the pledge cards and made a suggested gift on every card. What a furor, but it did greatly increase the giving.

Another memory of Dr. Young: We talked one day about teaching Sunday school and he said to me, "Lewie, you know the worst thing about being a minister is the inevitable return of the Sabbath. Having to preach every Sunday and when you have stayed at a church as long as I have, you've got to prepare a new sermon every week. Of course, when I go out of town, I get out an old one that went over well and use it. But when I am in town I have to come up with a new sermon every Sunday."

I am not sure the size of the church when Dr. Young arrived, but by 1950, when he was at his zenith of power and influence, we had

4,000 members—the largest, the strongest, and most influential congregation in the Presbytery and perhaps in the Southern church.
Dr. Young was old school, not wearing any vestments, preaching in a
swallowtail coat. Also, he would not marry divorced people.

When Dr. Young called on my wife, right after our first baby, they
talked about childbearing, how large she had gotten and how good it
felt for her to be slim again. Dr. Young, a very large man, said, "Well,
Jan, I got on the scale this morning and it showed 275 pounds." And
I said, "Tom Young, you are nobody's baby now." Jan loved that.

I was elected to the session before Dr. Young died. My father was
the chairman of the search committee to call his successor. I recommended he look at Paul Tudor Jones. Paul had graduated from Southwestern before I arrived, but I knew Tom and Jameson, his two
brothers. Jameson came to Washington to work on his doctorate. Since
my roommate Frank Campbell had volunteered for the Army, I had
an extra bed. Jameson and I lived together for six weeks or so.

When Paul Tudor arrived at Idlewild, I went to him and explained
I understood how it was to be a minister, going from church to church
and every relationship he established being church oriented. I said to
him, "You know, I understand a pastor's relationship with the parish-
ioners. I want to be your personal friend apart from your relationship
as my pastor." Paul was delighted, and we became close personal
friends. Until the time of his final illness, we had lunch together at
least twice a month, a joyful relationship that included his wife "T."
While the relationship was influenced by my being a parishioner, it
was far more than I had hoped.

Through our friendship I became even more involved in church
matters. Through Paul I became a member of the citywide Community Relations Committee. Also through Paul I became involved in
many difficulties of integrating the Presbyterian Church. Paul would
say, "Lewis, something is coming up at Presbytery next month; you
had better go." He persuaded the session to send me as a delegate,
and I would be one of his spokesmen on the floor. He could work
behind the scenes, and I, with the help of many others in our church,

could carry the ball openly. We were, for instance, able to persuade the Presbytery to adopt the resolution mostly enforced by all the congregations of seating African Americans as any other worshipers.

When Paul first began to preach about integration and brotherhood, I remember walking out of Idlewild one Sunday and Charlie Freeburg said, "Boy, that was another one of those grating sermons." Charlie was noted for his direct way of expressing himself. He meant the sermons grated on your conscience. Charlie and I agreed with the sermons, but knew the difficulty of the task.

After the sit-ins began, I was appointed to work with the Presbytery to resolve various issues. Dr. Millard, a saintly, retired minister from Evergreen Church, chaired the committee. We met in the Hill Board Room at Rhodes. Dr. Millard began the meeting with a prayer about brotherhood and the love of Christ. That could have introduced a reasonable discussion. I will never forget what happened next: A member of the delegation from Second Church spoke up and said, "We spent $4 million (or whatever number) on that sanctuary and we don't want any G.D. niggers desecrating it." I responded, "It is obvious that there is no point in discussing anything with this group." I moved that we adjourn, which we did.

Through the skilled intervention of Paul Tudor and Dr. Millard and others, Second Church did vote to seat them. That elder, who shall remain unnamed, helped lead the group from Second to form Independent Presbyterian, which has become a wonderful church, even though its name is a contradiction in terms: Presbyterian churches are connectional, not independent; they have to be members of a Presbytery, Synod, and General Assembly. Even though Independent does belong to a Presbytery and national denomination, it doesn't sound like it.

A group within Idlewild met privately to stir up trouble against the church's position and against Paul Jones as the minister. Paul and I discussed it and I don't know if he came up with the idea or I did, but we agreed that I would attend one of their meetings, which alledgedly were open to the public. When I appeared at the meeting, I was the skunk at the lawn party. I said, "Look, you have a right to your opinion, you can do whatever you want to do, the session would be glad to hear from you. We will give you an unlimited time to present your views and you just call me or call Dr. Jones and tell us what time you want to be there. We will have a session meeting with your views as the main item on the agenda." Then I left. The group broke up. Most returned to the church and remained members. A few moved to other churches where the desegregation policy was more to their liking.

At the apex of the racial disputes I was asked to represent the Presbytery in a lawsuit over the ownership of a church building in Jackson, Tennessee. The minister led a majority of the congregation out of the denomination and they attempted to take the building with them. We successfully sustained the rights of the loyal minority to retain the property. The judge went on to become a justice of the Tennessee Supreme Court. A leading Baptist, he told me of his fascination with the governmental structure of the Presbyterian Church.

During Paul Tudor's ministry, I was on the session, except when I went off in the rotation. I attended many Presbytery meetings, a few Synod meetings and one General Assembly. I've already mentioned my various duties as a Sunday school teacher. At one point, I became a local expert on Job and taught a six-week series of lessons on Job to adult classes. Then, I taught the series to other churches including Calvary, Grace-St. Luke's, and First Presbyterian in Tupelo.

When I joined the Board of Trustees, three trustees were—to put it kindly—in their dotage. They came to the meetings but could not understand the proceedings. I complained to Edward LeMaster, "Ebbie" as everyone called him, that we ought to get them to resign. Ebbie was too kind to ask them, but when he stepped down, I succeeded him and pushed through a proposal to change the church rules to prevent election of a trustee after 75 years of age and limit terms to three years, not life, the same as elders and deacons did. When I was over 75, someone suggested another term, but I refused. Idlewild Church has so much talent, longtime members need not hog those positions. After I served on the session into my 80s, I applied the same rule to myself as an elder that I had for the trustees. I miss being on the session and a part of church decisions, but it is a good rule.

When Paul Tudor retired he told me, "Lewie, I will not return to the church for five years. My successor needs to establish himself. It is unfair for me to linger around and overshadow him. Even if you die during this time, I will not conduct your funeral service." It showed how wonderful Paul Tudor was and how much he understood the dynamics of ministerial succession. What a selfless, kindly, thoughtful person he was. He lived long enough to come back to the church, but that was long after Henry Strock, his successor, thoroughly established himself with the congregation.

I chaired the committee to call Henry Strock. During the interim, church officers held a retreat during which I gave a sermon: "Idlewild's Future Challenges." Because of its excellent reception, I actually got to preach from the pulpit one time. My thoughts had elements of a sermon. I was extremely pleased and flattered by the reception of the congregation. I described the experience to my son, then in seminary, and he said, "Daddy, I know you did extremely well, and I wish I had been there to hear it, but I can't resist telling you what we all say in seminary." And I said, "What's that?" He said, "We all say, everybody's got one good sermon."

So true, and this also describes something of my relationship with my wonderful son. I hoped he would become a lawyer and follow in my footsteps. After he finished college, he told me he gave law much consideration. He realized that if he became a lawyer, followed in my footsteps, and did well, everybody would say his success was handed to him on a silver platter. If he fell on his face they would say, "Gosh, he must be the stupidest guy in the whole world, to have that opportunity and not be able to pull it off." Then he said, "What I want to do is go to seminary." I answered, "I am disappointed, but that is the highest calling any person can have, and I am proud you are going to do it." He has gone on to an outstanding career. He attended Louisville Seminary and graduated with high honors. He won the same fellowship to graduate school Paul Tudor had won at the same seminary. Lewie went to the University of Chicago and took a doctorate in

New Testament. Eighty-six students started their doctorate in theology at Chicago; he was the first to complete his doctorate after five years. His thesis concerning pseudepigraphy and the theology of First and Second Timothy and Titus was published. For more than 25 years, he has been professor of New Testament at Austin Presbyterian Theological Seminary. He loves teaching and excels in his profession. I am proud of him.

My oldest daughter was a Presbyterian elder, in Knoxville. My youngest daughter was active in the church in Clearwater. Because of family problems, she has been less involved in recent years.

When Corrine Nienhuis preached her first sermon at Idlewild, I congratulated her and I told her about my son's observation. When she preached a second time, she looked down at me in the third row and said, "The first time I preached, one elder came up and told the old seminary comment that everybody has one good sermon. Since this is my second, I am very nervous." She did well again.

Another Idlewild story sticks in my memory. John Coates, acting chairman of the church endowment fund, asked me to talk about the endowment fund. When I got up to speak, I looked out over the congregation and these feelings just popped out: "I love this church." It was from the heart. I do. I don't know of anybody who remembers that speech except the beginning. I continue to be active in the church.

I teach Sunday school every Sunday and I am reminded frequently of Dr. Young's comment about the inevitable return of the Sabbath. In my 60 years of Sunday school teaching I have learned much more than my class members. It has been a great experience, increasing my knowledge of and grounding in the Christian faith. I am extremely proud of Idlewild Church, a leader in the Presbytery and in the entire denomination. Idlewild demonstrates that the church has within its member people of conservative views of the Christian faith along with those who are liberal theologically. Dr. Young, Dr. Jones, Dr. Strock, Dr. Lowry, and now Steve Montgomery have dealt with that problem ably, and we have lived together as brothers and sisters in Christ through many years.

With Christianity under attack in Europe and the United States and growth limited to Africa and Korea and similar places, we must draw together as Christians instead of pulling apart. We all have a right to make our own interpretation and understanding of the Christian message, which is for all. Christianity has been received by people of different backgrounds, mindsets, circumstances, cultures with each bringing different approaches, but after all, we are all Christians. We all believe that God sent Christ to show us how to live, to act as our redeemer, to save us from our sins and give us the hope and prospect of eternal life. That's the basic message. Personal differences are based upon inevitable different attitudes toward life and toward faith. Yes, some people find Idlewild too liberal; others, too conservative. For the most part, despite our differences, we love each other and find brotherhood, and that is what Jesus came to teach us among many other things.

On my 90th birthday I received a letter from Leslie Ramsey Stacks, a member of one of my Sunday school classes when I taught in the Pioneer Department. She apparently saw an article about me in a Presbytery publication. I hadn't heard from her in close to 50 years, but she wrote me: "You have always been one of my role models. When I was a teenager, I took it for granted that a man who was an attorney and a politician would also teach Sunday school. It was not until I became an attorney myself that I had a clue how few busy professionals give as much time to their churches as you did. I was very impressed by the way you always put God and faith ahead of politics and popularity. I was a junior in high school when Martin Luther King was assassinated. I might not have known the details of what you were doing and saying in your political role at that time, but I had a firm understanding of your abiding grace and humanity in those most turbulent of circumstances. It was your example and that of my parents and some other folks at Idlewild that led me to believe that we were to always follow the will of God even when it is disfavored and might lead us to grief. The strife over the civil rights in Memphis in the 1960s certainly put such beliefs to the test, but you were one of the people who showed me that we can stand firm for what is right. I don't think I ever sat down and had a one-on-one conversation with you, and yet you have been a big influence on my life. You are one of the people who showed me what it looks like to be a faithful follower of Christ. You also showed me how much good one can do with a law degree. The reason why I left the ministry in the 1980s was because I found out it was impossible as a female minister to find a call and a place where my husband could also teach. When I tried to think of what else I could do that would be a faithful response to God, I thought of you and that led me to law school. I never saw law as a detour for ministry, but as a continuation. That was a gift to me and it has been invaluable."

Nothing has touched my heart as much as this letter. I remember Leslie, a bright, thoughtful and conscientious young woman. I had no idea of having so much influence upon her and perhaps she also was unaware at the time. She reminds us we never know our influence on people and the importance of influencing others in the best way possible.

The church has been a guidepost to my life, refocusing me when flushed with success and supporting me when facing difficulties and sorrow. A great deal of who I am and my community activities came from the inspiration and education at Idlewild Church. I know many people in the church are hypocrites, but the church holds many more good people than most other places. I sincerely believe the church, the bulwark of Christianity, Christ's instrument in the world, is here to stay.

SIXTEEN

SOLO PRACTICE
SNOWDEN & DAVIS

When I left the Canada firm, I arranged office space with an older lawyer, R. Lee Bartels; in return, I helped on some of his cases. Mr. Bartels' son, Billy Bartels, was a friend; we had gone to camp together. He died early in World War II.

I spent a year scrambling for business. During that time I represented a wife and infant son on a workmen's compensation claim in a wrongful death case. The man had worked on the line at Firestone, and it appeared that a defective machine had accidentally electrocuted him. The husband and wife were separated, but not divorced, at his death. She agreed the settlement would go to her infant son. I managed, over the strong objection of his family, to have the body exhumed. In those days, there was a lot of knee-jerk reaction to exhumations and autopsies. Pathological examination indicated he had been electrocuted. The condition of his body, particularly the fingernails and other signs of electrical shock was strong evidence; she got the maximum payment of $10,000. I made the maximum fee of $2,000, which made my year of solo practice successful.

One humorous incident about Lee Bartels concerned a long-standing receivership involving the old Memphis Building and Loan Association. Mr. Bartels represented a group of the creditors; Frank Glankler, Sr., represented the debtor. They proposed a settlement plan with a hearing to set a trial date. Mr. Bartels, always meticulous, represented many creditors, but others had their own attorneys. He had contacted them all and worked out a trial date with maximum availability for all the lawyers. He presented this to Chancellor Bejach in a chart.

Bejach glanced at it briefly, and then said, "I have discussed this with Mr. Glankler and we agreed upon a date," which Bejach specified. This date was completely unsatisfactory, according to the Bartels chart. At Bejach's ruling Mr. Bartels got very red in the face and as he walked out he said in a clear voice, "I didn't know that your honor had joined the law firm of Canale, Glankler, Loch & Little." A frightened hush came over the courtroom. I moved away because Bejach was not a judge to trifle with. He got extremely red in the face and then said, "Hand me back your chart and I'll see if that date is agreeable to Mr. Glankler."

Bartels was more than fair to me. I paid no rent and he wasn't demanding of my time. I shared his secretary, Mary Ann McNamara, who was most supportive. The Barretville Bank was his principal client. Years later I represented the bank and Paul Barret, Jr.'s., estate.

Another lift came from a lawyer who acted as a divorce proctor and a legislator. I filled in for him while the General Assembly was in session. A divorce proctor sat in on all divorce cases. Many cases were almost ex parte, one lawyer, and usually an absent husband, mostly routine work: "Where were you married? Have you been married before? Where were you divorced? Does your husband live in the state?"

One day, in answer to "Where were you divorced?" the plaintiff said, "I didn't get a divorce. I was married in another state before I came to Tennessee. Then I got married again here." I asked, "Did you tell your lawyer about this?" She replied, "Oh yes. He said not to worry about it." I arose and moved to dismiss. Judge John Wilson spoke up: "Both lawyers approach the bench." When we did, he turned to Mr. Passmore, the plaintiff's attorney, and inquired, "Did you know about this?" Passmore stammered and finally said, "She may have told me." Judge Wilson curtly replied, "I ought to hold you in contempt. I am going to dismiss the complaint and order you to refund the fee and pay the court costs yourself." The attorney was white, the plaintiff was black, and he knew she didn't need a divorce from the defendant. Perhaps she needed one from the former husband, because he was still alive but not in Tennessee. This showed why proctors were needed.

In the spring of 1945, Snowden & Davis approached me to join them to try tax cases. The firm, a tax boutique, had a number of contested tax matters, but no one with much trial experience. They made me a good offer. Both Judge Martin and Mr. Bartels recommended I take it. You might say I became a tax man by the backdoor by trying tax cases. My accounting courses in college and law school, plus two more tax courses, gave me some foundation.

John Snowden had been killed in World War II. Allan Davis was the senior partner, an excellent tax man with an accounting background. I worked with him from 1945 to 1949. I was already active in the American Bar Association, learning how other firms operated. In Memphis, most firms had no regular hourly rates. None, I believe, kept time. Most billed at the conclusion of the matter. One of my first reforms in my new firm: timekeeping and regular hourly rates (we added monthly billing after Donelson & Adams was formed).

We had some luck in our tax trials. An early one involved Bill Kent, a prominent businessman and major stockholder of Anderson & Tully, the Memphis timber company, now huge. Kent established several flight schools to train pilots during World War II and made his wife a partner in each, although her capital contribution was a gift from him. (Interestingly, Louise Campbell Kent was the only daughter of the renowned Dr. Willis Campbell, founder of Campbell Clinic and pioneer of modern orthopedics.) The real issue: Was the partnership a sham? This was before spouses were entitled to file jointly and get a rate equivalent to filing separately. We showed that his wife was an active participant in the partnership. The case was a family partnership case, which we tried and lost in the Tax Court, but won in the Sixth Circuit. By coincidence, the judge writing the opinion was Judge

McAllister. My Donelson grandmother was a McAlister (with different spelling). Judge Martin teased me, asking, "Who is the best judge you know besides Judge McAllister?"

This Sixth Circuit Court of Appeals case in 1948 was my first return visit to my old court. It got serious attention as one of the first such cases in the country and the first in Memphis. Unfortunately, the Culbertson case, another family partnership tax law case, was certioraried about two weeks earlier. The Supreme Court took the Culbertson case on appeal, and denied the government certiorari in Kent. I missed going to the Supreme Court, and never had another chance.

My second case for Bill Kent involved depreciation and other deductions on the flight training schools, and we were successful again, this time in the Federal District Court. I learned one lesson in that second Kent case, actually the Cohn case because Bert Cohn, his personal friend, personal lawyer, and partner in many of these ventures, was the named plaintiff in that case. I figured that Bert was a lawyer, and he understood the legal issues well and would be a great witness, so I put Bert on. He turned out to be a terrible witness. He qualified his answers and drew fine legal points; I got rid of him as soon as possible and put Bill Kent on the stand. Bill, the perfect witness, stuck to the facts; he clearly enunciated his position and his reasoning behind it. He seemed fully credible, not trying to adjust his testimony for what he thought the court might want to hear. (Actually, Allan Davis and I tried the first Kent case together. Davis participated with me in preparing the brief and made one cogent suggestion, which the court subsequently adopted. I had thought the argument too simplistic. I learned from that situation that courts appreciate simple arguments, particularly when very pertinent to the issue.)

The Eric Hirsch case, also a family partnership case, had an interesting twist. After we won the case and had been sustained in the Court of Appeals, we went back to the District Court to get a judgment for our refund. At this point, the IRS suddenly raised the issue of whether he had paid certain required payments on his tax estimate. Unfortunately for us, Hirsch was in the Coast Guard at the time the returns were filed and had accounts with several different brokerage companies. I am sure he had paid all of the taxes due. We found one payment from a brokerage house, but we couldn't find the others. Unfortunately, we had to take a reduction of the judgment.

I wanted to take the case back to the Court of Appeals, because we had attempted to get the payment records from the IRS; the IRS admitted, after the court allowed me to issue a subpoena, the records had been lost in a fire. Because the issue had not been raised at the original trial or at any of the previous examinations of the tax return, I felt we could win this case on appeal, but Hirsch had had enough. We took the reduced amount.

A different issue was involved in the case for J.E. Dilworth Company, a mill supply company with distribution all over the Mid-South and a subsidiary corporation in Jackson, Mississippi. In the late forties and early fifties, each corporation had its own tax exemption and graduated tax rate; you began at the bottom of the lowest rate with each new corporation and that produced a reduced overall tax liability. This resulted in a proliferation of corporations. The IRS contended that our client had created the subsidiary corporation only to save taxes. Our basic excuse was that a Mississippi corporation got a preference of 5 percent under Mississippi law on all bids for any state contract (Dilworth did a substantial amount of government business and this gave it a competitive advantage in Mississippi). In addition, we contended the importance of keeping Mississippi sales under Mississippi operations, distinguished from Memphis operations, because, in fact, the Memphis operations included North Mississippi and we wanted to keep the two offices distinct.

As was common then, the person who today would be the chief financial officer for the Dilworth Company was a woman, a bookkeeper. She was a smart person, but she was not a CPA; of course, CPAs in private business were rare. I carefully went over with her the proof as to how they had made a determination for allocating the overhead, and on direct examination she did extremely well. I waited somewhat nervously when the government's attorney cross-examined her.

He asked several perfunctory questions, and then he asked a long, involved question the gist of which was, "Isn't it true that at the year-end you and Mr. Dilworth would sit down and look at the overhead and see how much money that Mississippi corporation had made before the overhead allocation and you determined that overhead allocation to the maximum tax advantage of the two corporations?"

Before I could object, Judge Davies, the federal judge trying the case, said, "Don't answer that question, lady, he's trying to trick you." After that I knew we were going to win that case, and we did.

During this time, to get into Federal District Court you had to pay your tax, file a claim for refund, wait six months, and then sue. Because the defendant was the collector of Internal Revenue in Nashville, you had to file suit in the Federal District Court in Nashville, which meant a number of cases before Judge Davies, and I was successful in most all of them. Not exactly a pro-government judge, Judge Davies had the habit of sounding the docket, and you would go on that date and sit for the day to get your case set, an expense for my clients and a trip for me to Nashville. In one case, I was substantially ready for trial and didn't go up for the sounding of the docket on Thursday. The clerk called on Friday morning and said, "Your case is set for Monday morning." I had a fit. I called Judge Davies, and he said, "Mr. Donelson, you had a chance to be here and you chose not to be here; that indicated that you were ready at any time." I struggled and got ready. We went up and tried the case, and won. He decided it from the bench. When the case was over he said, "Mr. Donelson, aren't you glad I made you try this case?"

Allan Davis and I also won a major case for the Terminix Division of E.L. Bruce, which involved the deductibility of retreatment and repair expenses on houses treated for termites. Terminix is the largest termite treating company in the country, and E.L. Bruce was a large hardwood flooring company, one of Memphis' most prominent and largest employers. The Terminix Company, the franchisor, required every franchisee pay to an insurance company a portion of the revenue received from each treatment, which was deposited in a reserve account. When retreatment and repairs were required, the franchisee could request reimbursement from the reserve fund. It was not strictly a full dollar-for-dollar reimbursement, although if experience was good and retreatment and repair expenses were kept under control, it could be, but if they ran too high, the reserve fund could be exhausted and the franchisee would be at risk. At issue: how these expenses were handled for tax purposes, because the franchisee paid funds to the reserve when the original treatment was done. This is probably the only tax case I ever had won by trial tactics. There was no discovery, and you never knew the government's position until the trial.

The issue was complex. The Internal Revenue Service disallowed the deduction of repair and retreatment expenses, incurred for a bankrupt franchisee, then taken over by Terminix. The government's defense, a strong one, was that we would receive a reimbursement from the insurance company with whom the franchisee had made a deposit in that sale. We had not reported this as income, and appropriately so. In this instance, the franchisee had gone broke and the franchisor had taken over the operations and assumed its liability. The franchisor had not made the deposit. The bankrupt franchisee had. We had a complex defense of questionable validity. At one point I urged, and Allan agreed, to rest our case. When I said, "Plaintiff rests," it was like a stink bomb. We submitted proof as to the ordinary and necessary nature of the expenses for repairs and retreatment, the federal tax law standard for current deductibility. Clearly every termite company had to incur such expenses to stay in business. We proved our case; the government's burden was to show we had been reimbursed.

The government followed its usual practice of expecting the taxpayer to put on all of his or her witnesses, with the government proving its case with the taxpayer witnesses. We anticipated putting on Terminix's comptroller to explain how the repair and retreatment deposit was made by the franchisee and held by an independent insurance company and never received directly by Terminix. The insurance company would reimburse the bankrupt estate. As its successor, Terminix would benefit.

The government was caught flat-footed by our failure to put on proof about the reserve fund. Fortunately, it did not know who those witnesses were to be, and immediately moved for a recess. It received a one-day delay before resuming and placing on the stand the revenue agent, who tried to prove we had already been paid. I objected to this as hearsay. With the complications of the deposits being made by a completely separate company in which E.L. Bruce had no ownership interest, and with the franchisee company bankrupt, we determined that Bruce had a defense. We benefited indirectly from the reserve. Fortunately, the reimbursement evidence never made it in the record. As a result, we won the case.

Judge Boyd stated, "I do not understand clearly. I know something unusual is going on, but the plaintiff has certainly proved these expenses were ordinary and necessary expenses." We received letters from tax experts around the country, wondering how we had won. My only explanation was "trial tactics."

During the early 1950s, I had defended successfully a group of cotton men who traded in the futures market in a way that enabled them to create tax-free capital gains. Through Senator Kenneth McKellar, I obtained an appointment with the deputy IRS commissioner in Washington. The technique was complex; a simplistic version went like this: If you decided that cotton was going up, you would buy September cotton and sell one-half as much as you bought of March contracts. While these did not work in perfect tandem, they constituted a hedge, you might say, against a large loss. A long position held for more than six months was considered a long-term capital gain, and, therefore, under the law, you only reported half of that gain on your tax return. However, the short position, as a sale of something you did not own, was always considered a short-term loss; therefore you reported 100 percent of the loss. If you had a gain on the short-term position, you reported 100 percent of the gain. If you had a gain in the long position and an offsetting loss on the short, the result was a washout. Thus, buying long and selling short of one-half of their position, you had a loss that offset the entire gain because only

50 percent of the gain was reportable on the tax return, while 100 percent of the smaller loss fully canceled the gain under the tax code. Our clients had literally made hundreds of thousands of dollars on these transactions, which were in effect, tax-free, because of the use of short-term losses to offset the long-term gains. The total taxes saved were, for those days, considerable.

We fought all the way to the Deputy Commissioner's Office. The total tax saving involved was substantial and no one had the nerve to step up to that issue. At the hearing, I must have talked at least two hours explaining how this worked, with interruptions by the man who was chairing the hearing, and others. Few understood how cotton futures operated with the contracts—March, June, September, and December—or the more complex, varying cotton grades. They did understand the long and short situations and the tax implications of how long-term gains worked against short-term losses.

After my presentation, the IRS deputy commissioner said, "I don't see what is wrong with that. Guys on Wall Street have been doing this for years." This was a huge win and got much notoriety around Memphis among cotton men, the leading figures of Memphis business. This technique was similar to that used by today's hedge fund managers, but the tax loophole is gone. Now the rate is adjusted for long-term transactions without the 50 percent tax-free portion of a long–term capital gain.

These early triumphs from 1945 to 1954 show how I established the reputation on which we began the firm. I was young and aggressive and tried many cases that could have been settled. These successful trials added to the image of a firm that got results. A man came to me with a tax problem that I handled successfully. I asked how he came to me, he said, "Harold Rutstein recommended you; he said that you were very expensive but you were the best." I thanked Harold and told him to keep saying exactly that.

I also successfully settled a big case for the Mallory family, which involved South Memphis Land Company. Allan Davis had the creative idea that the tax basis of all the real property of South Memphis

Land was its fair market value as of March 1, 1913, not when purchased around 1905. This concept was correct. The code clearly states
that the tax cost basis of all assets held on March 1, 1913, the date the
federal income tax became effective, was its value on that date. We got
a favorable affidavit as to the value of the land on March 1, 1913, from
a real estate agent named Person (there is a street in South Memphis
named for him). Fortunately, he had died and there were no other
witnesses in 1947 to testify to 1913 land values in South Memphis.
Establishing our high value meant South Memphis Land Company
would be able to dissolve and distribute to their stockholders a large,
tax-free distribution, because the taxable income on dissolution was
only the excess of the 1948 value over the March 1, 1913, value.

Senator McKellar was a stockholder in South Memphis Land Company, having taken stock as his fee for incorporating the company. The
senator, as described earlier, was a relation by marriage. He became
highly interested in the case and got me an appointment with the top
IRS person in that division. After our conference, the IRS caved in. We
then dissolved South Memphis Land Company. Every stockholder
received a substantial tax-free distribution. Senator McKellar told me
this was his first real capital. Public officials were not well paid then.
He graciously invited me up for his "mortgage burning party" as he
called it, celebrating the payment of his debts.

In 1949, my senior partner, Allan Davis, died suddenly. We had
worked together closely for four years, and I became his right-hand
man. He must have had some warnings of heart problems; he had told
his clients if anything happened to him, they should come to me. Most
did. Allan was only 49 years old with the most creative tax mind I ever
encountered. Working with Allan was a joy. He taught me to be creative in tax planning. After Allan's death, I stayed with the firm for
five more years. Fred Brown and Stuart McCloy were older partners
in the firm. Because of Allan's legacy, I had the majority of the clients
and brought in the majority of the fees, but the older partners felt I
should receive less because I lacked seniority. Also, I doubted the future of tax boutiques. The big eight accounting firms were establishing

their own departments to handle tax disputes. Most large law firms were also establishing their own tax departments. It was going to be hard to live off the referral of tax matters, and I noticed that we were getting no additional business from most tax clients.

A client referred to me by another lawyer brought this home to me. I handled a tax problem for him. Later he called and asked a question that was not a tax question. I had asked if he had called the lawyer who referred him to me and he said he had not. I answered his question very simply, but when I called the other lawyer, his reaction made it clear he would not refer any future business. Tax is so pervasive; most businesses cannot separate out tax problems. My partners wanted to remain a tax boutique and did not want to build a larger firm with a broader base.

Snowden, Davis had grown, adding Sam Myar, Frances Loring, Donald Wellford, and Harry Wellford. We did well. I handled the tax mentoring of Sam Myar and Harry Wellford. In my training of Harry, I told him to call a client and tell him something he did not want to hear. Harry complained, "Lewie, you can do that so much better than I can." I responded, "Yes I can, but you've go to learn how to do it."

In April, Jan and I suffered one of the few tragedies of our most blessed lives. Our first child was stillborn. Jan was and remained all her life a juvenile diabetic. We were concerned about having any children. In this moment of emotional, personal stress, our faith stood us in good stead. Dr. T.K. Young was a rock of consolation, as were our parents, and my brother's steadfast comfort and counsel sustained us. Fortunately, Jan became pregnant again, and in September 1947 our first daughter Janice was born. She is one of the most gentle people of the world and a blessing to the whole family.

By that time, I was assistant scoutmaster of a scout troop at Idlewild Church, Troop 47. Charlie Freeburg was the head scoutmaster. Under our agreement, he handled scout meetings, merit badges, and such; I handled overnight hikes and camp-outs. Once when I was driving a truck down to Camp Currier in Mississippi, it broke down. Someone came along and agreed to ride the campers to the cabins. I stayed with the truck along with one camper, and we got the truck fixed in time to bring the troop back. You can imagine the risk of renting a truck shortly after the war when new trucks were unavailable and parts, scarce. We had some interesting experiences on our overnight trips. Everytime we went, a scout would cut his hand with an ax or step on a nail or get burned in a fire. All those campers who couldn't manage to cook their food would end up trying to eat it raw. These were fun days, and I enjoyed them. Some scouts became lifelong friends and acquaintances. Millen Darnel, our senior patrol leader, became a Presbyterian minister in Memphis. Coyle Shea, the scribe of the troop, became a well-known otologic surgeon. Others also became influential citizens in the community. After the young men began to return from the service, Charlie and I gave up our scouting responsibilities.

I also began to get more involved in the community. Edward Le Master, Jr., a longtime Idlewild friend and civic leader, asked me to join the board of the Travelers Aid Society. I moved up to president, and later regional vice president of National Travelers Aid. In 1949 we had a second child, a son, Lewis IV; and in 1954 our third child, another daughter, Loring.

Her name came from my mother, Katherine Loring Campbell. Her mother was Charlotte Loring Nicholson Campbell. The name came down through many generations from Charlotte Loring Putnam, wife of General Israel Putnam, a Revolutionary War general from Connecticut. Charlotte Loring Stone Nicholson, my great-grandmother, was from Ohio. When the Civil War began, she returned to Ohio; her husband joined the Confederate Army. She died during the war, never returning to Tennessee. My great-grandfather remarried a Kate Martin, likely another relative, who raised my grandmother. My grandmother was called Lora by her friends, because she didn't like Lottie. She named my mother Katherine Loring. We intended to name Loring Katherine Loring, but our close friends and next-door neighbors had a daughter named Katherine (Katie), so we decided one Katie was enough. Our Lori now uses the name Katherine Loring. Those early years of marriage and children were busy. I worked long hours and was seldom home. When Lewis was born he had colic for over six weeks. I tried to help, but Jan had a tough time. Lewis was born shortly after Allan Davis died. I was driving hard to hold his practice together, and Jan managed our young children and home life.

SEVENTEEN

MY OWN FIRM

B ecause we continued to quarrel over profits, I decided to leave Snowden, Davis in September 1954. Ben Adams had joined the firm one year earlier, and because of our friendship he agreed to come with me. Ben and I talked about including Sam Myar and Harry Wellford, but we were unable to reach an agreement with either one of them. Sam, a brilliant lawyer and rainmaker, died before he was 40. Harry and I remained good friends through politics and church. A fine lawyer, he went on the federal district bench and moved up to the Sixth Circuit Court of Appeals.

October 1, 1954, was the beginning date of the new firm Donelson & Adams. I love practicing law and I was good at it. My legal career and the growth of Donelson & Adams are integral to my memoirs. The initial plan was to separate the law practice from the rest of the story because I had two aspects to my public life: law practice and public and community service.

The origins of the present firm Baker, Donelson, Bearman, Caldwell & Berkowitz can be traced back to the 19th century. In 1888, James F. Baker, Howard Baker's grandfather, established a law firm in Huntsville, Tennessee. Howard's father, Howard Baker, Sr., joined his father and the firm opened an office in Knoxville. A major client for many years was the Southern Railway. In his almost 20 years of private practice, before his 1966 election to the U.S. Senate, Howard Baker was an able and successful trial lawyer all over East Tennessee. The firm, after several name changes, eventually became known as Baker, Worthington, Crossley & Stansberry. Howard, a true small town lawyer, did everything, including try a half a dozen capital murder cases. It is fun to ride around upper East Tennessee with him. He will recall a crossing accident, a train wreck, a land dispute from his years in private practice.

Bob Crossley, his partner in Knoxville, became well-known for his bar review course. When we merged, Howard's firm had offices in Knoxville, Huntsville, Johnson City, Nashville, and Washington, D.C. Howard returned to the firm after his tenure as chief of staff in the Reagan White House. Crossley left the firm before our merger. Stansbury left us to join a client. Bob Worthington is still with the firm.

We can trace the earliest roots of my family in the practice of law. My great- great-grandfather Samuel Donelson, brother of Rachel Donelson Jackson, was admitted to the Tennessee bar in 1796, the year Tennessee became a state. He practiced in the law offices of Andrew Jackson and John Overton. Legend has it that he went to a nearby town to try a case and was killed by Indians on the way back to Nashville. His eldest son, Andrew Jackson Donelson, my great-grandfather, whose history was described earlier, practiced law only sporadically after his admission to the bar in 1822. Until Andrew Jackson's death in 1845, he acted primarily as Jackson's aide.

My great- great-grandfather, A.O.P Nicholson, graduated from the University of North Carolina at Chapel Hill, studied medicine in Philadelphia, and practiced briefly, but decided he did not like it. He then read law and was admitted to the bar around 1825 and practiced law, except for two terms in the U.S. Senate, until the Civil War. After the war he became chief justice of the Tennessee Supreme Court until his death in 1878. My great-grandfather, William McAlister, was a practicing attorney in Nashville during the latter part of the 19th century. He also served as chancellor and as a justice of the Tennessee Supreme Court. So I had a great heritage in the law.

Donelson & Adams began with Ben Adams and me. We had a small office on the 15th floor of the Commerce Title Building. Ben was a native of Grenada, Mississippi; his father, president of the Grenada Bank. Ben attended Ole Miss undergraduate and law school with friends and connections in North Mississippi. In 1954, I had been in law practice 10 years and Ben, several years fewer. Our basic concept to build our law firm was to provide legal services to a business in almost every field. I had a good base of clients, some still with the firm today, including the Fisher family, the Abston Norfleet family, the Miller Quinlan family, the Purnell family, and the Mallory family.

Ben and I kept time and billed monthly. Our hourly rates were about $10. Many firms depended on retainers. When we opened, I had $100 per month retainers from Ozburn Abston, John T. Fisher Motor Company, Choctaw, and Purnell's, and $25 per month from Memphis Compress, Norcross Farms, and some home builders. Peggy Neal, our secretary, who came with us from Snowden Davis, started at $200 per month. Several income tax cases were in process. With many of my clients, major matters were billed separately. I probably made $20,000-$25,000 per year and Ben, much less. My hourly rate was $15 but I charged $10 for many regular clients.

For many years the partners held monthly billing meetings where each bill was discussed and agreed upon. This important learning process for our younger partners introduced them to a law firm's business aspects. Many of these discussions improved the fairness and acceptability of our fees. Profits were divided on a formula. Each partner was credited with 30 percent of an original fee for legal work, 20 percent for ongoing clients. The balance was credited to each attorney, including associates, for each working hour, weighted for that attorney's hourly rate for that client. This formula and its continued use for fixing compensation was a key factor in our growth. We based compensation on performance, not seniority. Able lawyers who suffered under seniority compensation were attracted to our firm.

This formula continued until after our merger with Shepherd Heiskell. Because I controlled much of the client base and the complexity of allocating the First Tennessee (then First National Bank of Memphis) fee, we shifted to the present tier system with subjective tier placements based upon originating, billing, and responsible and working attorney hours. We strove to reward performance. I suffer from the system now, but it works. As we have grown and added offices, this tier placement process became ever more difficult. When we started the system, a bonus pool allowed us to reward an annual performance which exceeded an attorney's tier placement. When the firm was small, no special compensation was awarded for firm administration, but with expansion this became an important component of tier placement and bonus.

In 1954, I moved beyond tax work. Ozsburn Abston had been involved in a protracted dispute with the Federal Trade Commission for obtaining a special discount from General Motors. Ozburn Abston, a large automotive parts company, operated stores throughout the Mid-South. The Robinson Patman Act was inspired by the aggressive tactics of the Atlantic and Pacific Tea Company, then the nation's dominant retail grocer, and was directed against large retailers who bought direct and got the price allowances usually given wholesalers. The company was a co-defendant in the investigation with General Motors. Frank Norfleet and I worked with the general counsel's office of G.M. on a pattern of operation to permit wholesale distributors to have ownership in stores that sold directly to dealers, garages, and car owners. The settlement required a complete restructuring of the company, converting stores into separate corporations in which the company owned less than 50 percent interest. This restructuring, a major legal task, was an exciting challenge. We visited the headquarters in Detroit, meeting with the general counsel and other top officials.

Donelson & Adams started based on three families, the Ozburn Abston Norfleet Family, the Fisher Family, which owned John T. Fisher Motor Company and Factory Motor Parts, Samuelson Tobacco Company, and the Mallory Family, which owned Memphis Compress and South Memphis Land. I inherited these clients from Allan Davis and developed the representation of the Purnell Family and their chicken processing business, and Choctaw, and the Miller Quinlen family. I developed a strong relationship with the L.M. Kirkpatrick family and represented a number of home builders including my friend Charles Freeburg, previously mentioned, Spencer & Riley, Smith & Turley, Morris Mills, Jack Renshaw, and others. I also did tax work, estate planning, and pension and profit sharing work for doctors' clinics. We were committed to extending our practice beyond tax.

One joy of law practice then was to act as counsel, not just a lawyer or technician for a particular job. My close personal relationships included the cornerstone families mentioned earlier. In some ways I knew as much about their businesses as they did. I also represented the Norcross family, Arkansas planters, and handled the father's and mother's estates and then the son's and the daughters'-in-law estates. In the Fisher family, I represented the father, the mother, and the children, and now one of the grandchildren. The same is true with the Ozburn Abston family. I represented the first generation and the second generation. I feel lawyers today have neglected to establish these close personal relationships.

I totally committed myself to the practice of law and never involved myself in side businesses or time-consuming deals. I worked long hours and many weekends. In the early days, the office was open on Saturday mornings. I often went to my clients' offices and occasionally to their homes, and thus became acquainted with entire families. I enjoyed this and it worked well. I felt close to my clients. In the process, we became good friends, and I became almost a part of the family. In the television drama "Upstairs, Downstairs," the family counselor was always called in to advise about major problems. Mine were especially warm and rewarding relationships and enabled me to give my clients better representation.

Today's lawyers are viewed as technicians for a particular task and, in the process, the role of being a true counselor and providing broad and wide-ranging advice has been greatly diminished, if not lost altogether. My nonlegal advice to many longtime clients was probably more valuable than my legal advice. It came from knowledge of the business, knowledge of the family, and then of course knowledge of other businesses and other families. Such knowledge is difficult to obtain unless you practice law with a broad range of clients. Those relationships and practices were a significant dynamic that made Donelson & Adams successful. Ben operated the same way. One practice we always followed was to go to the client's office; this establishes an intimacy and a much less formal professional atmosphere.

One problem in recent corporate scandals is the limited scope and responsibility of outside counsel. In large corporations where in-house legal counsel either choose or strongly influence selection, outside counsel never establishes the intimate relationship with the corporation and seldom has the strong relationship required to give unvarnished legal or nonlegal advice. If you look at some of these corporate scandals, the availability of sound legal advice was sadly lacking.

In tax practice, with the fear that a tax treatment might be called "fraud," we had a term to describe a tax proposal: "Does it pass the smell test?" If it didn't smell right, you shouldn't do it. I said to clients on occasion, "It may or may not be legal, but we don't want to do it, it doesn't smell right." It is a great principle for lawyers to remember.

Unfortunately, the accounting firms have usurped this role and are more frequently present in the client's office and are more often called on for what would be nonprofessional advice. Accountants have skillfully established themselves as consultants as well as accountants; whereas, we have now become lawyers, but not counselors. Lawyers are trained by the study of law and by the experience to give good advice. That skill is not confined to the law but applies to most business problems. The bar has allowed this tremendous asset to get away from us. CPAs, consultants, and financial planners all usurped this role to the detriment of the clients who no longer make full use of their lawyers' knowledge, experience, and wisdom. This has been in part due to the attitude of the organized bar that fiercely protected law practice from invasion by nonlawyers. In the process, though, the courts whittled away from law practice, general business advice, financial advice, estate planning, pension, profit sharing, and fringe benefit advice. These and many others have been abandoned to nonlawyers. Unfortunately, these have been fast growing areas.

Within less than two years, we needed more help. I continued my tax practice, including litigation, but moved rapidly into general corporate, partnership, and other kinds of business matters. Ben assisted in many tax issues, particularly trusts, estates, and wills. As new federal programs sprang up, Ben developed expertise in housing and real estate. We represented Russell Wilkerson and Bobby Snowden, and Jim McGehee, while he was with Marx & Bensdorf and then in his own firm, James E. McGehee and Company. Ben handled most of their work. He also did some chancery litigation. We hired Edward "Mike" Grogan to help with litigation and Elwood Edwards for support in general corporate, estate planning, and real estate. Elwood gravitated toward our numerous home builders, developers, and real estate clients and was good at dealing with them, including some I referred to him.

To promote the firm's growth and prosperity, older lawyers had to relinquish as much as possible to the younger ones. Gradually, the associates became acquainted more and more with the clients, which enabled them to take over the client, and the entire firm benefited. Because one lawyer can do just so much, having others to take over matters helps the firm grow and become more profitable. In short, Ben and I multiplied ourselves. This was done carefully to preserve the personal attorney-client relationship. Another lawyer changes this relationship, and the client needs to know the senior lawyer is still involved. We lost some clients; others drifted away. Hard-working associates produced additional revenue divided according to the production of each partner, determined under the described formula; the partners made more.

I taught the law and tax part of a chartered life underwriting course for 10 years, and for the next 10 years after that I taught the tax part and Ben taught the law part. I made numerous contacts with chartered life underwriters who steered me to clients who needed tax advice, particularly estate planning advice, and these contacts became a major source of our referrals. I got the Purnell family and their chicken processing business through Dick Clark, an insurance man, who took the course and became a close personal friend. He also involved me with Matthews & Whitfield, a road building and landfill company in Tupelo. This resulted in our involvement in land development projects in Alabama and Florida and also enabled me to get Mike Sturdivant as a client, a large cotton planter from Glendora, Mississippi, also in the motel business; A.B. Rozelle in Osceola; and several clients in the Missouri Bootheel; the Smith family in Jackson, Tennessee; and the White family in Union City, who were in the funeral home business, along with many others, including a number of doctors' practices.

Ben and I spoke annually to the Association of Cost Accountants, small accounting firms from towns in western Tennessee. These firms soon became a great source of referrals, not only for tax disputes, but for general representation. Through one of these accounting firms I began to represent then House Speaker (and later Governor) Ned McWherter, who owned a large beer distributorship in Dresden and Jackson, along with a nursing home and numerous other entities.

One particular tax case that we tried and won in the Tax Court came from referral by a cost accountant in Tiptonville. We won by arguing the tax law, strictly enforced, can create injustice. My client, a fine gentleman but unsophisticated, managed a cotton gin. The owners built a new and larger gin and offered him a partnership. He made a capital contribution, and the company had a fabulous year. Later the other partners offered to buy him out at what he thought a handsome profit, but when he received his statement on his share of the profits, he found that it was far more than he had been paid. He received about $15,000 but his K-1 showed his share of the profits at about $30,000. I argued with the revenue agent that this was totally inequitable, and equivalent to fraud. I'll never forget his response: "I have my oath to protect the revenues."

In trial I made my opening statement, then put Mr. Finch on the stand. He came across as I have described him, straightforward, honest, but unsophisticated. When the IRS attorney cross-examined him, the judge interrupted and said, "Are you telling me that you are trying to tax this man on $30,000 of income when you concede he only received $15,000?" The IRS attorney began an involved explanation, but the judge responded, "Not in this court." The incident typified the mindset of many IRS agents.

Cost accountants became a revenue source, particularly for tax disputes, many of which we settled with the IRS, but some like the Finch case went to trial. Because we were willing and ready to go to trial and frequently won, our ability to settle satisfactorily was excellent. We also got referrals from attorneys around West Tennessee, partly by making speeches about taxes at local civic clubs.

The firm continued to expand. Don Malmo joined in 1959, immediately becoming my primary associate for corporate matters. Don was married to L.M. Kirkpatrick's niece, Elma. Don gradually brought more of the Kirkpatrick family's business to the firm and took over a part of L.M. Kirkpatrick's legal work, including Kirkpatrick Coal Company and their other entities. They became a major client. Don had worked and served a stretch in the Navy as an officer before attending law school. In short, he was a mature and experienced man when he came to us. Don worked with me closely for many years. An excellent lawyer and popular with clients, he developed his own practice and eventually accepted a full-time job as CEO of Duncan Williams Company, a bond house, while continuing his own small law practice.

The following year Bob White joined us. Bob's father had been treasurer of Stratton-Warren Hardware, which Allan and I represented, and a member of the Idlewild Presbyterian Church. When Bob was about nine years old, he and his mother were in church when she fell over dead. On top of that traumatic event, when Bob was 12, his father died. Bob's older brother took over as his guardian, and I handled the estate. After a short period, Bob's brother had a breakdown. Then I took over as Bob's guardian. His share of his parents' estate provided adequate funds for his education, but it was unfair because his siblings had the benefit of a college education before their father's death; an example that some things that seem equal are not equal.

Bob went to the Baylor School in Chattanooga and to Washington & Lee for undergraduate and law school. He was Phi Beta Kappa when he graduated college. Bob was afraid to marry a charming young lady he was interested in when he graduated from college. He felt he could not afford to marry and worried about his family's history of mental illness, which afflicted all three of his siblings. When Bob graduated from law school, I urged him to go to Chattanooga where his roommate's father was a lawyer and eager for him to join the firm. I warned him if he came to Memphis, he would have his hands full with the older siblings. He came anyway. He was the only balance the family had. He never married.

Around 1962, we made our first merger with the O'Hearn & Keathley firm (Bill O'Hearn and Dick and Roy Keathley). Bill and Dick brought considerable expertise in the insurance industry along with litigation experience. Dick, who worked full time for an insurance company, became inactive in the firm. Roy, an able lawyer and a good rainmaker, has been with us ever since and built his own practice. Through one client, a Holiday Inn franchisee, he became counsel for the Holiday Inn franchisee association and expert in motel and hotel deals. He has represented the Sandestin Hilton from its beginning until today. In 1963 we added Maurice Wexler. Like Don Malmo, Maurice had worked for a number of years in the human resources department, personnel we called it then, of a large company. He brought maturity as well. When he applied, Maurice was in law school in Chicago, and I interviewed him during an ABA meeting in Chicago.

By 1964, we had nine lawyers, well above average for Memphis firms, with a reputation as highly expert in tax planning and tax matters. We also were well-known in corporate matters and in corporate acquisitions, with a large practice among home builders and developers. We did major amounts of estate planning work for West Tennessee, East Arkansas, and North Mississippi. I was 47 years old.

We developed our own specialties. Ben became expert in government housing programs, the best in the area, and handled most probate work. Elwood Edwards worked with the home builders and real estate developers. Mike Grogan continued in litigation. Bob White became an estate planning expert, perhaps the finest draftsman of wills and trusts in the city. Maurice, at my urging, became active in the ABA Labor and Employment Section and in EEOC work, serving on major committees. He became well-known nationally in the field and developed an excellent practice, including many national firms. One year he was specially honored by the section as one of its outstanding lawyers. Maurice went through a brief internship with me and developed several clients of his own, including Jimmie Foster. In his early days he did corporate work, acquisition and sale of businesses, securities and partnership law, and taxation, concentrating on employment law, especially EEOC matters. Roy Keathley's progress has already been described. We trained all six of these young lawyers. Each man had a broad internship and each was encouraged to develop his own specialties.

Perhaps the most notable tax case in the early days of Donelson & Adams was a tax civil fraud trial, involving Dr. Tom West and his wife. This case began during Allan Davis' lifetime and we won after a trial of over a week. Slowly working through the process, I brought it to the new firm in 1954. Dr. West was a prominent surgeon, and the IRS wanted to make an example of him. There was much gossip that doctors collected cash fees and never reported them. I believed and proved that Dr. West was the soul of honesty. He engaged me after the revenue agent had proposed a large deficiency and recommended criminal prosecution. Dr. West was so offended by the agent's attitude that he antagonized her completely and I had to persuade the agent in charge to give us a new revenue agent immediately. We got two, both from Chattanooga. I could not settle the case, although Justice agreed to drop the criminal but not the civil fraud charges.

We went to trial. I prepared a net worth analysis that proved the doctor had sufficient income to support the growth of his net worth. A net worth analysis begins with a balance sheet at the beginning of the first year for which the government is proposing a tax deficiency. It shows all the sources of income and deducts from them the living expenses, debt repayment, and capital outlay. This was supposed to reflect that the increase in net worth of the taxpayer at the end of the year had been fully accounted for by the revenue sources, less expenses. It sounds simple, but it is a complicated process. You not only have ordinary income, but capital gain income, gifts, loan repayments, loan receipts. Margaret West, the doctor's wife, was a bright person and we developed the net worth analysis.

Recurring loans Mrs. West received from her father complicated the situation. Her father, Grant LaFollette, a banker in a small town in East Tennessee named for her family, retired. In typical East Tennessee mountain fashion, he came to Memphis with about $300,000 in cash in a brown paper sack. The loan record was kept on the sack: "Loaned Margaret $15,000; Margaret paid $5,000, etc." It took us almost one week to prove the net worth. Mr. LaFollette had died, but we had taken a deposition to preserve his testimony. We had a strong case, and I was mystified as to why we weren't able to settle.

There was no discovery then. When the government put on its case, the revenue agent introduced an exhibit, which I had never seen, although we had gone through Appellate and Justice before filing suit for refund (years of agony for the Wests from 1948 to 1956). The government's exhibit proved to be a cash flow analysis designed to show that the Wests did not have the cash from his reported income and their loans to make the real estate purchases they had made. You had to reflect cash income from Dr. West's practice, cash loans from Mr. LaFollette, cash income from sales of capital assets, and cash outlay for living expenses, real estate purchases, loan repayments, and any other cash disbursements.

I told Mike Grogan, who assisted me at the trial, to stall in every way possible while I studied the exhibit. I had only a short while to analyze it; fortunately, the question of when you added and subtracted was not easy to determine. The agent had erroneously subtracted on three entries when he should have added—three entries totaling $75,000 for a $150,000 differential. On cross-examination I started down the exhibit. First item: Why did you add this, why did you subtract that? This went on for each item. When we came to the first erroneous entry, I asked how this was different from the items above where you added, or vice versa. He would defend this entry. Then I would start over again, why did you add, and why did you subtract?

After over an hour of comparisons, the agent finally admitted, "I might have made a mistake." On each erroneous calculation, we got a reluctant concession. These concessions wiped out any unexplained income difference. The case was over, although the publicity on the victory never equaled the lurid details of the charges. The court gave us a 100 percent refund of tax, interest, and penalties. This great victory added to our growing reputation.

Dr. Bill West, their son, now of the West Clinic, tells this story about the big event. Dr. Tom West took the family on a cruise following the trial to recover from the strain. Margaret felt responsible because of her father's cash loans that complicated the cash flow determination. It was the Wests' cash flow, not Mr. LaFollete's, that we tried to establish. Errors by the revenue agents in trying to reflect these loans and repayments produced the alleged deficiency.

I cabled Dr. and Mrs. West about the total victory. They had a victory dinner on the ship with champagne. Bill West was under 10, but he began to sip surreptitiously from the almost empty glasses. He went sound asleep and had to be carried to the cabin to sleep it off. The trial put an end to talk about doctors cheating on their cash fees and brought in other doctors and dentists with tax problems. In all honesty, it may have caused them to be more careful about reporting their income.

Meanwhile, our nontax practice grew. We represented a dozen substantial home builders and developers. During that time, every corporation had its own tax exemption; our home builders had multiple corporations. Maintaining their minute books was a major task. We never lost a dispute over these multiple corporations. As mentioned, I won a tax case for J.E. Dilworth where the IRS attempted to deny a separate corporate exemption for a subsidiary in Mississippi. With home builders, a separate corporation was easy because each new tract of land formed a natural entity.

We also had several failures to file tax cases that we disposed of with fines and suspended sentences. The art was to persuade the Department of Justice to bring the prosecution in the Middle District of Tennessee, where the atmosphere was much more favorable. Of course, there is no defense except incompetence. You either filed or you didn't. Judge Boyd, in the Western District of Tennessee, was extremely tough in criminal matters. We established connections in the Department of Justice in Washington to assure the cases were brought in the District Court in Nashville where Judge Gray was more tolerant. In most cases we settled them with a fine, and, in some cases, with a fine and a suspended sentence. I don't think we ever had a failure to file case where the taxpayer received jail time until many years later when I represented Tommy Burnett.

I did some tax fraud work in addition to the West case. I got some fraud cases reduced to civil tax deficiencies with penalties, but three went to trial. I associated John Hooker, Sr., a distinguished criminal trial attorney, on two of these cases. John Hooker was one of the icons of the bar, politically powerful in the Democratic Party. Well-known and popular, he could have easily been governor, which his son later futilely attempted several times. Each one of my tax fraud clients was guilty. I thought we might be able to win the case of a woman who failed to report interest earned on personal loans made to a friend in business. The difficulty was the substantial amounts of money involved. She decided to plead guilty.

I remember one case in particular. A man who was not a regular client called me and said a special agent wanted to look in his lockboxes. I asked, "Lockboxes? How many do you have?" and he said, "Five." I replied, "Well you do understand that whatever you tell me is confidential, but I need to know what's in the lockboxes." He said, "Cash."

After some thought, I said, "Go down and open the lockboxes and take out all of the cash. I don't want to know how much it is. The revenue agent will raise hell because you did that, but at least he won't know for sure that you had the boxes loaded with cash." The government did a net worth on him, and I tried to refute the net worth, but it was clear that a lot of unreported income was involved.

When we appeared for arraignment, a visiting judge, Judge Chandler, was sitting on the bench. During that time, most criminal cases in federal court were bootleg cases.

The first bootlegger to appear entered a guilty plea and the judge said, "I'm going to fine you $200." A ripple went through the courtroom because Judge Davies, who usually presided, gave a year and a day for such guilty pleas. With the prospect of only a $200 fine and no time, there was a rush to plead guilty. When maybe the third one got up, Judge Chandler said, "I'm going to fine you $200," and the bootlegger said, "Your honor, I just haven't got $200, I can't pay it," and the judge said, "I'll let you pay it off at $50 a month." Then the stampede really began. I turned to my client and said, "We should plead guilty. You'll get a fine, but you won't get any time, that's the way I read this judge." He said, "I'm concerned. I don't know. Do you know how we could find out anything about this judge?" I said, "He's from Oklahoma City, and I have a friend out there, Jimmy Fellers. I'd be happy to call him." I put in a call and didn't get him right away. Meanwhile, our case came up, and I asked the judge to delay it until the afternoon. I talked to my friend in Oklahoma City and he said, "The judge won't give you any time on a federal criminal tax case. He'll give a heavy fine, he may fine you $10,000 on each count, but he won't give you any jail time."

We returned to the courtroom, but the judge didn't appear. Finally the bailiff came out and said, "Mr. Donelson, would you come to the judge's chambers?" The government attorney went with me and Judge Chandler stated, "During this recess, I received a call from Judge Davies, and he requested me not to dispose of your case. I told him that if I couldn't dispose of that case, I wouldn't dispose of any of his cases, and if he had that little confidence in me, then I was leaving." We had missed a golden opportunity and ended up going to trial. Because he decided to plead guilty, he received a sentence of three or more years.

I did associate John Hooker, Sr., with these cases; a friendship developed through this work. John would call about tax problems. An assistant attorney general of the U.S. had gotten involved in a criminal investigation for assisting in the settlement of criminal tax cases for some friends and was also being charged with criminal tax evasion. I was interested in hearing about this case, and I gave John some advice. We managed to get most of the tax problems settled, but we could not settle the criminal charge for securing dismissals for friends in return for payment, which amounted to a bribe. The assistant attorney general went to jail in a highly publicized prosecution.

I never had the privilege of participating with John during the actual trial of a case. Back in my Snowden Davis days, probably about 1948, I represented a gasoline distributor, C.E. Davis, in Dyersburg, who sold gas to an Army base. The issue: Were those sales subject to the state gasoline tax since they were made to the U.S. Army base? John Hooker, Sr., had a similar case for Esso (now Exxon). We paid the tax and sued for a refund. I participated with John Hooker in that case, and we won the case on a motion for summary judgment based upon briefs and oral argument on the grounds that a sale to the U.S. was not taxable under the statute. During that trial we developed a mutual respect and friendship.

One more fascinating tax case was the valedictory of my tax litigation period. I represented the L.M. Kirkpatrick family, one of whose holding assets was the Caney Creek Coal Company in Western Kentucky. Congress passed a law in the mid-fifties doubling the percentage depletion allowed for coal. I pointed out it was punitive to operate a coal mine as a corporation because all tax-free money from the percentage depletion allowance was trapped in the corporation. When it came out of the corporation, it would be taxed as an ordinary income dividend.

I warned them the value of the coal leases would arise when the corporation was dissolved. They assured me coal leases were merely leases and each carried substantial royalties that were competitive. With the royalties, they could not be sold for more than the assumption of the existing royalty payments.

We dissolved the corporation, and, sure enough, the IRS came in and appraised the value of the coal leases and assessed the stockholders' substantial deficiencies, arguing that the coal leases were worth $1.5 million. The agents developed a technical engineering report on the value of the lease covering the width and depth of the coal vein, the amount of the overburden, the quality of the coal, and then included the current market prices of the coal to come up with a $1.5 million valuation. We had one shareholder pay the tax and bring suit for a refund as the lead case for all stockholders. This case was to be tried in the Western District of Kentucky. I thought it might be a good idea to have a jury trial. Everyone in Kentucky talked about coal, coal leases, coal mines, and how much royalty you had to pay on a coal lease. I thought jurors would understand that leases represented the full value of the property because of the royalty payments.

When I reached Owensboro, Kentucky, Stuart McCloy, my former partner at Snowden Davis, had a tax case with a jury. The jury bombed him and I thought perhaps I misjudged the temperament of western Kentucky jurors. Although Stuart's case had a different issue, I went in and suggested to the judge I would waive a jury, recognizing that it would take a week to try the case with a jury and without one, it could probably be tried in less than three days. The government attorney who had won the other case felt confident and he would not agree. The judge reminded me that I could not do it without my opponent's consent.

I found a local lawyer who did work for the company. Neville

"Abe" Moore had practiced in West Kentucky all of his career and knew everyone in the district. He helped select the jury, and when we were finished, I thought we had a good jury. As a matter of fact, the government lawyer came forward and said he would waive the jury now. To the judge's amusement, I switched my position, saying after going to so much trouble to select a jury we might as well go ahead. We did. The government lawyer was able, and he tried the case hard. I teased one of my witnesses, Walter Wright, the named plaintiff. I said, "If he'd asked you if you were running around on your wife, you would have nodded your head just like you did to everything else he said."

We got our proof in and were able to show the royalty payments under the lease were competitive and no one would have paid more. The case went to the jury, and the jury came back with a value of $50,000 on the coal lease, a tremendous victory for us. As Ben and I left the courtroom, the judge got on the elevator with us and said, "Mr. Donelson, you mind if I ask you a question?" I said, "No, your honor, of course not." And he said, "Did you offer to settle this case?" I said, "You know I did; I never go to trial without trying for a settlement." He said, "Do you mind telling me what you offered as the value of the lease?" I responded, "$50,000." He laughed and said, "You know, sometimes these juries stumble on the truth." This conclusion enhanced our reputation as successful tax lawyers.

During the late fifties and early sixties, Ben and I were committed to public and community service. Ben followed in my footsteps on the Budget Committee of United Way. He became involved with the YMCA, University of Mississippi, St. Mary's Cathedral, and other charitable organizations, ultimately incorporating Trezevant Manor and serving on its board.

During late fifties and early sixties, the Ozburn Abston Company, having changed its name to Parts, Inc., which was more descriptive of its business—wholesale auto parts distribution—began to grow. The company bought numerous other warehouse companies and opened new warehouses in other cities, including Baton Rouge, Johnson City, and Jackson, Mississippi. Frank Norfleet, executive vice president of the company, and I enjoyed ourselves during these acquisitions. I would be the hard-driving bargainer; Frank, the nice guy who came in, settled the disputes, and closed the deal. One day I said to him, "Frank, let's change things and let me be the good guy." He thought that was funny as the devil, and so we did. He played the hard-driving guy, got the cheapest price possible, and I came in and closed the deal, offering them a little more money to smooth things out. We both got a big kick out of that.

My understanding of the Abston-Norfleet family dynamics was a major factor in crucial decisions. At Ozburn Abston, Dunbar Abston, Sr., Frank Norfleet, and I discussed all major business decisions. I participated and my advice carried weight. Frank was a stepson. Dunbar, Jr., was a blood son. Everett Norfleet was a stepson, but not a part of the business. Field Ozburn, the company founder and Dunbar's brother-in-law, and his wife Mignon had no children. I knew them and advised them all. I had a unique knowledge and an honored place in the family.

I urged Dunbar, Sr., to adopt Frank and Everett because he treated them as sons and because, as heirs under the provisions of his will, Tennessee inheritance declared them to be class B beneficiaries. The inheritance tax on class B beneficiaries was burdensome. Although they were long since grown, we went into Chancery Court and made it official. Their natural father had been dead for many years. Dunbar had been reluctant to ask them, but they were delighted. When we got outside the courtroom, Frank whipped out a couple of baby bottles and bonnets, which they put on, and we took a picture of them sucking on their bottles. Passersby were mystified, but it was hilarious.

I remember vividly the opening of the new headquarters on Pauline Street in the late 1950s. A big dinner was held and automotive parts people came from all over the country. Field Ozburn, no longer active in the day-to-day business, was beloved in the industry. The night was filled with praise for him and they called on him for a few words. I knew him well. I said to Jan, "He won't be able to say a word," and I was right. He cried to a standing ovation, an unforgettable memory. Field and Mignon were a wonderful couple. When he died, she was too ill to attend the funeral. As we passed the Baptist Hospital on the way to Elmwood, she watched from the window.

Mignon's estate provided an anxious situation. I had drawn her will and sent her a copy. She called and said it was satisfactory. Dunbar read it over and approved it. She asked if she could go ahead and sign it. I said, "I guess so." I stayed on the phone to supervise the process of proper execution with the two witnesses. When she died and Dunbar brought in the will, I realized that it was on Xerox paper, which was then distinctive. Probate Judge Sylvanus Polk, who was very meticulous, would raise questions. I got Bob White busy and he wrote an excellent memo citing authority that you could use printed wills bought at a stationery store. Wills could be written on paper sacks or any other material. As long as they were properly executed, they were valid.

I went to Probate Court loaded for bear. First National Bank was executor, and Joe Sims, head trust officer, was with me. It was a large estate. When I finished my opening statement and handed the will to the judge, he felt it, recognized the Xerox paper, and said, "Mr. Donelson, you know perfectly well that the court doesn't accept Xerox copies." He threw the will down on the bench. I replied in my humblest manner, "Your honor, that is not a copy. It is an original which was prepared on the Xerox." Then I cited my authorities and handed in my brief (or Bob White's brief). After scanning it, he said reluctantly, "Very well, you may proceed with your proof." When I finished, he quizzed the witnesses thoroughly. This was in the days before notarization made witnesses unnecessary. Finally, he admitted it to probate.

One other incident with the Abston-Norfleet family: Dunbar, Sr., had a policy that they should not fly together, but all were going to Little Rock for an OCY meeting. OCY stood for Ozburn-Crow & Yantis, a company of parts warehouses. I was along. The plane circled Little Rock, and the pilot announced he could not get the landing gear down. Dunbar immediately said, "I told you we shouldn't fly together and we've got Lewie here too. No one will know anything about the business if the four of us are killed." The pilot shook the gear loose, and we landed without incident.

This long relationship, ongoing today, was unique. I was more than a lawyer. I was a counselor. I participated in and advised about all of the major decisions and was considered an essential part of the business. I knew as much as anyone because I had acted in this capacity for many years.

During those years when we reorganized Ozburn Abston Company and forming Parts, Inc., Frank and I became close. We traveled together to the outlying stores, mostly by car, and had many opportunities to share our ideas. Frank served on the old County Court. He headed up the first organization overseeing health care facilities. In the ensuing years, we were involved in many civic and charitable endeavors. If one of us was called upon to help with a problem, we would call each other. Working together, mostly behind the scenes, many problems were solved.

Frank and Dunbar, Sr., were a dynamic combination. Frank was a go-getter, interested in growth, a great salesman, a great cheerleader, a charismatic figure, and Dunbar was the practical, down-to-earth, cautious, member of the team. Dunbar saw that they didn't grow too fast and Frank pushed new ideas and growth. In the process, Frank became well-known among various warehouse distributors around the country and was instrumental in forming the National Automotive Parts Warehouse Distributors Association. He was the first chairman, and for a couple of years I was the general counsel for the association. This proved to be impractical, because I was in Memphis and the headquarters was in Chicago. Finally, they got their own person. During Parts' expansion, I learned much about bargaining and trading, and by using that experience, I was engaged to buy, merge, or sell other companies.

In our early years, we established the first pension plans among Memphis businesses, including doctors. We represented Dr. John

Shea in Memphis Otology Clinic. We were originally engaged in the mid-fifties to obtain a ruling that his Otology Foundation was a 501(c)(3) corporation and entitled to a tax-exempt status. The issue was his ability to control the foundation research for his private benefit, a difficult subjective question, hard to disprove. For months he tried to have the exemption approved. I finally arranged a hearing before the two women who headed up that division of the IRS. Dr. Shea, a brilliant surgeon and a fascinating man, charmed the two, who were so impressed with his proposal that by the end of the meeting, they would have contributed to the foundation. Approval was obtained, and I represented John Shea and formed for him the first professional LLC in Tennessee.

John, an intriguing client and a surgical inventor, created several new operations that tremendously advanced the field of otology and were copied all over the world. He traveled and taught others to perform the operations. In later years, he reported, "What I do now mostly is correct mistakes made by the doctors trying to implement my invention." A bright man, John was a poor investor with more bad deals, particularly oil deals, than anyone can imagine. I remember telling him, "John, you don't need a lawyer, you need a guardian." His CPA, Lucian Minor, said, "John, don't you know that no good deal ever left Texas?"

John was involved in an oil program in Tulsa offering scheduled annual drilling programs. The investor made annual investments on each year's drilling program. The investor could drop out at any time. Another client with investments in the same program, and one of Lucian Minor's clients, also an investor, compared notes and discovered different returns for the same investment in a particular year's program. Bill Quinlan, my client, called and revealed his findings. I checked with John and found he had received an even higher return for the same invested amount for the same period. It appeared the amount of return received for the program related to whether they reinvested the following years. We called the Tulsa oil program and they brushed us aside.

We engaged my Oklahoma friend, Jimmy Fellers, to represent our investors. We filed a lawsuit with the federal court in Tulsa, and they agreed to settle, paying all of our clients in full. A lawyer friend in New Orleans had a client in the program who was also in on the settlement. Unfortunately, the program went on for at least another 10 years. Then I read one day the whole thing blew up and many prominent figures, including athletes, Hollywood actors, and others were caught in the loss.

We undertook an interesting tax problem for Price Curd, a local businessman, in various joint ventures with the Ritter family in Marked Tree, Arkansas. He wanted separation from them in a tax-free manner, if possible, and I extricated him in a most satisfactory fashion. As a result, C.A. Dawson, the longtime farm manager for the Ritter farming operations, asked if I could extricate his numerous operations and partnerships, which I did.

Dawson, a legend in Arkansas cotton planting circles, came from Iowa over 50 years before, at Ritter's request, to take over the farm operation. In our dealings with the Ritter family, we heard this story about Dawson. Don Malmo and I were working on the matter together. They described the scientific way of farming with records of the first frost and the last frost, daily records of the weather, and the chemical components in the soil, and other such data.

Don asked, "How do you decide when you are going to plant in the spring? Do you look at all this, and then are you able to determine when you are going to plant?" They answered, "We do look at all of it, but what we really do is, Mr. Dawson goes out in the field one spring day, picks up a clod of dirt, crumples it in his hand, sniffs it a few times, then he licks it and says, "We'll plant today."

The Ritter family typified what many early timber cutting people who came to Arkansas back at the turn of the century did. They cut the timber, established a farming operation, built the town, and, basically, owned the town. The Ritter family owned the bank, Cadillac and Chevrolet dealership, the telephone company, the farm equipment company, the grain elevator, even the ice plant. Their influence over the town was pervasive and probably remains so today.

Several lawyers approached us to merge our practices. One was

Bill Farris, but his practice, primarily zoning and other matters related to state and local government, didn't properly mesh with ours. We spoke with Leo Buchignani and Eugene Greener, but could not reach a satisfactory arrangement. Our first merger was with the Keathley firm, described earlier.

The major elements of our growth were the representation of Parts, Inc., because during this period it grew rapidly and bought a number of businesses; the representation of Choctaw, which grew rapidly as well; and Purnell's, which also experienced tremendous growth.

During the late fifties, I put together for some clients led by Morris Mills, one of our home builder clients, a conglomerate called Mid-Continent Corporation, a combination of real estate companies, including a brokerage company, some real estate holdings, home builders, and some developers. We took the company public, one of the first small public offerings in the Memphis area. Although the company never took off as hoped, in the end we liquidated and did all right on our investment.

In 1964, I incorporated Guardsmark, Inc., the security guard company. I had known Ira Lipman because his father, Mark, did a service for Parts. I watched him question employees caught with their hand in the till. It was eye-opening; he was extremely skillful and seldom failed to get a full confession. I also knew Ira through politics. He was active in the establishment of a Young Republicans Club in Memphis. After forming Guardsmark, Ira would call me every month to report his sales growth. In early January he called and said, "Lewie, come on over here, I can't figure out what happened, we didn't make any money." I explained that he failed to take into consideration any overhead when pricing his product. He had figured out the guards' pay and added a profit margin, but did not include rent, telephone, utilities, office personnel, and office supplies. Ira will tell you today, I taught him to understand a profit and loss statement and a balance sheet. But Ira actually went to the University of Memphis and took courses in accounting and became an expert in financial matters.

When Guardsmark did its first private placement with Stephens Brothers of Little Rock, it was an exciting deal that financed growth. The security services business had only begun to take hold, but investment bankers viewed it as a growth industry.

We went to New York for our second private placement from a venture capital group. Excited, we thought we had hit the big time. When it was completed, Ira arranged for a limousine to take us to dinner at the 21 Club. When we got to 21, I told Ira to let the limousine go, but he wanted the limo to carry us out to the airport. After a magnificent dinner, we went to the airport. At LaGuardia we discovered our flight had been canceled, but a flight out of Kennedy into St. Louis would allow us to make a connection into Memphis. The limousine had waited at LaGuardia and Kennedy. Ira didn't have enough cash left to pay for the limousine. Before credit cards, limousine companies didn't take checks. I said, "Ira, I have this air travel card which you're supposed to use to charge your airline tickets but they tell me you can get $100 on it." I went in and begged and begged and finally got $50, enough for Ira to pay the limousine driver. We arrived in St. Louis late, missed our connection, and ended up spending the night in an hourly motel, worst fleabag you ever saw, and a great comedown from our dinner at 21. That deal set Ira on his way. He grew the company successfully into a leading security company, with Ira as "the spokesman" for the industry.

During this time I learned another lesson about the practice of law. I served on the board of directors of Guardsmark, Inc., a semipublic corporation after its two private placements with outside stockholders. Over my opposition, they moved the headquarters to New York. I went up frequently to attend board meetings.

At one meeting, I thought the proposed acquisition of a security company in Connecticut unwise. The price was too high, and the company was not currently equipped to expand the acquisition to make it more profitable. Ira Lipman was furious. I explained if he wanted to buy it and to have me represent him as his attorney, I'd be more than happy to do so, but as a director I had to vote what I felt was right for the company and its shareholders. I submitted my resignation as a director, which he promptly accepted. In the process, I lost the legal business, although Bob White continued to represent Ira personally. Leo Bearman, a few years later, got the business back. This emphasized the difficulty of a company director, particularly one with public shareholders, or nonfamily shareholders, with a conflict of interest. As a director, you were responsible to the shareholders. As a lawyer, you were responsible to your client. I decided never to serve on another board as both attorney and director of a company with stockholders outside of management.

A couple of years later, about midnight on the Fourth of July, Ira called me and said, "Lewie, you were right. It was unwise to move to New York. We weren't ready." He moved back to Memphis, but after the company became a major success, he moved back to New York and now runs the company from there. It was big of him to make that call, and I was truly appreciative.

Ira and I remain friends and he has been most gracious to me. Jan and I were invited to a big dinner in New York to announce the creation of a new chair at the Wharton School at the University of Pennsylvania through a gift from Guardsmark, and a celebration of the company's 40th year. I am proud of his outstanding achievements. He has proven to be a real friend.

I began to represent Billy Wilkerson and the John T. Everett Company. Billy and his wife Jean became our closest friends. We lived next door to each other. His company expanded rapidly and bought companies that manufactured hardware items. Don Malmo and I worked together on these deals. Billy Wilkerson bought a screw company, a lawnmower company, a hinge company, a hardware screen company, a steel cutting company, a metal door company, and others. The biggest problem arose from a lawnmower company that required tremendous capital. Mowers were sold for three or four months per year, but you had to have a huge inventory ready. Many customers, hardware stores, and other retailers wanted payment terms to match the seasonal sales demand. You didn't get paid until fall for mowers sold the previous winter. The cost of carrying the inventory and then the accounts receivable were punitive and the capital requirement heavy.

The company's growth outran management available to run these plants and the capital to finance the inventory and accounts receivable. We formed a holding company called IMC (Industrial Management Company) to parent these diverse operations and supply the capital for growth. Billy, a great salesman and a visionary in putting companies together, needed a comprehensive plan to provide the increasing capital needed.

I had developed one technique to finance these acquisitions that addressed the capital requirement. Billy's holding company, IMC, would buy the assets (less the machinery and equipment) and assume the liabilities. I formed a group of investors to buy the machinery assets, most using borrowed funds. We leased these assets to the company at a rent that would retire the debt in three to five years. When the debt was paid, we would swap the machinery and equipment with the company in a tax-free (at the time) exchange for stock. It worked well. We had interest and depreciation to offset the rent. There was no tax on the exchange. The techniques increased the company's capital.

The company, however, desperately needed more capital. We talked about a public offering. The cynical phrase then was, "Go public or go broke." They made money, but rapid growth meant capital needs to finance inventory, and accounts receivable far outpaced net profits after taxes. I learned a hard reality for fast growing small businesses. The tax burden on a small corporation (far heavier than now) made rapid growth for a small business difficult. The company's after-tax profits could not provide new capital and surplus to support the inventory and accounts receivable needs.

I was certainly responsible, in part, for the collapse of the company by buying in fully with Billy's dream. We never got the public offering ready. The banks called the loans. As new counsel for First Tennessee, I was in a difficult position. The banks asked me to take over as acting CEO of the companies. I mistakenly agreed. The situation was dire;

several million dollars worth of checks had been written and signed, but not mailed. My dual responsibilities to the bank and to IMC put me in an awkward position.

In retrospect, I believe the banks would have agreed to much tougher demands. They did stay the course. I sold almost all the various manufacturing companies. These contracts would have paid all creditors in full and left John T. Everett Company, the core hardware brokerage company, intact. Nothing else would be left for the shareholders.

I took off with Jan for a long weekend and much needed rest after weeks of constant work. Unfortunately, a lawyer with three small claims put the company into a Chancery Court receivership. He did not contact me before filing. The results were the creditors got 25 cents on the dollar instead of 100 percent, and the shareholders, nothing, rather than an ownership in the John T. Everett Company, an unnecessary tragedy. It was my first hands-on experience with a major bankruptcy, which are feasts for lawyers. The bankruptcy bar, small, but close-knit, do scratch each others' backs. That experience taught me to avoid the bankruptcy or a receivership process if possible.

It was a personal financial disaster. My debt in the machinery deals was substantial. I showed a minus net worth because Jan owned our house. When Billy asked me to sign a note unrelated to the machinery deals for the company, I was probably the only note signer who could pay it. I told Jan about it and she was sympathetic, as always, and agreed to help Billy. The bank was also helpful by loaning me enough to pay off my outstanding loans, including the large unsecured one with three other makers. One fellow note signer paid his share immediately. Another one took several years, but paid his share in full. The third paid virtually nothing, so I paid 50 percent. The bank was patient; fortunately, in less than five years, I had repaid it in full.

It was a bitter lesson. I told Jan I would never be rich and I was going to quit worrying about it. It freed my mind. Many losers were clients and friends who took their medicine and remained clients and friends. Although this representation turned out badly, this type of attorney-client relationship was typical of mine with my major clients.

Tupelo connections came through Dick Clark, who took the previously mentioned CLU course. The connection to Matthews & Whitfield, the road contracting company, produced intriguing issues. Dick moved to Mobile and became vice president and then president of Pan Coastal Life, a small insurance company in Mobile, owned by a promoter personality named Red Wilkinson. Red became interested in developing an island in Mobile Bay, Pineda Island, which could be filled in for housing development. Through Dick he got in contact with Matthews & Whitfield, which undertook to raise the island's level sufficiently for safe construction. I got involved via Matthews & Whitfield's attorney and got to know Red Wilkinson. After much effort and expense, the Pineda Island project never took off, but through that project I met developers in Fort Lauderdale led by Andy Manno. His two partners, Chuck Hoy and Bob Gordon, a Choate graduate, did real estate developments around Florida, mostly buying land that needed fill and then building.

In the process, I represented their company, U.S. Land Company. Doing a development near Cape Kennedy, and another at Venice, I tried to help them get financing for a high risk project. We talked to a representative of the Central Teamsters Pensions Fund, then under investigation. The union official arrived in Teamsters style with a girlfriend in high heels, shorts, and a fur coat. We never worked out anything with him; two months later he disappeared on a flight from Miami to Nassau.

We talked to a L.A. mortgage lender. An older guy, he looked me in the eye and said, "Son, money doesn't have little beady gray eyes," and I thought to myself, "Yeah, but you do." I opposed my client doing business with him. Finally, we got financing elsewhere and proceeded.

I could tell many tales about Matt Matthews and his partner Henry Whitfield. Matt Matthews and I became close friends during our many travels. Talking to Matt one day about an associate with whom I wasn't too happy, he said, "Lewie, you know when you should fire somebody, don't you?" and I said, "No," and he said, "First time you think of it." I have remembered that for years. You spend so much time in salvaging a problematic employee and only save one out of 10, and the process is not worth it. It is sound advice, but tough to follow.

Matthews, a hard-driving, able contractor, served with the Corps of Engineers in Korea. One day we were wasting time down in Fort Lauderdale. We walked into a clothing store, and he bought four suits. I said, "You've got worlds of suits. Why in the world do you want to buy four more?" He said, "Until I was out of the Army and got my first real job I never had a new suit in my whole life. When I go in a clothing store now and realize that I can buy as many as I want, I just can't resist." The man lived hard and drove hard and died young.

Also through Dick Clark, I did legal work for Red Wilkinson. One day while trying to sell a project to a group that was building a country club in Anniston, Alabama, he told me what he would get those people to do for him, and I asked, "Red, what are you going to give them?" He said, "Tongue." That deal did not happen.

Red bought control of a little insurance company in Elba, Alabama, named Emergency Aid Life Insurance Company, formed during the Depression to provide burial insurance. Red had 52 percent of the stock, but Alabama Governor Jim Folsom's family had the other 48 percent. Folsom blocked Red from voting his stock. Jim Folsom, a flamboyant politician, six foot six inches tall, ran as a typical Southern populist: "I am for the poor people, I am one of them."

Red asked me to figure out how to get around that court order. I came up with a plan where I would form a company, a perfectly legitimate company with five or six of my friends as stockholders, and pay him a down payment of $25,000 on the stock with a note for the balance. He would be able to buy the stock back at an agreed price. This would give us a modest profit over a period of years. As we were true owners of the stock, all he had was a repurchase option. The price would repay our note and return our original investment plus a guaranteed profit.

I formed a company named Cherry Investment Company, a Tennessee Corporation. I took the stock to the headquarters in Elba, Alabama, for the annual meeting. I had it reissued in the name of my company and walked into the annual meeting and voted in a new board of directors with myself as chairman of the board. I hired two bright young fellows to run it, a chief executive and a financial officer, and I supervised the running of the company for the next three or four years, going to Elba every month for a board meeting.

I tried to persuade Jim Folsom we could turn the company around and make real money, but he never would believe me. He blocked me in court. No court ever issued any order for or against my voting the stock. I put Jim back on the board. Emergency Aid Insurance Company grew rapidly and became profitable. Finally, at the end of almost four years, I had an offer from a big insurance company in Birmingham, and we sold it. My investors made a nice return on their investment. I received good director's fees and a decent return on my part of the investment. Red Wilkinson made a profit and the Folsom family probably got the first real money they ever earned, over $400,000 in cash. After it was all over and Jim got his check he said, "You know, if I had listened to you, we probably could have made some real money out of this deal." And I said, "Yes, we could have, Governor."

Once I sent Don Malmo to attend the board meeting. The meeting room was smaller and narrower than my present office. Folsom was a huge guy. As Don described it, Folsom sat opposite Don and pointed his finger directly at Don's nose (Don claimed it was about one inch away), and asked, "Who's that little bitty SOB over there?" Don hastily explained who he was.

Jim, thinking he would kill me with kindness, invited me to a party at the governor's residence the night before the board meeting. I arrived, and unfortunately, Jim never arrived. It was an enjoyable party, and everybody looked after me very well.

The next day we rode to Elba and back for the meeting. On the return trip, the governor said to the driver, "Stop in this next town. It's wet and we can buy something to drink." The driver pulled over and the governor said, "Why are you stopping here?" He said, "I thought I would walk up and get it." The governor said, "Oh, no. Just pull up right in front." We were in the governor's car, license tag No. 1. "Give them something to talk about." We did. Sure enough, he drank two bottles of warm sherry and was pretty far gone by the time we got back to Montgomery. We arrived and were greeted by a black man named Winston, whose official title was manager of the executive residence. When I asked someone who Winston was, he said, "He's the man to see." The governor asked a couple of questions and Winston replied, "I took care of that, Governor, and I took care of that other thing, and the speaker said so-and-so." Here was a black man in Alabama around 1960 with remarkable status. Going to the airport I asked the driver, "Who in the world is Winston?" He said, "He is the manager of the executive residence with the contract for all of the gasoline for state cars. He gets a certain markup off of it, a fraction of a penny per gallon on every state gasoline purchase."

Poor Don Malmo traveled with me all over Alabama defending us in lawsuits in Mobile and Cullman and federal court in Montgomery, where we appeared before the famous Judge Johnson, author of many early desegregation rulings. The governor's lawyer said many derogatory things about me. When the hearing was over, I went up to the lawyer and said, "Step outside and say those things again, and I'm going to whip you, and if you won't do that, I'm going to sue the hell out of you for libel." Don says, "Here I am, paired with Big Jim, who was about 6'6", and Lewie is paired with Jim's lawyer who was about Lewie's size." It was a unique legal matter in wild and exciting times.

In the late 1950s and early 1960s, two cases involved the federal excess profits tax. One was for Schneider's Modern Bakery, which I tried and won. The issue was to show whether profits were excessive, and we demonstrated to the court the profits were a part of normal growth. Their growth could be anticipated and they were entitled to adjust the base to reflect that Schneider's paid inadequate salaries to its executive owners, which artificially increased profits. We also represented a man who made carburetors for stock car racers. I don't think he ever appreciated what we did; he got by without any kind of excess profits taxes.

Through another insurance agent, I contacted Jones Manufacturing Company in Humboldt, Tennessee, which made various products from cotton linters for mattresses, liners and other products. Jones was, and is, a family owned company. The founder had three sons, who owned and operated the company. Wallis Jones, the second brother, was the financial man and my principal contact. We worked to restructure the business to reduce its overall tax liability and put more profits in the hands of stockholders. I did a reorganization plan for them and they were very happy. The family was a good client, whom we still represent today.

Boswell Johnson was the chairman of Britling's Cafeteria. The company name was Blue Boar Cafeterias, with cafeterias in Memphis, Birmingham, Nashville, and Louisville. This large operation had many complex tax problems, multiple corporations, partnerships, profit sharing plans, and other tax planning. Boz married Daisy Fisher, another client, who owned John T. Fisher Motor Company, Samuelson Tobacco Company, and Bluff City Cigarette Company. I represented Daisy's previous husband before his death and the Fisher family for over 60 years. Boz and Daisy's divorce was ticklish, but with full consent of both parties, we managed it. I represented Boz until his death.

Johnson also owned an interest in Toddle House, a particularly delicate situation because Boz had a letter from J.C. Steadman, the principal stockholder and chairman of Toddle House. The document stated Boz Johnson owned half of Steadman's interest in Toddle House. Steadman's stepdaughter and principal heir was the wife of a close friend. In fact, I had introduced my friend to Steadman's stepdaughter. When Steadman died, I had the difficult task of showing the letter and persuading his heirs of its authenticity and of how to divide the interest. They responded well. Mrs. Steadman said her husband hinted at such a possibility. We then sold Toddle House to Dobbs House, which went public. I bought stock for $8 a share, selling it at $12. Jan's father bought more than I did, about $2,000 worth, and kept it until his death, when it was worth over $300,000. Shows you what a good investor I am. But that was 30 years later.

EIGHTEEN

REBIRTH AND GROWTH OF
THE REPUBLICAN PARTY

$\int$ ometime in late 1951, I attended a cocktail party where Allen Redd was a guest. During the party I sounded off about how the Democratic Party had left the South, eliminating the two-thirds rule and our voice in selecting a candidate. I complained of the Democrats' move left on most political issues and of labor unions' tremendous influence on the party. I also decried how it was almost impossible for a Southerner to be considered for the presidency and that Democrats gave the South a token vice presidential spot to salve wounds and preserve the one-party Southern vote.

I took off on the detriments of that one-party system to the South. I said all elections were decided in the party primaries, often contested not over issues, but personalities, and a lack of competition produced a lower quality candidate and officeholder than we deserved. I believed continuance of the one-party system would doom the South to perpetual inferiority in the national picture. Even despite the changes during World War II and the Roosevelt administration's remedies to freight rates and other trade issues, we needed to do something about the one-party system.

Not long after, Redd called and asked me to have lunch with him. I agreed, expecting a new client. When we met, he ventured, "You ought to be a Republican. I am trying to organize some Memphians to revive the Republican Party in Shelby County to create a true two-party system."

I explained, "That's a big move for me. I'm almost like Andrew Jackson's great- great-grandson, and it never occurred to me up until now that I might not be a Democrat."

I promised to think it over, and I went home and talked to Jan. I believed the two-party system was crucial for the South and I was more in tune with conservatism and nonregulatory policies of the Republicans than the Democrats who preached big government, business regulation, and lots of handouts. Jan agreed. I did explain that if we became visible as Republicans, we would give up publicly supporting Democrats. After considerable thought, I called Allen and agreed to be part of the new group.

In early 1952 the Republicans held their annual county convention in a Chancery courtroom. Harry Wellford and I decided to attend the meeting. We arrived well ahead of the scheduled meeting time, but we were locked out. This began our long battle with Lieutenant Lee, whose name was George Washington Lee. He had been a lieutenant in World War I, one of the few black officers in that war, and took over from Bob Church, Jr., whose father had been a prominent black leader in the late 19th century. His group, called the Lincoln League, had made a pact with Mr. Crump. Lee and his supporters controlled the party for purposes of patronage, post offices, and so on, but gave their votes to Mr. Crump in the general election. This increased his political power. The league had no interest in seeing the Republican Party gain power and strength. Most black voters had become Democrats because of the Roosevelt reforms, leaving only a hard core of Republicans. Called the Black and Tans, a term dating back to Reconstruction, most of them were black; there were a few white Republicans who held jobs at the post office and other federal positions during the years a Republican held the White House. They looked forward to reaping those benefits during the Eisenhower presidency.

After Eisenhower carried Tennessee and ran strong in Shelby County, Allen Redd and others formed the New Guard Republican

Association to revive and broaden the Republican Party in Shelby County. Allen was the moving force. Arch and Sally McClure were major players. Arch, who was with Ralston-Purina, subsequently rose to become its president. There were Alex and Mimi Dann. Alex was from Maryland and probably a renegade Democrat like myself. Walker Wellford, Jr., his nephew Harry Wellford, and Walker Wellford, Sr., had been some of the few white Republicans in Memphis not involved with the Black and Tan Republican Party. Others included Buddy and Sally Thomason, Leo Buchignani, Newton and Linda Allen, Bob James and his wife Pat, who became a real tower of strength. Tom and Elise Turley were extremely active. Elise acted as the secretary of the group. The Tennessee Republican Party in 1952 consisted of the first and second districts Upper and East Tennessee, Knoxville, and the black vote in Shelby County.

Mattie Peterson, who had been associated with Walter Judd, a congressman from Minnesota and a former Christian missionary in China, told us about the Republican Workshop. We would persuade people to have a gathering of interested citizens in their neighborhood. The workshop representative would talk about how the political system, the party system, party primaries, conventions, and the nominating process worked, concluding with a discussion of the positions of the two parties, comparing the two. Another session focused on the importance of a two-party system. Women ran the Republican Workshop: my wife, Jan, Elise Turley, Helen Allen, Sally McClure, Linda Allen, Mimi Dann, and many others. This was a party building tool, and we began to recruit precinct workers all over the city. No true precinct organization existed in the Democrat or the Republican Party.

Those young women and others organized hundreds of neighborhood meetings and organized precincts. They recruited poll workers, poll watchers, and telephone teams to get out the vote, and organized rides to the polls.

Mr. Crump's death in October of 1954 left a leadership vacuum, although some of his henchmen carried on for a number of years. Most businessmen were still wedded to the old Crump machine, fearing reprisals. In 1956 we had difficulty getting people to run as delegates to the national convention. We focused on the new suburbs, the middle-class neighborhoods, not the more affluent areas. We picked up many interested Republican workers, men and women in all areas of the county outside the predominantly black precincts, small-business people, white-collar workers, professionals, truly mainstream America. This surprising organization included areas all over the city and the county, and some of our precincts; we had captains and as many as 10 block workers. Gradually, we put together an organization that continued for years.

In 1956, we ran a candidate for congress, General W.A. Danielson, a retired commanding officer at the Army Depot. Gwen Awsumb ran for the state legislature. In those days, all Shelby County legislatures were elected at large, and the top nine candidates won. Gwen ran 10th. We had no money and no paid workers; the Republican campaign headquarters would be in our library, manned by the women I mentioned.

In 1956, we elected three Republicans to the State Executive Committee. This was a freak situation. Lieutenant Lee had a slate; we had a slate. Our slate: Helen Allen and Jan Donelson, Tom Turley, and Harry Wellford. The way the ballot looked, Helen Allen and Jan were under Lieutenant Lee's name. Tom Turley was under Lieutenant Lee's name; Harry Wellford and Lee's candidates were on the other column. We were down at the courthouse to watch the counting of the votes. I spoke quietly to Jan and said, "You're going to win." And she said, "What do you mean? Lieutenant Lee's getting all these votes." And I said, "Yeah, but these other candidates aren't getting votes." Jan and Helen both won easily. Lieutenant Lee won the most votes of anybody, but Tom Turley was also elected. Harry Wellford was the only loser on our slate. This gave us a position on the state committee and an opportunity to make our case heard.

Jan had a close college friend who lived in Maryville, and her husband Bill Felknor was a strong Republican. He introduced me to the Koella family. Through them we met some other very active Republicans in Blount County. One was on the state committee. We also got to know Ed Bailey, an active Republican in the Sixth District in Lexington, Tennessee, and some Republicans on the State Executive Committee from Nashville. Our voice began to be heard in the committee.

Gradually the attitude of the Republican State Executive Committee changed. The realization that the real Republican base could be established in Shelby County and spread into West Tennessee gave a new complexion to state politics. With Bill Brock's election in 1962 the Third District became more Republican. We gathered support from Roy Hall, Mr. Republican in Madison County. The Davidson County GOP members shared our views. By 1960 the tide had turned. Party-building Republicans outnumbered the old guard led by Guy Smith and Carroll Reece, Republicans with no interest in statewide growth, who seemed satisfied to continue as a minority party.

Through the influence of General Everett Cook, a close friend of Eisenhower's during World War II, I was named by Citizens for Eisenhower as state chairman for Tennessee in 1956, my first vehicle to establish a political presence around the state. I picked up friends, appointed chairmen in each of the counties, and began the rudiments of a statewide political organization, including Chattanooga where the Brock family was active. I recruited supporters in Nashville and throughout West Tennessee. Henderson County, where Lexington is located, a traditionally Republican county, has demographics similar to East Tennessee. It was the only county west of the Tennessee River that Carroll Reece won in his race against Estes Kefauver. During that 1956 campaign, I made a deal with Lieutenant Lee to provide funds to get out the vote; Eisenhower got almost 50 percent of the black vote in Shelby County that year. He carried Shelby County, winning the state easily. When the Republicans added Shelby County to the Third District where the Brocks and others put an organization together, the possibility of a nonpresidential Republican candidate carrying Tennessee became real.

As soon as I was appointed state chairman for Eisenhower, I endeavored to contact Guy Smith, Tennessee State Republican Party chairman. He refused to take my calls. When I went to Knoxville, I called on him; he refused to see me. I was mystified. I finally realized that my appointment was a shadow of things to come, when the first two congressional districts would no longer control the party. The change was evident when the White House began to contact me.

The ironic twist in the story occurred in 1964 when the Goldwater forces and the new Republicans gained control of the party structure. At large delegates to the convention were to be chosen by the state committee. Jan had served 10 years, and I had taken her place. A Knoxville Republican contacted me about getting Guy Smith named as a delegate. I had the pleasure of telling him, "If Mr. Smith will call on me personally I will consider the appointment." He did and he was appointed, but his days as a party leader were over.

In 1958 and 1960, we won the precinct caucus contests by substantial margins, and got our candidate elected as county chairman, but the State Executive Committee continued to ignore us at first. Gradually Tom Turley, Helen Allen, and Jan began to gain support and Chattanooga, Nashville, Jackson, and Henderson County joined our cause. We sometimes compromised with old-line white Republicans, such as Millsaps Fitzhugh, but our grassroots organization got stronger each year. The Republican Workshop continued its neighborhood by neighborhood progress of recruitment. After five or six years we had loyal workers in every white precinct, small businessmen, druggists, filling station operators, housewives, professionals, doctors, dentists, architects, engineers, and school teachers, unafraid of the Crump machine. They were interested in better candidates and a two-party system. We could turn out the vote.

After Mr. Crump died, he had not prepared any successor and no other leader arose to take his place as heir apparent. Many who held office in 1954 after he died continued to run, and they organized themselves into the, one might say, residue of the Crump organization. In 1958 or maybe 1960, the Crump slate ran on the slogan "Keep Memphis Down in Dixie," an overt racist slogan. Nevertheless, the blacks continued to vote for the Democratic slate overwhelmingly. We continued to run candidates for Congress and ran slates in 1958, 1960, and 1962 for the state legislature. In those days the New Guard Republicans pushed desegregation, and the Democratic politicians supported segregation.

These events did not go unnoticed by blacks, but when you ran as a Republican those courageous positions were too frequently forgotten. Around 1956 an old college friend, John Spence, invited me to speak on the race issue at his church. I strongly advocated desegregation and other civil rights pointing to its strong Christian basis, negative effect on the economy, and the bad image of the South. I was a novice. I knew John Spence was a newspaper reporter, but I didn't connect that with a speech in a Unitarian Church. The next day, his newspaper ran a front-page story on my talk. The hate calls far outnumbered the supportive ones. I learned my first lesson about the press, but I stood my ground.

After Brown v. Board of Education, our cocktail parties were filled with what I called "nigger jokes." One night, leaving a party with Harry Wellford, I said, "I'm sick of those jokes." He agreed. We committed ourselves to say simply when someone started telling one, "I don't want to hear it." I don't know if we converted anyone, but we certainly muffled that talk among our social crowd. Many quietly thanked us for speaking up.

Around 1956, Allen Redd died. Not long before his death he called and invited me to have lunch. He told me he had a serious heart condition, and the doctor told him that he did not have long to live. He wanted me to promise to continue to be active in the party. He died shortly thereafter. His request was a solemn event for me and I felt strongly about it. We changed the name of our group from the New Guard Republicans to the Republican Association; I served as its president up until 1962 when Bob James was elected county chairman, after his narrow defeat for Congress. Then the association was swallowed up in the party.

By 1960, the Republican Association had taken control of the party in Shelby County, and with sufficient support on the state committee, our victories at the local level were not overturned at the state level. The real turning point was the 1962 election of Bill Brock to Congress from Chattanooga. We had more or less made peace with the upper eastern Tennessee Republicans. We had successfully gained the support from a number of Republicans in other areas around the state, and we were able to organize a tremendous effort for Vice President Nixon and Henry Cabot Lodge in the 1960 election. In 1962, Bob James ran for Congress and lost by less than a 1,000 votes, and Bill Brock was elected in the Third District in Chattanooga, a watershed year for Republicans in Tennessee. Brock's win established that area as a Republican district and gave statewide candidates another lift. Brock was re-elected three more times and succeeded by another Republican, Lamar Baker, who served several terms until Watergate did him in. But the district was solidly Republican again with Zach Wamp. Bob James' strong race did the same thing in Shelby County that Howard Baker's 1964 race did statewide. It established believability. By 1962, as president of the Republican Association, I had become the principal spokesman for the Shelby County Republican Party. Following Bob James' defeat, he became county chairman and the association was dissolved. Winfield Dunn, I believe, succeeded Bob, then Harry Wellford and Alex Dann. What we started in 1952 had grown into a strong Republican organization. Tennessee was truly a two-party state. With our victories in 1966, 1968, and 1970, we began to fight over the spoils. Jan was turned off. We had gone 14 years with no state or local victories and got along beautifully. We were truly a band of brothers and sisters. These bonds were strong, built in the fire of struggle and defeat. We truly loved each other. The party grew many new leaders and workers arose, but those originals were special. Even today the memories of those days bind us together in a special way. The friends Jan and I have made in politics have enriched our lives and broadened our horizons.

In 1964, another important year for the Republicans, Dan Kuykendall ran for the Senate, against Albert Gore, and Howard Baker ran for the Senate to fill the vacancy left by Estes Kefauver. I was on a committee along with John Waters and George Ed Wilson from the state party to persuade Howard to run. I had known Howard's father and his stepmother, who succeeded his father in Congress, but had not known Howard Henry, as East Tennesseans tended to call him. He agreed. I had been acting as state campaign chairman for Kuykendall. Dan selected me because of the statewide connections from the 1956 Eisenhower campaign. My organization efforts were well under way, and we merged the two campaigns. Although we made some noise and headway, the Democrats considered us a joke. They were shocked when Howard Baker lost by less than 50,000 votes and Dan ran well. In Memphis, Bob James ran again against George Grider for Congress, but lost. We ran a full slate of candidates for the state legislature; no victories, but we were real contenders at last.

By 1964, control of the Republican Party in Shelby County was finally settled for good. Harry Wellford and I went to see Lieutenant Lee to work out an understanding. We took the position that we represented the majority of Republicans in the county and wanted the majority of representation in the party structure. We offered Lieutenant Lee a significant minority with adequate representation, including election as a delegate to national conventions, but he rejected that proposal. We said to him—probably I said to him, "If you are not willing to make a reasonable compromise, move over because we are going to take over the party and freeze you out." Lieutenant Lee was a memorable character, as I noted earlier.

In 1964, we were totally dominant in precinct caucuses and that year's Shelby County Republican Convention. Lee's power had vanished. Bob James and I were elected as delegates to the convention in San Francisco. Lieutenant Lee took his case as usual to the State Executive Committee and lost. Then he appealed to the national convention. Jan and I were with Keith and Peggy Spurrier in Carmel, California. Keith and I were playing golf at Pebble Beach when we heard of Lee's contest. As the only contested delegates at that convention, we appeared before the Credentials Committee and made our case amid nationwide TV coverage. We won. I heard from friends at Choate and Georgetown whom I hadn't contacted for years. The convention was fun, with no incumbent president or clear primary winner. Goldwater won, but Rockefeller and Scranton contested to the end. Several roll calls were necessary for the final nominations. I made more Republican friends, especially from Tennessee, among the delegates. My daughter Janice was a 17-year-old page. Lieutenant Lee disappeared from the scene. The influx of conservative Democrats drawn by Goldwater further solidified our base in Shelby County and in rural West Tennessee.

During the 1964 election, we learned that in the Republican primary, East Tennessee overwhelmed the vote in the other part of the state. The Republican primary in Shelby County was beginning to grow. In the general election, we learned the importance of mitigating the over- whelming Democrat black vote in order to win in Shelby County. If a Republican in a statewide race carried the first three districts strongly, reduced the losses in Middle Tennessee, broke substantially even in West Tennessee, and carried Shelby County, this combination would produce a victory. That would be the blueprint in Winfield Dunn's gubernatorial victory in 1970, to be discussed later.

We also saw the Republican Workshops had produced a genuine precinct organization, which the Democrats did not have.

In Howard's 1964 Senate race, he got strong majorities in the First and Second Districts, held his own in Shelby County, and lost in Mid- dle Tennessee. His weakness was in rural West Tennessee and in Middle Tennessee. The most important part of that race was that he established believability among political watchers, including major business leaders who were quietly Republican but reluctant to back a party viewed as a certain loser. His race said that a Republican could win a statewide race. Recognizing the potential of victory, our finan- cial supporters began to grow.

We also learned that, particularly in Shelby County, presidential years were very different from off years because they involved a much larger vote. Bob James actually got more votes in 1964 than he got in 1962 but lost by a substantially higher margin. The turnout was much larger among Democrats in presidential elections. We saw an opportunity for a turnover in a federal elected office in off years.

That off-year strategy proved true in 1966. Dan Kuykendall ran for Congress against George Grider who defeated Bob James in 1964. Dan won. This victory proved the strength of our precinct organization. The election of Republicans to the legislature from Shelby County and particularly Howard Baker's 1966 win in the Senate race showed that the balance of power in Tennessee had begun to shift. Tennessee was up for grabs in every election and on its way to becoming a Republican state, nationally and on the state level.

Before the 1966 election another major change strongly affected Tennessee politics. In Baker vs. Carr, the one man, one vote rule was ordered by the U.S. Supreme Court. Tennessee had a specific provision in its constitution that required it to reapportion every 10 years, but this had not been done since 1910. The Supreme Court remanded the case to the three-judge federal district court in Nashville that had originally decided the case, with instructions to adopt a reapportionment plan for the state. I represented the Republican Party at that hearing. I prepared two plans that met the constitutional standard. Computers were virtually unknown. Developing a plan that was sufficient to meet the one man, one vote requirements took a great deal of effort. I learned the art of reapportionment: to spread around your strength to get maximum effect. There's no point in carrying one district by 80 percent and losing another by 55/45 when a small shift in voters could produce two 55 percent votes in favor of your party. I enjoy fiddling with figures to create a plan. I tested myself by preparing the most favorable plan possible for the Republicans, then a more reasonable plan: I used the extreme techniques of gerrymandering to achieve maximum benefit for the majority party, an art practiced all over the country as incumbents persuade the legislatures to adopt plans to keep their seats safe. With so little turnover, these provide only small shifts in party strengths in Congress and the state legislatures.

When I arrived in the court, at least 20 lawyers represented various interests, cities, the governor, the Democratic Party, labor unions, Farm Bureau, and so forth. I could not believe it when the court asked if anyone had a plan to present, and I had the only plan. Perhaps the lawyers thought the judges would prepare a plan, or that the court would give specific instructions as to what they wanted done and allow time for the development of plans. I offered the court two plans, one of which I called a Republican plan and the other, a fair plan. They questioned me in-depth about these two plans to provide reapportionment for both the Tennessee House and Senate.

The court took the matter under advisement, and after a period of study, adopted my so-called "fair plan." The Republicans captured the state House of Representatives for the first time in history, a major change. The plan also required election by individual districts rather than at large within the county. Both blacks and Republicans suddenly were able to elect legislative candidates, a shocking impact in that first year, 1966. In Shelby County, two blacks were elected to the legislature, the first since the Reconstruction era. Four or five Republicans were elected to the House and two or three to the Senate. Those new Republicans from Shelby County became in 1966 the absolutely essential votes to gain control over the House where the division was equal, with one Independent who voted with the Republicans. Bill Jenkins, a First District Republican who later became a congressman, was elected speaker. Ultimately, that court decision enabled the Republicans to capture seats in Davidson County and other places around the state where Republican strength had been minimized by gerrymandering.

Later the General Assembly passed two other plans for the Senate and one other for the House which we were able to have declared unconstitutional. It wasn't until after the 1970 election that then-Speaker McWherter told me he finally realized drawing reapportionment plans was a technical task requiring careful mathematical determinations. He promptly brought in people who knew how to draw up these plans. The Democrats, since then, have skillfully minimized Republicans' strength. The party did not capture the state House again until 2008. After one Senate victory, Republicans were not able to capture the Senate until the last election. In statewide races, Republicans have won the overwhelming majority since 1970. This shows the power of skillful gerrymandering. Bob Walker helped me with these cases, and subsequently became the expert on reapportionment. He turned that over to John Ryder; it wasn't exactly a piece of lucrative business. In those days, it was done for the party with no pay for it, only favorable publicity.

NINTEEN

OTHER CIVIC WORK

Meanwhile, I was active in several civic organizations. Through Bill Kent, my client for whom I had won two big tax cases, I served on the Budget Committee of Shelby United Neighbors, the predecessor of the United Way. Bill was the chairman for the first couple of years, and then I succeeded him as chairman. Bill began careful businesslike reviews of various agencies. One example of the depth of our review: We noticed a substantial undesignated accounts receivable, unnecessary for the agency. We suspected the director was lending herself money. I called the president of the agency, a friend, and told him of our suspicions. He replied, "We have total confidence in our director." I said, gently, but firmly, "I urge you to investigate because we are going to call it to the attention of the SUN Board." He reluctantly agreed to investigate. The next day he called back, thanking me profusely for our warning. She had borrowed without the board's knowledge. I'm sure the incident had a salutary effect upon the entire SUN organization.

I rose through the ranks to become president of the United Way, or of Shelby United Neighbors as it was called then. Some board members were dismayed to see the United Way leadership was 100 percent white. With the support of A.E. Hohenberg, Charles Goodman, Reggie Wurzburg, and others, we decided to integrate the board. It was difficult. While we easily put suggested members on the board, other members resigned and refused to serve with blacks. Nonetheless, it went forward without serious incident, the first significant desegregation effort in which I was directly involved.

Through Paul Tudor Jones, I served on the Community Relations Committee. Hollis Price and Paul served as co-chairman; Rabbi Jimmy Wax was another influential member of that committee. One key to success was that Frank Ahlgren and Ed Meeman, the editors of both newspapers, and the managers of all three TV stations were on the committee. The media leadership agreed not to announce our plans in advance. This tremendous concession came because they put the good of the whole community above their commitment to a free press. Such an agreement would be impossible today, when the press feels the duty to publish all the news as soon as they have it above all other consideration. The committee was able to integrate, without a single incident, buses, the library, the zoo, water fountains, restrooms in public buildings, restaurants, movie theaters, hotels, and, finally, public schools. It was a remarkable achievement unmatched in the South.

Over the years, the committee developed a process that worked superbly. I was co-chairman of the committee with Vasco Smith, whose wife Maxine was executive secretary of the NAACP, when we decided to integrate the restaurants on a certain day. Two black couples and two white couples would go to a restaurant. They would be seated separately at two tables for four, with a black couple and a white couple at each table. The restaurant would have been notified of their arrival and a plainclothes policeman would be there in case of trouble. The next day the *Commercial Appeal* and the *Press Scimitar* and the TV stations would announce that yesterday the restaurants had been integrated without incident. Every major step toward integration went off in Memphis without demonstrations, no booing or hollering, rock throwing or any kind of violence. This incredible record was a testimony to good planning and strong committee leadership. It was also evidence Memphis was not as racist as many Southern cities. Atlanta, Jacksonville, Birmingham, Mobile, Jackson, Mississippi, New

Orleans, and even North Carolina towns like Charlotte never achieved any such result. Our actions followed the difficulties in Little Rock. The committee was equal in membership, whites and blacks, and introduced me to many black leaders.

When we pulled off integration of the public schools, our last effort, probably around 1962 or 1963, a couple of reporters from up East came to Memphis looking for trouble. One from *The New York Times* interviewed me and asked, "How do you think this happened in Memphis?" I said, "Good planning and good leadership, but it also points out Memphis is not what I would call a redneck community. It's more of a plantation-type community. A number of the businesses, at least in the early days, were cotton and timber, and the attitude of those people who worked with blacks on their land was an attitude of paternalistic interest, racist in some sense, but not in the sense that many rednecks viewed blacks as economic competition and socially inferior." His theory was that Memphis had lived so long under Mr. Crump and doing what Mr. Crump wanted (this was almost 10 years after Mr. Crump's death) that when leadership announced they had done something, nobody objected. In any event, he was clearly disappointed at our success.

Regrettably, he viewed the occasion as a nonstory. It was an amazing story, and I tried to tell him of its importance and significance. Any success story was contrary to his image of the South. What an example it could have been if the Eastern press had given our success full coverage. Unfortunately, Memphis did virtually nothing to publicize this and exploit the positive image of the city.

In the early 1960s, Frank Clement, then governor, appointed a committee of 100 to plan the future of Tennessee; it consisted of politicians, officeholders, businessmen, and civic leaders. Clement included me. I had gotten interested in the Tennessee financial structures, especially the pernicious aspects of the state's heavy general sales tax. This resulted in lower-income citizens being taxed a much higher percentage of income than upper-income individuals.

Interestingly, my great- great- grandfather, A.O.P. Nicholson, two-term U.S. Senator and for 10 years chief justice of the Supreme Court of Tennessee, was chairman of the Committee on Revenue at the convention of 1870. As chief justice, he probably drafted the language in that constitution, subsequently used by the Tennessee Supreme Court in 1932, to prohibit a graduated income tax. The case, Evans v. McCabe, was written when Supreme Court justices did not have law clerks. The superficial opinion does not even mention an earlier case of Bank of Commerce v. Senter, which held the corporate income tax to be constitutional, nor a case that held constitutional the taxation of dividends and interest from stocks and bonds, the so-called Hall Income Tax. The Supreme Court's decision in Evans v. McCabe was based upon language in the 1870 constitution that said the state shall not tax the income from stocks and bonds, which are taxed ad valorem. The Supreme Court held by inversion that this permitted no other form of income taxation. In short, to permit the income tax on dividend and interest precluded a tax on any other income.

What I saw was a steadily rising sales tax and the long-term negative impact of a regressive tax structure that held the bottom levels of our society down. I was convinced an income tax was the proper solution. Every state surrounding Tennessee had an income tax, all passed around the same time as Tennessee's sales tax. The Tennessee tax structure did not grow as rapidly as inflation and required constant tax increases to meet the needs of the dramatic growth in government after World War II. I argued for an income tax to provide the state with a new revenue source and more funds for education and other fiscal needs.

After several committee sessions, I raised the revenue question. After a strong speech on the inequities and inadequacies of our tax system, I made a motion and the committee adopted a resolution recommending an income tax. The only result of this resolution: the death of the Committee of 100. Nonetheless, tax reform became a major interest of mine and it remained a live issue in Tennessee until the end of 20th century.

Another project of mine was the Rivermont Club. It was probably

Bailey Campbell's idea to create a downtown social club with dining and other facilities. We came up with the location on the South Bluff, a magnificent site, with a view straight up the Mississippi River and the Arkansas bottomlands. Bailey and Frank Norfleet and I were the original organizers; we involved Billy Wilkerson, my close friend and next-door neighbor. We had some meetings, built up enthusiasm, and our wives started selling memberships. They did a fantastic job. We sold enough memberships to buy the property and build a building. We built an apartment hotel where members could live or have guests visit; we hired a maitre d' to organize the club. Operations began out of the old Brinkley Snowden home on Central. Unfortunately, we had a lot of trouble with the building. Bloomfield, our builder and a speculative type builder, did not provide a quality building. But he got the building built at the price we had agreed upon.

Unfortunately, the club did not really take hold, and we struggled. We couldn't rent the apartments. We tried various appeals and approaches, but Memphis was not ready for a downtown social club, and particularly one located "way down on the South Bluff." The result did initiate development of the South Bluff, but not soon enough to save the club.

We struggled for a while, and representing the club, I sold the property to Kemmons Wilson, who was interested in our land. He built a wing on the front. At the end of that long struggle, as we closed the sale, somebody said, "Lewie, you ought to get a legal fee for all your work." I responded, "My legal fee is being out of this trap." A good idea and a great start, but somehow we never could make it work.

TWENTY

THE FIRM BEGINS TO GROW: CREATING A MODERN LAW FIRM

In 1964, Norfleet Turner, then chairman of First National Bank of Memphis, approached me about becoming outside counsel. I told Norfleet of my interest, but questioned him about the bank's current firm, Shepherd, Heiskell, Williams & Wall. The bank paid them a retainer of $12,500 per year which I told Norfleet was ridiculously low. We did not want to provide such a subsidy to the bank. He said, "We will refer you a lot of business." I responded that I wanted the bank to pay us adequately for our work, and while I hoped he would refer us to a lot of business, each one would have to stand on its own feet. That sort of broke off the negotiations, but in a couple of weeks they resumed.

Norfleet and I reached an agreement: The bank would pay a retainer of $25,000 per year. At year's end, we would agree on the remainder of the bank's annual fee. He asked us to merge with Shepherd, Heiskell who provided their legal work, primarily loan documents and major collections. He retained us in anticipation of the bank's expansion and future acquisitions, not an area of expertise of the Shepherd, Heiskell firm. We agreed to do that merger. Elwood Edwards did not join the new firm, in part, because of his concern about adding Shepherd, Heiskell as partners. Ben also had reservations, but we decided it was a good move, which proved to be correct.

At the time of the merger, our firm consisted of Ben Adams, Mike Grogan, Elwood Edwards, Bill O'Hearn, Don Malmo, Dick Keathley, Roy Keathley, Bob White, and Maurice Wexler. Shepherd, of the Shepherd, Heiskell firm, retired, and Longstreet Heiskell became of counsel. The attorneys who joined us were Ernest Williams, Jr., Ramsey Wall, Bill Kirsch, Ernest Williams, III, Frierson Graves, Marvin Ratner, and David Williams. Marvin Ratner left shortly to go with another firm, and Bill O'Hearn went on the bench.

Our gross had been considerably higher than the Heiskell group for the three preceding years, but our allocation formula made the merger easy. Surprisingly enough, the Shepherd, Heiskell firm did not keep time records, bill monthly or get retainers. I became managing partner and we selected the Heiskell, Donelson, Adams, Williams & Wall name. Longstreet Heiskell was a distinguished older lawyer. The Heiskell name was a well-known name among the Memphis and Tennessee bars.

As mentioned earlier, my great- great-grandfather was A.O.P. Nicholson, a United States Senator when Tennessee seceded. He and Joe Heiskell, Longstreet's grandfather, became friends in a Civil War prison camp.

This merger with Heiskell, almost our equal in size, went smoothly despite a few difficulties caused by different personalities and cultures. With immediate success and the rapid rise in incomes of the Heiskell partners, there were few complaints. The Shepherd, Heiskell lawyers began to keep time records, bill monthly, and greatly increase their billings.

The process of settling the bank's fee was difficult. The first year I negotiated with Norfleet. He enjoyed the negotiations as much as I did. I told him what I wanted. He pretended to faint. I asked him what he thought the bank ought to pay. He quoted a figure. I had the number of hours worked on bank business for every lawyer and their hourly rates. I did some figuring and said David Williams would not even make the minimum wage under Norfleet's figure. After more haggling, we settled on a figure that brought our gross fee up close to

$100,000. My partners had hoped to get an amount equal to our rent, which I exceeded. The merger of the law firms was effective as of October 1, 1964. We moved into the then-new bank building on March 1, 1965. This fee negotiation continued every year while Norfleet remained chairman.

After Norfleet retired, Allen Morgan, Sr., took over as chairman. He wanted to work out an agreement to give the bank a discount against our regular rates, then bill monthly, and receive monthly pay. This has been the general basis ever since.

During Morgan's tenure as chairman, the bank issued a substantial bond issue to increase its capital. I worked on that project with considerable assistance from Don Malmo, Boyd Rhodes, and Bob Walker. Salomon Brothers handled the bond issue. When time came to sell the issue, we had not finished with the documents. The accountants were late. We postponed the proposed closing. Allen told me if the market changed in those two weeks, he would get on me for our delays. Two weeks later we closed and, fortunately, the market had moved favorably to the bank. Salomon had this unique practice where on the day of the closing when you actually priced the issue, everybody gathered in a big room with a little table in the center and someone got up representing Salomon and someone got up representing the issuer, and they negotiated the price. Allen and I agreed on our plan, but I had the excitement of negotiating the price with the Salomon representative. I enjoyed that experience.

On another occasion, I was in Morgan's office for a discussion about a bank problem. He asked me to stay after the others left. He said, "Lewie, I need to name a successor in the next six months," and he talked about the potential ones. I knew most of the top executives well. There were the two Mitchells, Billy and Early. Early was head of the bond department from which both Norfleet and Allen Morgan had come. I knew Henry Haizlip, John Whitsitt, Bob Rogers, and various others, and we discussed each one and he solicited my opinion. I would frequently say, "He is a great banker." Allen would reply "No Lewie, you do not understand, I am not trying to find a great banker. We've got lots of great bankers, and we want to use them, and we will. I need to find a great CEO who can speak for the company, who can relate to the public and to the shareholders. He needs to be a great executive with an ability to plan and envision future growth." He mentioned Ron Terry and Cullen Kehoe, but I was not too familiar with either one.

Not long after, Allen told me he had decided on Ron Terry. I was surprised, but Terry turned out to be a brilliant choice, leading the bank to new heights of profitability and dramatic growth. I was impressed with how thoroughly Allen knew his people, their strengths, weaknesses, and potential. He clearly understood what the institution needed. I was flattered for Allen's show of confidence in my advice, which definitely was not legal advice. This exemplified the existing relationship between the bank CEO and the outside counsel.

Allen Morgan encouraged me to grow the law firm. He pushed to make First Tennessee the biggest bank in the state and wanted us to be the biggest law firm. We were growing rapidly but had not seriously considered creating other Tennessee offices. Allen also talked about his vision of a big securities firm—we called them stock brokerages—in Memphis. I was almost 20 years older than Ron and had represented the bank longer than he had worked there. Ron and I developed a special relationship.

Ron Terry had not been CEO many months when one day he said to me, "Lewie, I am going to do something very drastic." I said, "What's that?" He said, "Norfleet and Allen concentrated on growing the bank and we have grown tremendously, but I want to concentrate instead on making the bank more and more profitable. Growth will be slower but profits will be much higher in relationship to our capital." Profit was the touchstone of Ron's years as CEO. He never got into a growth contest with UP, which grew much more rapidly, but the bank's profits far outshone any other bank in Memphis and Tennessee. Timing is critical. When he decided to change policy, the bank cut back on loans to reduce risk and to cut expenses, which did result in increased profits. This occurred before that serious real estate collapse in the early 1970s. First Tennessee was uniquely able to weather that storm whereas UP, NBC, First American, Third National, and Commerce Union all suffered serious losses. At one point First American and UP were in shaky financial condition. His vision proved to be superb and his timing was perfect.

During the late seventies, the bank formed a real estate investment trust (REIT). There was a nationwide craze for REITs and many banks formed them. The real estate recession put all at risk, and many in serious financial trouble. Involved in the formation of the REIT, I had some familiarity of its operations. It had many specified requirements that had to be observed to obtain tax benefits. Bob Walker and David Williams took over most of the day-to-day dealings with the REIT, because real estate lending deals could be handled by our banking group, experts in such matters.

When the troubles began, Ron said, "Lewie, we are going to need somebody to watch for all of our real estate loans that may have some difficulties, and Henry Haizlip asked me to ask you to help him." I said, "I'll get someone on it right away." Ron said, "He wants you to handle it personally." I did. Henry and I had known each other a long time. His parents and mine were contemporaries and good friends. Henry and I had frequent dealing during the settlement of REIT and other bank loan problems.

I would show up for a conference about a loan and be asked, "Are we in this much trouble?" I would answer, "Henry thinks so." Henry Haizlip was the chief lending officer of the bank. First Tennessee came through much better than most large banks in Tennessee, but the bank had troubles, many related to the REIT.

Henry called one day and said, "Lewie, there is going to be a big seminar about real estate investment trusts up in New York, the troubles they have, and what everybody is doing about it. I am going to take a couple of my people up there to it and I want you to come and bring somebody else, but it's at your expense." It was a command performance. I went, and probably Boyd Rhodes came along. Many REITs had overreached and were in trouble up to their eyeballs.

Many had made loans inappropriate for REITs. The REITs were designed to be real estate owning entities that paid annual returns. Many REITs had invested in condominium projects where you sold the condominium, but without any further annual return.

The first morning, we came down for breakfast at the hotel and Henry said, "I tell you what I will do, Lewie, I will match you for the breakfast." We matched and I won. We were busy all that day and that night Henry said, "I want to go to 21 for dinner." I knew immediately what he had in mind. We went to 21 and had a lovely dinner with lots of wine. After dinner, Henry said, "Lewie, I will match you for the dinner tonight." The bill must have been $800 to $1,000 minimum, substantial then. We matched and I won again. Henry never asked to match me on anything after that.

The person running the REIT told me about one loan. I asked about the security. He recited the amount and then paused. I said, "There's got to be more." Unfortunately, there was not and that loss represented the largest single loan loss the bank had ever had.

Bill Matthews, the Union Planters Bank chairman, had been recruited to salvage Union Planters from its multiple loan difficulties. Bill stopped me one day and he said, "Lewie, I do not understand it. Every time I come down here, your bank has all the security and I am sitting here with an open note, no security." I said, "That's easy, Bill. We've got good lawyers." A couple of days later, Bill called me and asked, "Do you think you can take on the representation of Union Planters Bank?" I said, "Bill, you know I cannot do that, I can't represent Union Planters and First Tennessee at the same time."

Frierson Graves, then a longtime partner, had been assistant city attorney, and then city attorney. He loved the job but it paid little and consumed much time. One day I said, "Frierson, Wyeth Chandler thinks you are wonderful, and you have been lifelong friends. Why don't you get him to get you a good job instead of that city attorney's job? It doesn't pay anything much." He said, "What are you talking about?" I said, "How about general counsel for the Light, Gas & Water Division?" Frierson thought about it for a minute and said, "OK, that would be fine." I spoke to Wyeth, who arranged it. Frierson did a tremendous job and became an expert in utility law. He helped LG&W become a leader among the TVA distributors. The Light, Gas & Water Division tried to start a coal gas project, and Frierson and Don Malmo spent weeks and months on it. We got a large fee, although the deal never materialized.

David Hansen, the head of the Light, Gas & Water Division, and I got to know each other during that project. Memphis had a serious ice storm and freeze. Jan and I had been in Nashville. When we walked in our front door, I heard a horrible sound. The pipes had burst and water was spraying everywhere. The next day I was talking about it and somebody said, "The worst thing was, knowing you, you would not even know where to turn off the water," and I said, "Yes, I did too." I picked up the phone and I called David Hansen and said, "Get somebody out here right away," and in 10 minutes someone was there.

Initially, we handled all the bank's acquisitions. The first acquisition was a tiny little bank in the Nashville area, White's Creek Bank. We felt the antitrust rules prevented our acquiring a larger bank in Nashville, and it would be difficult to get approval from the comptroller, the Federal Reserve, and the FTC for a larger merger. Buying a smaller bank was a very serious mistake. First Tennessee never got a foothold in the Nashville market from this tiny base. Our original acquisitions in Chattanooga and Knoxville and in the upper East Tennessee area were much larger operations. By then we understood the monopoly rules would not be strictly applied except for buying a bank within our immediate market. From 1965 to 1982, we made acquisitions in Jackson, Dyersburg, Greeneville, Johnson City, Maryville, and other cities.

Lee Welch, who was hired as inside counsel, handled more of these transactions. One day he called me and said, "We are about to complete the acquisition of such and such a bank." I had not been involved, and I asked, "What do you want me to do, Lee—come down and raise my hands and say amen?" He said, "That is right!"

The year of the Heiskell group merger, we grossed about $600,000, and we began to grow rapidly. Bill Kirsch and the two younger Williamses began to grow their businesses dramatically. Bill Kirsch's excellent trial skills and the Williamses' growing expertise in banking and finance companies gave new dimension to our practice. From 1964 to 1968 we hired several associates. Auvergne Williams, Jr., stayed briefly. Charles Clement left after a year to join Holiday Inn. Mike Pleasants stayed with the firm for many years.

As First National Bank of Memphis bought additional banks, the name no longer fit the institution, and after much study, First Tennessee Bank became the name. Ramsey Wall checked corporate records and found no conflicting uses. We proceeded to publicize the name with massive advertising and spending.

After all the publicity, I got a letter from Brad Reed of Bass, Berry and Sims, whom I knew slightly. (We became friends several years later when we served together on the Tennessee Higher Education Commission.) He represented a group who owned a corporation called First Tennessee Corporation, which had been incorporated before First Tennessee National Corporation. He requested we cease and desist from using the name of First Tennessee Bank. He really sought a payment for relinquishment of rights to the name. I was horrified. I went down to see Norfleet Turner, and he was equally horrified. I told Norfleet I thought when we bought the bank in Jonesborough, which had the No. 1 charter in Tennessee, they owned a corporation called First Tennessee Corporation as a subsidiary. He agreed. Norfleet and I fumbled frantically through those files and, sure enough, we found it. The bank did own a corporation called First Tennessee Corporation, incorporated long before the Nashville group's corporation. I wrote the lawyer and called his attention to our ownership of that corporation. I did not get a letter from him, but my own letter returned with a note on the bottom that said, "I'll be damned." It was a scary moment, but we escaped by the skin of our teeth. The record keeping then in the secretary of state's office was miserable; it is not much better with a computer. You needed to be extremely careful in relying on anything from that office.

During Norfleet's term as chairman, the bank had a dinner cele-brating its 100th year. Representatives from the banking industry came from across the nation for the festive occasion. I sat with the then-chairman of the First National Bank of Boston, and we talked about valuations of banks and prices of banks. He said, "The terrible thing is that even though I've been in the banking business my entire career, if I look at the financial statement of a bank, I don't have the remotest idea of the bank's condition. Standards for loan loss reserves and other accounting policies are so vague that unless you know ex-actly those policies, it's difficult to determine a bank's worth." That was an interesting lesson and helped improve our due diligence in buying a bank.

One of my first hires after the merger was Bob Walker in 1968. I interviewed him walking to City Hall. At the door, I said, "Bob, tell them you're hired." He told me when I hired him on the spot, not consulting anyone else, that he had a moment of doubt, wondering if he wanted to be in a firm where one person called the shots. He did join and has no regrets. Bob was called into military service the next year, but returned to the firm after its completion. Bob worked with me several years and did some bank work. He began to develop small bank clients. Ron approved it and Bob has built his practice on start-up banks and small, growing banks. By investing in some of them, Bob has done well financially.

In 1969 and 1970, we organized our hiring. Many other firms al-ready recruited associates in the fall of their final law school year. I wanted us to do the same. This horrified some older partners who were concerned about whether the firm would have enough work for them. In 1970 we hired Boyd Rhodes. Then in 1972, we hired Mike Richards and John Speer. In 1973, we hired Charlie Tuggle, Hardy Mays, Kent Wunderlich, and an associate who has left. These excellent new associates gave us a strong base to handle bigger matters. The older lawyers multiplied themselves by delegating.

Don Malmo, Bob Walker, and Boyd Rhodes built their own prac-tices after working under Ben and me. John Speer established his own base after several years under Bill Kirsch. One thing I tried didn't work well: We rotated new associates from corporate to tax to litigation as interns, but litigation was so protracted they could not be extricated after their allotted time.

The firm, informally, had corporate, tax, banking, real estate, and litigation groups. In January 1975, I submitted our first 10-year plan. Maurice Wexler, who apparently saves everything, dug up a copy of this plan. We had 12 partners and eight or nine associates. My plan was not well received by the partners. I usually dealt with reluctance by not taking a vote. Gradually, I began to institute the changes. Several years later at a partners' meeting Maurice concluded we had followed most of the plan.

I predicted we'd have 40 lawyers by 1985, but I was conservative. We had the Nashville and Knoxville offices, and our gross income had grown to $7.5 million. We agreed on our need to strengthen our litigation section. We considered possibilities and finally settled on Leo Bearman and his son Leo, Jr., both superb trial lawyers. Leo, Jr., is the best in Tennessee: bright, extremely able, a prodigious worker who believed in careful preparation. I was working for Governor Alexander as commissioner of Finance and Administration. The Bearmans came to Nashville and we talked. They wanted assurance of my return to the firm. I promised, and they joined us. Leo, Sr., had been primarily an insurance defense lawyer, but his skills extended far beyond that. One Leo, Sr., legend will suffice. Leo, Sr., defended an insured person. The insured was drunk and his vehicle came weaving down Trezevant, ran up on the curb, and hit a woman, seriously injuring her. On cross Leo, Sr., asked her, "Did you see the car coming?" "Yes." "How far away was the car?" "[It was] at least a couple of hundred yards." "You say that the car was swerving back and forth." "Yes." "Why didn't you get up in the yard out of his way?" He argued basically "the last clear chance doctrine," that she had the last chance to present injury to herself.

When we established litigation, corporate and securities, tax, real estate and banking departments, the plan envisioned a firm manager, a management committee with a chairman, and additional support staff for financial and timekeeping records. It called for quarterly firm meetings, monthly partner meetings, and biweekly department meetings. The plan urged the recruitment of enough new lawyers to allow senior lawyers time to develop new business. Low overhead may be nice for current profits, but it punishes growth. The plan emphasized that the firm was a team, not a group of lawyers sharing offices.

My 1975 plan anticipated increasing expertise and of more clearcut departmentalization within the firm, but not additional offices. It called for better defined management structure and for annual recruitment with increased monitoring of young lawyers by older lawyers.

Sometime before 1975, the famous Patty case came down. It basically held that all of the state's usury statutes were unconstitutional because they violated the constitutional provision limiting interest, thus creating chaos among banks. We had a full-scale meeting in Ron Terry's office where I was a principal player. The firm was looked to for advice. We called various lawyers around the state who had drawn documents for the bank's various branches and found the idea of legally permissible interest varied from lawyer to lawyer. I had been telling Ron we needed a standard loan document and a standard interest rate policy statewide. I urged our firm's involvement in preparation of these documents. These calls proved a uniform policy was desperately needed. When I walked out of the meeting, Jack Donelson, a bank officer, said, "What I most like about you is how you handled yourself in that meeting. You didn't say *you* are in a bunch of trouble; you said *we* are in a bunch of trouble. Your attitude was how to get the matter straightened out and protect ourselves for the future."

I became involved in legislation to correct the problem and to get a constitutional amendment to permit it. I appeared at a number of those hearings, and one time I was on a panel discussion about the usury issue with the Tennessee Banking Association attorneys. Lt. Gov. John Wilder, in his usual scholarly fashion, presented a series of detailed questions about how the new law would work. He asked a long question, and the lawyer representing the Tennessee Bank

Association gave a long involved answer. Milton Hamilton, majority leader in the Senate, sitting on the platform with me asked, "Lewie, what did he say?" And I said, "He said, 'No.'" Everybody died laughing. Lawyers do have a tendency to explain the situation so thoroughly that no one knows what they said. One of my strengths as a lawyer is to keep it simple and understandable to the client. Ron Terry said to me one day, "I have the best lawyer in the world, David Williams, to analyze the legal problems with all the pros and cons, and you to tell me what to do." Maybe it was arrogance, but I was never afraid to give an answer. One friendly enemy said, "Often wrong, but never in doubt."

In 1975, we hired two additional associates and targeted the hires for a specific area of expertise: Rob Liddon for bank lending work and real estate type work, and Ken Kenworthy for pensions, profit sharing, and fringe benefits. Both are now experts in their fields, and our business expanded in these areas with more lawyers to support them. (Tragically, Ken was found to have a cancer in his lung in October 2006 and died in March 2007. A health fanatic, he worked out every morning and swam laps. He hadn't smoked in over 20 years, but it was a smoke-related cancer.) When I visited his wife Sherry after the funeral, she produced a file Ken had maintained over his years with the firm. I opened it and on the top was a handwritten note with instructions I had given him when he joined us. Following that were several notations outlining what he had done in response.

Maurice Wexler, with his expertise in client development, after several years of training began to concentrate on EEOC matters. At my suggestion he became active in the American Bar Association in this area as I had done in the tax area and Ernest Williams, III, even more successfully, in commercial code law. Both built excellent practices, in part from bar association connections and their highly visible participation with these bar association sections.

By 1975 we were the second largest firm in Memphis, behind Armstrong Allen. We recruited on campuses; Mark Glover was one such recruit. We added two to three associates per year.

In 1976, we made a major breakthrough in hiring the first African American, Allan Wade, to join a major business type law firm. I had known his father, a member of the cabinet of Winfield Dunn. I told Allan that we hired him to be a lawyer and not to make a career out of civil rights. Allan proved to be an excellent lawyer and worked without difficulty all over West Tennessee with white clients who possibly never dreamed of working with an African American lawyer. One day when we finished up in Dyersburg, the client took us to lunch at the bank's dining room. I am sure Allan was the first African American to eat as a guest in that dining room, and no awkwardness arose. Allan became the premier business, tax, and estate planning African American lawyer in Memphis, serving clients of all backgrounds. He proved to be an able trial lawyer, winning several major cases, including a huge tax refund for the Duncan Williams estate. He left the firm about 10 years ago to open his own law office. He became counsel for the City Council and an influential Memphian.

By the end of 1978, the firm was well established with over 20 lawyers in corporate, tax, estate planning, real estate, bank lending, and EEOC and labor practices. Hardy Mays and Charlie Tuggle rapidly matured into excellent corporate lawyers, providing depth in that area to allow us to handle larger and more complex transactions. Roy Keathley and Don Malmo also developed their own practices. Roy, through his representation of Frank Flautt and Jeff Mann, became an expert in franchise problems and counsel for the Holiday Inn Franchise Owners Association. He also had a number of real estate development clients. Don Malmo concentrated in the corporate and tax areas and gradually accumulated a number of business clients. He assumed the responsibility for the Kirkpatrick family representation. Don also helped me with numerous acquisitions for Billy Wilkerson. Bill Kirsch established himself as a fine trial lawyer, especially in complex matters. John Speer developed as the major lawyer for the bank in its collection problems. David Williams became a superb attorney on all loan and bank lending matters.

Management had been organized with a board and a managing

partner. Don Malmo, Roy Keathley, and Maurice Wexler all took turns at the job. None decided to continue beyond one year. When I went to Nashville in 1979, Bill Kirsch became chairman, and during these years the firm slowed its growth, missing my driving force.

We also hired Mark Glover in 1979 to further strengthen our litigation area. Even though in Nashville, I actually hired William Fones in 1980. His father had been a longtime friend of mine. William was hired to be our tax expert and certainly proved that with a vengeance. He is, in my opinion, the finest tax lawyer in this city.

The Bearman merger mentioned earlier provided us with two outstanding trial lawyers. Leo, Jr., is also a brilliant scholar, be it Shakespeare or Sherlock Holmes, and possesses a deep sense of community responsibility. He has won major cases for our clients over the years, including First Tennessee. In his most noteworthy case, he successfully persuaded the Tennessee Supreme Court to strike down a statute that seriously inhibited city growth. He also successfully defended a tobacco company in a products liability case, a rare and significant victory. He recently secured another great triumph in a difficult patent licensing case for Medtronics. He also won a significant victory for the city of Memphis and MLG&W, securing a dismissal of a water rights case brought by the state of Mississippi. The court, after a three-year delay, ruled the state of Tennessee is an essential party, and the case must be filed directly in the Supreme Court. Leo, Jr., keeps us the frontrunner in litigation and has enabled us to build an excellent litigation department, an essential ingredient for any great law firm.

One offshoot of Frierson Graves becoming general counsel of MLG&W was that we acted as bond counsel for the division. When MLG&W issued a large bond issue to purchase the steam plant, Frierson asked me to handle it. Borrowers' counsel doesn't have much responsibility. I was in New York in the Brown & Wood offices reading the documents. I came to one convoluted paragraph and asked, "What does this mean?" The Brown & Wood lawyer read it over and said, "Damned if I know, it was in the form when I came with the firm and I left it in there." I replied, "If there's one thing that frosts my butt,

it is long, wordy, complex forms with provisions no one understands."
It stayed in. Frierson and I handled the big bond issues for MLG&W.
We turned this business over to Allan Wade. When Allan left, he took
the business with him.

George "Buck" Lewis joined us in 1980, Ben Adams, Jr., in 1981. In
1981, I returned to the firm from Nashville. I had become well-known
throughout the state, and particularly in Nashville. When I left, Governor Lamar Alexander said, "Lewie, you may not be the best lawyer
in the state, but you are certainly the best-known, and you ought to
start spreading your law firm over the rest of the state." The law firm's
development after my return will be detailed in a later chapter.

THE CITY COUNCIL AND THE SANITATION WORKERS' STRIKE

A fter the 1966 election, *The Commercial Appeal* pushed for a change in Memphis city government. The commission form of government, put in by Crump around 1910, was considered an innovative and progressive new structure at that time. The system provided for the election of five commissioners, with each managing certain parts of city government. One would preside as mayor in meetings and act as ribbon cutter and spokesman for the city on appropriate occasions. When adopted, it wasn't a bad form of government for a city the size of Memphis, but as the city grew larger and more racially diverse its structure was no longer appropriate. No blacks or Republicans had ever been elected to the commission. Members were not widely dispersed in the city.

The Press Scimitar also pushed for a council-city manager form of government. The city manager would provide day-to-day professional and nonpartisan management, and the council with citywide representatives would make legislative decisions and control the purse. The city management form of government did not work for Memphis. A racially divided city needed one spokesman to provide leadership and be the focal point. Also, city managers tended to be less sensitive to political realities. Memphis needed a city council elected from districts to assure representation for all segments of the community.

The City Commission did not want a change in the form of government. The newspapers became frustrated and finally called for a town hall meeting. This was held in the auditorium and a Charter Commission was elected. At that time in Shelby County, blacks, particularly in the NAACP, were organized, and Republicans were organized, but Democrats, relying on their base strength and remnants of Crump machine officeholders, were unable to turn out many supporters at the meeting. As a result, the overwhelming majority of the newly elected Charter Commission, referred to as the Program of Progress (POP), were Republicans and blacks.

The commission operated in a professional way, with the city attorney as legal adviser and a professor from the University of Memphis to help analyze the issues and present options. They heard advocates of various forms of city government, along with other special programs to be included in the charter. The main issue was whether to select the council city manager form of government or a mayor–council form of government.

Republicans elected to the Charter Commission initially were of an open mind, but we became convinced that with the strong racial division and the growing black population, Memphis needed the mayor-council form of government. We made one compromise: to provide for a chief operating officer for the city who would perform the functions that might have been expected of the city manager, but with less public visibility and much less power.

We made fateful decisions. Perhaps the most significant one was to decide whether to have all council districts or some at-large representatives. A compromise provided an excellent solution. The charter would provide for seven districts and six councilpersons at large. This meant every citizen would vote for a majority of the council, the six at-large and the seventh, the councilperson from a district. This meant a healthy political mix. Some councilmen would be responsible to and elected from the whole community, some from their districts. It assured black representation and representation from all areas of the city. It enabled the city to have several leaders from certain areas with more than their share of excellent officeholders. The first council included four members from Precinct 57, Gwen Awsumb, Downing Pryor, Jerred Blanchard, and me. The election would be nonpartisan with no party designation on the ballot, no party primaries, and run-offs if no candidate received a majority.

The newspapers and TV coverage of the POP committee overwhelmed the opposition of the City Commission. The Charter Commission meeting and deliberations were covered by the press in great detail. The coverage outlined the issues and highlighted the discussions and the reasons behind the decisions. This represented a peak in public interest in city government in Memphis in my lifetime. The momentum was so strong that the City Commission folded under the pressure and agreed to put the new charter on the ballot. They made one or two minor changes, but it went to the voters substantially as the POP committee had agreed and passed easily in early 1967. The mayor-council election was set for the end of September; the run-off, 30 days later.

The Charter Commission brought attention for the first time to black political leaders, including Dr. Vasco Smith, whose wife Maxine was secretary of the local NAACP; Jesse Turner, head of the Tri-State Bank; and Dr. Hollis Price, president of LeMoyne-Owen College, all established leaders. New faces emerged, among them A.W. Willis, Russell Sugarmon, and Ben Hooks, able young lawyers. I got to know them during those hearings and this helped us work together on difficult issues ahead. From the Community Relations Committee, I already knew Smith, Turner, Dr. Price, and several powerful black ministers, but through A.W. Willis, I came to know Bishop J.O. Patterson, presiding bishop who brought the Church of God in Christ to national recognition. Ben Hooks had Republican connections and came out of the Lt. Lee organization. Ben was eventually appointed to the Federal Communications Commission through the influence of then-Senator Howard Baker. He was the first minority appointed to a major federal regulatory agency.

After the charter's adoption, the next task was to find candidates;

and I was chairman of the committee. After much effort, I persuaded seven people to run if I also agreed to be a candidate. I talked to Jan, who was unenthusiastic, but supportive. I called the seven together and told them, "I am going to run. No one can back out."

Henry Loeb had been mayor. He planned to run, as did A.W. Willis. They ran against incumbent Bill Ingram. Ingram was one of those occasional freaks of politics. A relatively unknown lawyer when appointed as City Court judge, he decided to believe a black defendant instead of a police officer. Many black defendants got off under what you might call Ingram's judicial reign. Word spread around the community that Ingram was the black people's friend. He rode that reputation in the black community, then on a populist platform to victory as mayor. His term as mayor was undistinguished, and surprisingly, he took several actions that the black community considered unfavorable. Unfortunately, Ingram took away black votes from Willis, who might have run more strongly. Loeb won easily. In districts where blacks could be elected, A.W. Willis and Russell Sugarmon, very able representatives, weren't considered "black" enough. This marked the beginning of a trend in the black community to elect weak, unqualified candidates who played the race card, which pushed many able black candidates out of the political arena.

The council races were intense; every position required a runoff. I was in the runoff against Frank White, a former Democrat state senator. With the election at the end of September, I decided to start on Labor Day with a visit to the then-new Lakeland Amusement Park. With little talk about the election, I got a poor response. Voters had not focused on the election and did not expect old-fashioned, hands-on campaigning. My son went along and after we finished, he said he'd never run for anything. During the Crump era there was no campaigning, although from 1956 on, door-to-door canvassing and some handshaking began. In 1967, Memphians began to experience the personal touch in politics.

For the most part, I enjoyed campaigning. I went door-to-door, primarily in areas in which I had no personal connections, such as Frayser and the black community, including one housing project. Several times I stood outside of Montesi's and shook hands for an hour. After one such session, I told Jan, "I am so sick of my own name; I might even change it." I would say, "My name is Lewis Donelson and I am running for city council-at-large position four." I thought I was reasonably well-known in the community because of my chairmanship of the United Way and president of the Republican Association. I also had been a delegate to the Republican National Convention in 1964 and received national publicity. In addition, I was a lifelong Memphian, as were my father and my grandfather with the same name, but even after I told a person my name, there was no glimmer of recognition. If you concentrate on the names, it is surprising how many you could remember. What a hit when, to someone on the way out, I said, "I sure hope you vote for me, Mr. So-and-So," calling the name.

Milton "Pinky" Simon of Simon and Gwynn was my PR person for the campaign; Irvin Bogatin, my campaign manager; and Bill Brakebill, my finance chairman. Because my public image was Republican, I worked to reach out to Democrat voters and to the black community. Because of my position on the Community Relations Commission, my public stand on integration, and my campaigning in the black community, I did extremely well for a Republican.

Pinky Simon came up with an effective slogan that depicted the image I wanted to project and the way I felt I would behave as an officeholder: The slogan was "Courageability." I have always believed the public yearns for people to speak out and take courageous political stands. Yes, times have changed, but I still believe the public is receptive to political courage. All the advice from political consultants and professional campaign managers is to follow the polls, not take any unpopular positions, and if you don't agree with the popular position, then try to avoid any position. In short, say what people want to hear. I believe this is the dry rot of the present political system. My personal experience confirms that. One TV station aired a forum with the 26 council candidates. I remember many tough questions. One was, "Would you vote for a tax increase?" Twenty-five said "no," and there was one "yes"—mine. "I would vote for one if I thought one was necessary," I said. Financing government is a foremost responsibility of officeholders.

Another question: "Would you be in favor of an open meeting law?" I said I would not. I believe all public business should be conducted in open meetings, but open meetings tend to inhibit communication among council members and reduce the possibility of reaching a consensus needed to achieve the best results. The same ratio: 25 yeses and one no. In the runoff election I got more votes than anyone, 65,076. Political pandering is pervasive today. Officeholders are sometimes punished at the polls for courageous stands, but I still believe the public respects courage and will listen to the politician who takes an unpopular stand, but explains, with skill, his reason.

Most of the candidates whom the POP committee persuaded to run, won. The winning at-large candidates were Wyeth Chandler, Jerred Blanchard, Downing Pryor, Philip Perel, Tom Todd, and me. The district winners were Bob James, Gwen Awsumb, Billy Hyman, H.A. McBride, and three black winners: Fred Davis, Jim Netters, and J.O. Patterson, Jr. Fred Davis and Jim Netters were most effective councilmen. Netters, pastor of Mount Vernon Baptist Church, is an honorable and compassionate man. He built Mt. Vernon into a great church. Fred Davis, then an idealistic and energetic young man, brought to the council a wonderful innocence and enthusiasm. He made a great councilman and was the first black councilman to be elected at large in subsequent years. I became good friends with them both. J.O. Patterson served in the state legislature and participated only marginally on the council.

Then Jan and I had what proved to be a great idea. Jan invited all the council members to a seated dinner at our home, unheard of in Memphis at the time. Initially, it was a little bit awkward. Everybody stood around at first, even the black people did not know each other well. I had met McBride, Hyman, Patterson, Davis, and Netters during the campaign, but they were virtually unknown to me. James, Pryor, Awsumb, and Blanchard were friends; Perel and Chandler were acquaintances. James, Perel, Hyman, and McBride, all business-people, brought a fiscally sound approach to city problems. All the members were high quality people of integrity who were sincerely concerned about the welfare of the community. The party was a smashing success.

As we were standing around looking at each other, Fred Davis arrived, late as usual on what he used to call "CPT or colored people's time," walked in the door and looked around and said, "Ooowee East Memphis," and everybody laughed. The ice was broken. We had a Ping-Pong table at the house and a lot of them played that evening. Wyeth Chandler loved to tell the story. Originally, he was awkward, but by the end of the evening he was playing Ping-Pong with Fred and having a great time. It helped begin the bonding necessary for the baptism of fire ahead.

Shortly before we took office, two sanitation workers were killed when the compactor mechanism of one of the trucks was accidentally triggered. There was no insurance for their families because they were not covered by workmen's compensation. The commission, which was winding down, did nothing. That lack of action left feelings of bitterness among the sanitation workers, which we would inherit.

An important dynamic of that first council was created by six at-large councilman, each elected by the whole community with responsibility to all Memphians. Today, without at-large positions and only super districts, the council's ability to develop consensus and take actions for the welfare of the entire community is diminished. Too much parochialism and concern about individual districts make it more difficult for members to think of citywide needs.

We took office in a burst of favorable publicity and with a lot of enthusiasm. Downing Pryor was elected chairman. I was named chairman of the budget committee because of my tax background and my experience on the United Way Budget Committee. I chose that assignment because city government had been without budget reviews and open budget hearings for many, many years, or even overall budget review by the commission. The commissioners lobbied and log rolled among themselves to get more money for their departments, presenting proposals with few details and without specific items. We needed budget hearings open to the press and public with every department's budget under detailed review. Every department would be invited to present a budget and answer questions. The press was most interested, with full TV and newspaper coverage of budget committee meetings.

Terribly busy, I seldom had time to eat lunch. On one occasion I ate raisins and peanuts with a Coke during the budget hearing. Jan, watching it on TV, said I would take a mouth full of peanuts, and then chew and chew and chew and chew until she said to the television, "Lewie, for heaven's sake, stop chewing." You're not conscious of the camera and the results can be embarrassing.

The budget hearings were an eye-opener. We found many unnecessary things, many employees with jobs without useful purpose, and many programs that needed to be discontinued. We cut the budget substantially. We not only listened to the presentations, we gave presenters feedback on what we liked and what might be cut. We also gave them a full opportunity to respond. Many commented they liked leaving those hearings knowing where I stood and where the committee probably stood.

With the exception of one year, I was chairman of the Budget Committee my entire term on the council. This powerful job gave me tremendous insight into city government and major control over its direction.

One year, perhaps the first, Myra Dreifus presented a proposal to provide funds to feed breakfast to children who otherwise would not have eaten. We appropriated $500,000 for that program, which became a national program. I've often said I don't have many good ideas, but I recognize a good one, and that was one I recognized.

We also had responsibility for the budget of city schools, and we reviewed this budget, not with the same minute earnestness given the city budget, but with considerable detail and care. I often questioned educators about programs for bright students. I supported efforts to help those in need of additional help, but I always felt strongly that if you do not encourage bright students and use the most talented people, the city is doomed to decline. These students are the source of progress. They have new ideas. They are the essential ingredients for a great city. During my first close look at education, I was appalled by the overhead encrusted on the school system with only a small portion of the money going to classroom instruction. We immediately learned the difficulty of firing teachers. I didn't do as much to streamline the school budgets as I did the city budgets. They were harder to deal with. We put up less than half of the money.

Then the state provided about one-half of the funds. The city schools received their share of the local sales tax divided on a per pupil basis. The city schools also received their share of the county property tax allocated to schools, again on a per pupil basis. City school property taxes provided the remainder of the education funding, which became substantial as many more assistant principals were needed for discipline, along with more teachers and teacher aides in poverty areas.

Busing began; white flight exploded. The city system struggled to meet the crisis, but solutions were scarce and public support, weak. When minorities exceeded 60 percent, school quality declined markedly. This was not strictly a racial problem; it was a poverty problem compounded by single parent families and drug addiction. Without a coherent plan, the School Board and the school system argued these factors required more money per pupil, but failed to make the case with the state or the city. And so the Memphis City Schools drifted toward disaster. The importance of education is easy to recognize in general, but specifics for improvement are harder to define and implement. Education improvement doesn't bear immediate fruit, and education failure takes years to become apparent. In city school funding, it was hard to see where the money went. I finally obtained close to a line-item budget to enable analysis of expenditures and the possibility of cutting the fat in school administration.

I spent somewhere between 75 to 100 hours on the city budget each year. My regular council activities took between 30 and 40 hours a week, and during the sanitation workers' strike, more than that. I was freed up to do what I thought was right, because I had no intention of running again and did not plan a political career. I loved practicing law, and I was in the process of building a law firm. Because of the size of the firm and my many connections in the community, I frequently recused myself. Sometimes I would say, "The proposal to some extent impacts banks; I do represent a bank, but I feel that I can vote on this without any reservations." Times are different, but it's amazing how well this was accepted. I don't recall that my recusing myself or my explaining my connection with clients turned into a big issue.

The overwhelming issue of the first year of the City Council: the sanitation workers' strike. As background, Pryor, Blanchard, Awsumb, and I had been on the POP committee. We felt the charter would provide a strong mayor-council form of government. The charter gave the mayor the contracting power. The council was designed as the legislative body with control of the purse strings and review and approval of budgets and policy decisions, but the day-to-day operations resided with the mayor, who appointed directors to head up the divisions of city government, with the council's approval. If you had asked us whether the council should get involved in a labor dispute, we would have said, "No." Unfortunately, none of us envisioned what was to happen.

In our third week, the Public Works director came to the Tuesday morning sessions, informal meetings to review the agenda and meet with the mayor. He informed us the sanitation workers had gone out on strike that morning. We knew of unrest over the sanitation workers' deaths and the absence of any benefits. As I mentioned, the old commission had done nothing. On taking office, the new council appropriated $10,000 to the families, then the maximum under workmen's compensation. We knew of efforts to organize the workers into a union, but felt protected by the Tennessee law which held governmental units could not recognize unions. Our education began that morning when Director Charles Blackburn explained the triggering event. If it was a rainy day, the workers were required to come in, but if it was raining too hard, they would be sent home without pay. The foremen, all but one white, however, did receive pay for such a day. That incident fueled the building fire.

We learned later that other workplace issues desperately needed attention. For example, most sanitation workers came to work by public transportation. When they finished, no shower facilities were available for them to clean up and change clothes. Garbage was picked up at the back of a house in the alley or back by the garage, usually in the rear of the house; the garbage was dumped into tubs, the tubs were carried out to a truck and, by the end of the day, the sanitation workers were dirty and smelly. The next week the workers came to the council chamber requesting to be heard and created a disturbance.

A televised debate was arranged between a union representative from Washington, P.J. Ciampa, and Mayor Loeb with Paul Tudor Jones, Idlewild minister and co-chairman of the Community Relations Committee. Ciampa's language was so objectionable and offensive that many citizens who might have been sympathetic with the union were appalled. In fact, his conduct so offended Dr. Jones that he did not participate in the ensuing struggle. The original attitude of the council was overwhelmingly that the dispute was none of our business. The mayor had the contracting power; a Supreme Court case clearly held the city could not recognize the union. The mayor had gone into court and gotten an injunction barring picketing and other activities.

The white community overwhelmingly supported the mayor and his refusal to negotiate, even black council members did not seriously press the issue. As events unfolded, the racial connotations became more and more evident. Sanitation workers' pay was low, but more offensive were the working conditions, previously discussed. The rainy day policy had been changed, but no shower or dressing facilities had been provided. Some talk began of a pay raise at the beginning of the city's fiscal year in July. The sanitation workers received strong support from many black ministers, but few other unions became involved, and the NAACP was never that active. The quarterback of the ministerial support was the Reverend James Lawson, a bright Vanderbilt divinity student and protest organizer at Vandy during the turbulence of the late fifties and early sixties. He sincerely believed conflict was the only route to progress in race relations. He conceived the sanitation workers' slogan for banners and chants: "I AM A MAN." Daily marches and daily council meetings tried to deal with the problem, but a solution proved more and more difficult as the division became more and more bitter. Within a few weeks, all three black council members and three whites could see this was no longer a labor dispute, but a racial issue, tearing the community apart and destroying the image of Memphis. A settlement was urgently needed.

A difficult issue to overcome: how to deal with the union despite strong state legal prohibition against recognition. Jerred Blanchard came up with a brilliant idea. He said, "We won't recognize the union, but we will enter into a memorandum of understanding with the union. We will have a contract with the union, but just outline the terms under which we will deal with the sanitation workers." This technique was ultimately used to settle the strike. The model was used again all over the entire country by Jerry Wurff, the national president of the American Federation of State, County, and Municipal Employees, AFSCME, as it is known. Thirty-five states then either had state laws or state court rulings that prohibited governmental units from recognizing unions. While the press acted as though Memphis was a backwater town, many of these laws and rulings were in the northern and western states. This technique saved the union and let it grow to become one of the nation's most powerful.

To ameliorate the racial connotations of the working conditions, I proposed a resolution that the city become an equal opportunity employer, and a second resolution that we set up a civil rights commission for the city that would hear complaints from employees. Neither got much public support. I remember meeting with Mayor Loeb about another matter. As I was leaving he said, "Look here, Lewie, on my desk there's 130 letters about your two resolutions, 128 of them against, and 2 of them for. What do you think of that?" My response was, "I didn't think we were elected to count letters."

As weeks passed and the strike continued, the city became bitterly divided. Everywhere the mayor went (he never approached the black community) he received standing ovations. The union issue allowed latent racism in the community to surface. I was surprised at its virulence. Yes, there was white support for the sanitation workers, a delegation of white ministers called on the mayor urging him to settle and a smattering of whites appeared in the marches. Some council members became increasingly alarmed.

I had always considered myself to be persuasive, and I struggled hard to develop a majority to settle the strike. The principal barrier was the correct legal position that contract issues were not the business of the council, and that we had no right to overrule the mayor. As the strike went on and the marches continued and the national publicity grew, those of us who pushed for a settlement realized more and more how vital a settlement was for Memphis. How frustrating not to reach a consensus. We agreed on money demands with a vague consensus on the Blanchard memorandum. But another issue arose: a checkoff. We couldn't do that, but I pointed out that a payroll deduction, like the one provided for United Way, was possible. This is not as effective as a checkoff because a payroll deduction required each employee to sign a request to deduct union dues from a payroll check.

One amazing and generous response remained secret for many years. I had made it clear that the city budget was totally committed, with no money for an immediate pay raise. Abe Plough called and said, "Lewie, I know that you need money for an immediate pay raise and I will provide it. But no one must know." He continued, "Just call me and tell me how much the settlement will cost until July 1, the beginning of the fiscal year, and I will send a check to cover it." When we settled, he did. Suddenly, there were several million dollars I pretended to find in the budget, and no one questioned me. Until Abe died, I never told anyone, even council members, about this. Of course, Mr. Anonymous, as he was called in the community, was so well-known that many suspected the money came from him.

One night during a secret meeting at Fred Davis' house, I came up with a possible solution. I suggested that council members who wanted to settle the strike, despite feeling such action was not our responsibility or authority, would vote for it if the mayor agreed, even if the mayor denounced them for taking such a position. Three council members agreed to do this, and when we called the mayor, he refused.

Fred Davis, chairman of the Public Works Committee, held a public meeting to listen to the strikers and hear their protests. Jim Netters and I were also on the committee. The hearing in the south wing of the old Ellis Auditorium was almost filled. After a long and tumultuous hearing, our committee voted to recommend to the council to settle the strike, proposing a five cent raise immediately and another 20 cents at the beginning of the next fiscal year, July 1, using the memorandum of understanding and payroll deduction techniques.

Fred, young and inexperienced, allowed the meeting to get out of hand a couple of times, but he had courage. He spoke up for his beliefs, popular or unpopular. In those early days, I vividly remember our voting on a difficult strike issue. We voted in alphabetical order, Davis then Donelson. Fred said, "Aye," and I said, "Aye." Fred turned to me and said, "Lewie, one of us has got to be wrong." That was Fred. He made many courageous votes and became more and more popular with both the black and white communities in the years he served because of his reputation for courage and integrity. In the years since, Fred and I became a duet to remember the strike; we have made at least 50 appearances in the last 25 years. I have come to admire Fred Davis extravagantly.

Chairman Pryor called a meeting of the council to hear the report of the Public Works Committee; it was a packed meeting. Fred made introductory remarks and then said, "We are proposing to the council to give the sanitation workers a raise of five cents, immediately." Someone in the back of the room jumped up and said, "The nigger done sold us out for a nickel!" When order was finally restored and our proposal presented, the attitude of the workers and the council's reaction to the unruly behavior and insults may have switched some votes, but the motion failed by seven to six. Fred was devastated, and our last, best chance to settle the strike was gone.

The strike proceeded, the marches continued, and the national publicity escalated. Local ministers persuaded Dr. Martin Luther King, Jr., to lead a march. This produced another negative reaction from some council members who could not be persuaded this was a racial issue, not a labor issue. Most council members were not racists, but anti-union. They also were conscious that the council would exceed its authority if it attempted to negotiate a contract over the mayor's opposition. Loeb's intransigence in this case and in a few other issues set a tradition that changed the dynamics between the mayor and the council. On difficult issues, the public tended to look to the council rather than the mayor to handle the issue. This schism distorted the original intent of the Charter Commission.

Wyeth Chandler, a former councilman, who succeeded Loeb, skillfully dealt with the council. The next mayor, Dick Hackett, fairly skilled in dealing with the council, was so politically cautious he wanted the council to take on some issues that he preferred not to handle himself. Willie Herenton attempted to restore the balance, but primarily developed a wall between himself and the council as he struggled to regain his powers under the charter.

During the Loeb administration, we agreed to a strong policy of annexation. The council took the lead in this matter, and its actions made it appear that I was doing the annexation because I had no intention of running again. I was willing to go down and talk to the people in Whitehaven and Raleigh and "beard them in their dens."

In my mind, this psychological shift in the relationship between the council and the mayor moved power toward the council. The charter amendment eliminated at large council seats and created super districts in their stead. Both the shift and the amendment weakened perceptibly the effectiveness of the new form of government. We have no one on the council elected from the whole city with a feeling of responsibility to the whole city. The present system encourages council members to be parochial in their interests and their votes, voting for what's popular in, or of benefit to, their district without regard to the overall welfare of the city. This tendency became particularly pernicious when making decisions affecting the whole community. The public good sometimes requires a representative to vote for the benefit of the whole community, not a particular constituency. The tragic conclusion of the sanitation workers' strike reminded council members of their mistake when they had been unwilling to overturn the mayor, which set a precedent that encouraged councilmen to do so when they felt it was necessary, and gave them legal cover for their action.

At the first King march, violence came not from King or his supporters but from a group of young blacks who started the rock throwing. The Memphis police responded strongly and gave the press pictures of them using force to subdue the rioters. The violence ended quickly; the march broke up in confusion. Dr. King, although not responsible for the trouble, was humiliated.

The city, or at least those involved, waited in confused anticipation as to what would happen next. At the next morning's council meeting, one said, "We'll showed them today we're not going to put up with any violence in this city." I said, "Unfortunately, while true, the public image of Memphis is that we broke up the march by police force, and I'm afraid this is one of the bleakest days in Memphis history." I was right. National publicity was tremendous, and all negative. Memphis was depicted as a racist backwater community; the strike issues remained at a stalemate. The federal mediator came in, and we agreed to meet with him and union representatives. Dr. King agreed to return to Memphis, anxious to prove he could stage a peaceful march.

Dr. King returned. The mayor had obtained renewal of an injunction against the march. Lucius Burch and the Burch, Porter law firm, including Mike Cody and Charlie Newman, handled a lifting of the injunction. The day before, in the late afternoon, the attorneys finally worked out an agreement about conditions for the march.

By that time Dr. King was at the Lorraine Motel, and James Earl Ray was ready. Fred Davis, Jerred Blanchard, and I met with the federal mediator and the union representative in the Claridge Hotel. Someone called and told Fred Davis to turn on the television. We did. The television reported Dr. King had been shot and rushed to the hospital. Quickly, it became clear he was dead. We immediately began to plan with the mayor how to deal with the anticipated disturbances. The mayor asked the governor to call out the National Guard. The Tennessee National Guard, on maneuvers in Mississippi, rolled into Memphis to patrol the streets. The mayor put on a curfew; rock throwing and Molotov cocktail tossing occurred. The violence was primarily in the black community. East Memphis was relatively quiet. The demonstrators apparently believed they hurt white merchants in the black community.

James Netters and I agreed to meet to discuss the situation. We met that night in the parking lot of Seessel's grocery store across the street from Idlewild Presbyterian Church. We watched armored trucks rolling down Union Avenue, a very low point in the city's history. The violence in Memphis was much less pervasive and destructive than in Detroit, Cleveland, Washington, D.C., and other cities. As the center of attention, Memphis was inundated with negative news coverage.

In effect, the strike was over. The mayor caved in under national and local pressure. Jim Manire, the city attorney, and I negotiated a settlement with the union using a memorandum of understanding and the payroll deduction which the council had suggested earlier and came up with a money settlement virtually identical to that proposed by Fred Davis' Public Works committee. The city was in shock and racial feelings escalated. The strike and its bitter fruit exposed the depth and breadth of white racism in Memphis.

My dear friend, John T. Fisher, the oldest son in the Fisher family and with whom I had been very close, especially after his return to run the family automobile agency, organized a gathering of prayer and reconciliation. Held in Crump Stadium, then our largest outdoor venue, people of both races packed the arena and spoke of their sincere desire to heal and move the city forward. I was proud of his risky and courageous initiative. He continues to be a great citizen of Memphis, working quietly for good causes.

Following that gathering and its aftermath, many positive results emerged. One was the creation of MIFA, the Metropolitan Inter-Faith Association, a church-based movement to provide charitable service. Another initiative sprang up: the Memphis Food Bank, another influential organization. Many other efforts began to improve communications and relationships between the races. Some continued for years and greatly enhanced biracial friendships. One group went on for at least 20 years, meeting weekly to discuss how to improve racial relationships in Memphis and working to do so.

The Breakfast Club, which met periodically, was organized by Ron Terry, bank chairman, and me as outside counsel for First Tennessee Bank. This group included the presidents of all the banks, the president of the Chamber of Commerce, and a number of outstanding citizens and business leaders who met to discuss how to revive the city. The Peabody hotel had closed before the sanitation strike. We agreed reopening The Peabody would help revive downtown. The Breakfast Club managed to get that done, with all the bank presidents committed to provide the necessary financing to do that. The Belz family, with its background in the lodging industry and involvement in franchising, particularly Holiday Inns, was persuaded to take over purchasing and reopening the hotel. In behalf of the group, I investigated. I talked to a Boston man who renovated classic old hotels there, including the Parker House. He taught me that if you are going to do such a renovation it must be first–class, not a fix up, but a reproduction of the original grandeur. The Belzes did that, and the hotel is a tremendous success.

The impact of the strike on Memphis, however, was devastating; it took at least 20 years before the city recovered. Nashville moved ahead of Memphis, and Memphis lost its premier place in Tennessee and among leading cities in the South. Memphis also lost some jewels Mr. Crump had assembled in International Harvester, Kimberly-Clark, and Firestone. FedEx had just begun, AutoZone was not yet conceived, and the cotton business had shrunk to a few large and powerful cotton shippers of which the Dunavant Company was the most dynamic.

The council moved on to other problems, one of the most significant of which was annexation. The city had not expanded its borders for many years. Raleigh, Whitehaven, and Frayser, vibrant communities, acted as integral parts of the city except for political considerations. The council held training and planning sessions with John Osman at then-Southwestern (now Rhodes College) to discuss issues. Certainly one was the importance of including those areas as actually part of the city. People in those areas made their living in Memphis and yet did not contribute to its economic support by paying city taxes.

From that series of meetings, discussions of long-range plans for the city and the need for a strong annexation policy came about. We did add Whitehaven, Frayser, and soon Raleigh, and areas of East Memphis, a highly controversial decision resisted by residents of Whitehaven, Frayser, and Raleigh. I remember a violent protest in Whitehaven. I was a principal advocate of annexation and primary council spokesman. A Whitehaven man who'd had a few beers watched me on television, got mad, called my office, and said he was going to kill me. He called a couple of times. I was out of town. After the second time, my secretary went down to Frierson Graves, then assistant city attorney, and asked him what to do. He answered, "The next time he calls ask him his name." I thought that the silliest idea ever, but the next time he called she asked his name and he gave it. Frierson sent the police to pick him up and throw him in the jail. He was drunk. When I came home, Frierson said, "What do you want me to do with this guy?" I asked, "Is he sober?" He said, "He's totally sober now. He's been in the holding pen for over 48 hours." I said, "Send him on home."

I had become inured to threats because of numerous calls. My wife bore the brunt of them. At first she tried to reason with callers and defend me. She realized that didn't work. She was too sweet and polite to hang up, so she'd hold the phone away to avoid listening. Then she'd hold it back up; if the person was still talking she'd put it down again, and if they weren't talking she'd say, "Are you still there?" If they didn't answer, she'd hang up. One time she hung up with a person still on the phone, and the woman immediately called Gwen Awsumb. Gwen called Jan and said, "What in the world did you say to that lady?" Jan responded, "I didn't say a word to her. I held the phone away from my head and didn't listen to a word she said, and when I thought she had hung up, I put the phone down." That experience made Jan nervous about ever putting the phone down until she was sure the person was off the line.

The council sent Wyeth Chandler and me to appear before a Whitehaven group opposed to annexation. I made my presentation and arguments in support of annexation, which would require Whitehaven to pay its fair share of city operating costs in order for Memphis to have adequate tax base to benefit all who lived and worked in the city. A few boos and hisses, but mostly stony silence. I sat back down beside Wyeth and he said, "Lewie, I don't see how you can stand not to tell them what they want to hear." I said, "I'm not running for another office, and I can tell them what I think without any worry about being re-elected."

Several years later when the new charter was adopted for the county with a county mayor and county commission government, a group led by Henry Haizlip asked me run for county mayor, and I told him, "I'm barely smart enough not to do that." Then I said, "I don't think I could be elected because I'm not that popular out there." He said, "Everybody knows you and you could be elected. Do you mind if we take a poll?" I said, "I'm not going to run either way, but you can take poll if you want to." He came back a week later and said, "We took a poll, and you were right." He didn't show me the poll, and I did not really want to see it.

After the sanitation workers' strike, because of my leadership in efforts to settle it, my influence with the council and the mayor greatly increased. Jerold Moore was the chief administrative officer of the city, a position created to provide the benefits of a city manager without losing the benefits of having a mayor as the focal point for the city. He frequently called me about upcoming issues and invited me to meet with the mayor for discussions. Loeb was a reasonable person concerned about the welfare of the whole community. He was certainly not in the least racist, but slightly paternalistic toward blacks, and we got along extremely well.

Free from political realities and with no desire to be re-elected, I was often chosen by the council to handle difficult issues. A young black man took his uncle's car without permission. The uncle reported the car stolen, not knowing his nephew was involved. The young man led police on a chase all over the community and into the county where he was stopped, severely beaten, and died. The assailants were sheriff's deputies. I suggested it was unknown whether police or sheriff's deputies did the beating. County Mayor Skip Nixon challenged me, saying if county deputies were at fault, he would publicly apologize and buy me a dinner. When I was proven right, he neither apologized nor bought me a dinner.

The council sent me to see how to improve racial relations. I went to various communities. One thing was most interesting. I was talking to the priest at St. Patrick's Church on Linden. He said, "We used to have policemen on the beat who walked the neighborhood and established rapport with the community, and the community, particularly the good element of the community, looked to these cops for protection, advice, and leadership. Now the police ride in squad cars. Nobody knows who they are. It's a different person almost every time without any connection with the community. It's become a case of policemen as faceless enemies." It was a perceptive comment showing the difficulty of policing a large city, and gives a glimpse of the sources of hostility toward the police. Police brutality, particularly in arrests of black citizens, exacerbates the situation. Such incidents get big play from the media, but police department protection and support of the community are not publicized, lost in the world of bad publicity. The killing of the young black man generated rioting, violence, and fires in Memphis, further adding to a bad national image.

During the strike, Jesse Epps rose to head of the union. He proceeded to organize the hospital workers. I had to negotiate with him and one of his aides on a wage increase. The second year when wages for the sanitation workers arose, I set up a conference with Jesse Epps. I said, "Jesse, you know I'm striving to keep Memphis' expenses under control. So I'm going to offer you a raise of . . . ." I forget what it was, seven or eight cents, something like that. And I said, "I have another (I don't know what it was, but we'll say a nickel) that I can give you, but what I want you to do is raise Cain about the original proposal, and I'll hold the line, then you insist on more. Toward the end of the budget process, you can announce you obtained an extra five cents from the city." He thought the idea terrific, and that's what we did over the next two years. The last year, I thought it was all settled, so I told Jerold Moore what to offer in addition to what we had publicly announced, using the same procedure. He called me about 3:00 one morning and said, "We are negotiating with the union. I told them your final offer." I said to Jerold, "That's all we've got. We can't afford any more." Jerold said, "They want to hear it directly from you." I said, "Put them on the phone." He said, "Oh, no, they want to hear from you in person." I got up and went downtown, and I met with them, and gave them my standard speech: "Here's what we have, here's what the budget is, here's how much revenue we're going to get, here's what I can offer, and that's all I can afford." They said, "Fine, we just wanted to hear it from you and understand what you were saying." This indicated their confidence in me; they believed I told the truth. I don't know if that always works, but it certainly was a very happy conclusion to a difficult problem.

Another accomplishment on the City Council was to persuade the county to take over John Gaston Hospital, which served the whole county and many others as well. It was ridiculous for the city to support a hospital that served the county. I talked to Bill Farris, then on the County Commission, and he agreed. With his help, I persuaded the county to take over the hospital.

Before then I had been involved with the problem of John Gaston's service to citizens in East Arkansas and North Mississippi who went without paying. Medicaid was not a law; it had just begun. I was most concerned about Arkansas citizens, a great burden, but Mississippi residents proved an equally heavy one. After much negotiation, I worked out an agreement with Arkansas to give us around three or four days' take from the dog track. Unfortunately, when the hospital passed from city to county, the agreement was lost. Years later we reinstituted efforts to collect reimbursement from Arkansas. Ironically, when I became chairman of The MED, I inherited the problem from the county viewpoint.

Another major issue during my council term was the routing of I-40 through Overton Park. My wife was strongly opposed to an interstate going through the park. I felt the completion of I-40 important to the economic development of Memphis, especially downtown. The 240 and 440 loops are long, somewhat circuitous routes downtown without easy access to downtown shopping, and were particularly in sad shape after the sanitation workers' strike. Businesses deserted downtown in droves, and downtown shopping never revived. This condition existed in many cities as shopping centers went up in suburban communities. In Memphis this imbalance was particularly acute because downtown is at the west end of a one-sided city with its back to the river. Downtown life is vital to a city, especially shopping. I felt that since buses already traveled through the park, originally as streetcars, even before my birth, an expressway would not be such a tremendous change. I now recognize the tremendous volume of traffic that interstate highway would have carried and the ecological impact it would have had on Memphis and surrounding communities.

The council voted repeatedly to push for the highway's completion. Charles Newman, representing I'd say a group of little old ladies in tennis shoes, successfully prevented it. The bus route through the park is now gone, and the park remains one lovely unit, a tremendous asset to the community. In recent years it's slipped in desirability and usability, with police limiting access to the park. It's especially sad for me having grown up near the park, as I discussed. When my children were growing up, we frequently went for a walk there after Sunday school. I wanted them to experience the woods and the majesty of the Southern forest.

The Memphis park system was tremendously vital when I was young. Mr. Crump established independent commissions and allowed them to do their work. He rarely interfered with the operation of the Light Gas & Water Division, which provided excellent utility service. He also kept hands off the Park Commission, which provided a wonderful park system. We had more acres of park per citizen then than virtually any other large city. We have long since lost that title, although including Shelby Forest and Shelby Farms might make Shelby County one of the top few. Overton Park and Riverside Park are two jewels, strategically located so that all communities can benefit. Riverside is now called Martin Luther King Park, an appropriate designation. Unfortunately, the city has done too little to maintain our parks; they have declined in appeal and value. Martin Luther King Park should be an important asset to the community, and it has not been in recent years.

When I was elected to the council, I gave up other civic duties, except for teaching Sunday school. I became inactive in the Rotary Club, resigned as a member of the Board of Trustees of Rhodes College, one resignation I regret. I was on the Rhodes board when we had to decide whether to preserve the architectural purity of the campus. It was a difficult decision even then. The original cost of building in Gothic style with stone was 30 percent greater than traditional construction. Now it's pushing 40 percent. After much agonizing we stayed with the architectural purity, a great decision. Dr. Peyton Rhodes, president after Dr. Diehl's death, did an outstanding job, and despite having been a physics professor all his life, was a good fundraiser. His successor, David Alexander, a Rhodes alumnus with a doctorate and an ordained minister, was primarily an educator. He focused on academic excellence, strengthened the curriculum, improved the quality of the faculty, and raised professors' salaries. Unfortunately, David was not a businessman; he proposed and pushed through deficit budgets using endowment funds. I was much opposed. This was not a factor in my resignation from the board, which was based entirely on my having time to practice law while on the City Council.

As a member of the City Council, I became well-known. Everybody spoke to me on the street because I was on television so frequently, especially during the sanitation workers' strike. I once asked Kaye Pullen, a reporter for Channel 13, later a close friend of ours, "Kaye, why is it any time we come out of a meeting everybody sticks a mike in my face?" She replied, "Lewie, don't you realize you have an unusual talent?" I asked, "What do you mean?" She explained, "You have the ability to say something in 30 seconds, and that's all TV people want."

A good friend and I were in San Francisco working on a deal and staying at the Mark Hopkins Hotel. I told him about the incredible power of television, and how I couldn't go anywhere in Memphis without being recognized. The next morning going down to breakfast somebody got on the elevator and asked, "Mr. Donelson, what are you doing in San Francisco?" And I said, "I'm out here on business." He commented, "I'm from Mississippi. I see you all the time on television."

Even now, and I've now been off the City Council for many years, I'm well-known in Memphis. I've had some exposure on television since that time, but even now people tell me, "I remember seeing you on the City Council." I remain proud that my fellow council members voted me the "most valuable member." I believe no one else has received such an award, and it came from those who shared that same baptism of fire.

While my service on the City Council was eventful and stressful, it was rewarding. It gave me a better understanding of the community, the political processes, and the other forces that make the city work. I was uniquely able to advise clients of problems that had political connotations. I learned how to get things done. While I worked an average of 40 hours per week on council matters, I still put in over 2,000 billable hours per year for the firm, but the sacrifice was worth it. No other Memphis lawyer had the special knowledge of the community and a very strong law firm to back him up. I believe that my council experience was one of the elements of our subsequent dynamic growth.

TWENTY-TWO

THE WINFIELD DUNN MIRACLE AND AFTER

One of the things I could not separate myself from while I was on the City Council was my continued participation in Republican politics. I continued to serve on the Republican State Executive Committee and was involved in political campaigns, previously described.

Because of media attention generated by my service on the City Council, surprisingly, enough Republican friends in East Tennessee urged me to run for governor. This is always flattering and an ego boost; I considered the possibility despite Jan's intense opposition, but I never got my own consent. When Winfield Dunn, a practicing dentist and Shelby County party chairman, came and said he wanted to run I offered him my support. I said, "You have relieved my mind because I've been thinking about running and hadn't been able to get my own consent. You have solved the problem."

Winfield, a fine looking Lincolnesque type man, tall and thin, very well spoken, was absolutely a superb candidate. His father had been a Democratic congressman from Mississippi, which gave him some political experience. Without a doubt Winfield was the best campaigner I've ever seen. He loved people and that was evident. When he spoke he looked people in the eye and showed them his interest. His innate integrity shone through and those who heard him knew he spoke from the heart. A poll in December 1969 on potential gubernatorial candi-

dates revealed Winfield's name recognition was about 2 percent, including in Memphis.

Politics 40 years ago was much more the field of amateurs, at least
in Tennessee. We raised less than $100,000 for the primary. Winfield,
such an effective campaigner, made friends and got votes wherever
he went. He worked hard in East Tennessee, especially the First and
Second Districts, to build his support. The early primary favorite was
Maxey Jarman, who had more money than Winfield and an impressive background in business. He made a most appealing candidate
for Republicans, but his appeal was his résumé, not his personality or
his ability to deal with people. As I noted earlier, my analysis of the
vote and my prediction of Winfield's victory proved correct. Maxey
came into Shelby County with a 15,000-vote lead. Shelby County gave
Winfield a 42,000 majority; he blew away Maxey.

After his primary victory, Winfield picked up more support and
some more money. His Democratic opponent was John J. Hooker. I
have mentioned my friendship with his father. John, Jr., became more
and more erratic as the years progressed. By 1970, he had run and lost
several different political races. He captured the Democratic nomination during the end of Buford Ellington's last term. Buford and Frank
Clement had leapfrogged each other and served in different terms in
the governor's office. John J. Hooker was closely associated with the
Kennedy family, who were viewed in Tennessee as extremely liberal
Democrats. His campaign was quite liberal and somewhat erratic,
creating a real chance for Winfield to win. Howard Baker's victory in
1966 proved that a Republican could win in the statewide race; this
gave Winfield believability. Because of Winfield's charm, the plausi-
bility of a Republican victory, and Hooker's erratic character, Winfield
won almost easily.

We flew to Nashville after the election to participate in the celebration. It was already apparent that the changing of the guard had
occurred when the Highway Patrol was knocking itself out to be
accommodating to the newly elected Governor Dunn and his supporters.

To show you how naïve we were about state politics, I suggested that Winfield announce his campaign on the steps of the capitol. I thought it was a public place where nothing or no one could prevent us from doing so. No one did; however, I learned later that we were supposed to get permission for a rally on the steps of the capitol building.

When Jan and I went to a rally for Winfield in Brownsville about two weeks after his election, I pulled up in front of the meeting place to let Jan out. I turned to the trooper standing there and asked where to park. Although I did not know him, he said, "Mr. Donelson, leave it right there. We'll take care of it." The world had changed.

Despite his political inexperience, Winfield proved to be an excellent governor, primarily because of his magnificent touch with people. I realized immediately after the election that we needed to start on the budget for the next year, to be presented by the first of February. Winfield had not yet appointed a commissioner of Finance and Administration on whom that job would normally fall. I spent time with him in Nashville helping prepare that original budget and got to know Jerry Adams, deputy commissioner of F&A and a tremendous help in preparing the budget. Governor Ellington was cordial and provided as much assistance as possible to help ease the transition.

We were talking with Ellington about political matters in Tennessee and the name Ray Blanton came up. Television had just begun to have tremendous impact on politics; most candidates spoke with Tele. Promp.Ters. Governor Ellington said, "You know that blank look that Blanton has when reading from the Tele.Promp.Ter?" I said, "Yes." He responded, "That's for real." It was a sad prophecy. Blanton wasn't an evil man, but he proved the Peter Principle and rose high above his level of competency.

I prepared that first budget because the commissioner of Finance and Administration had not been appointed. Harry Wellford, Dunn's campaign manager, went on the federal bench almost simultaneously with Winfield's taking office. I became known as Winfield's principal adviser. During the campaign, I met every Sunday afternoon with Winfield to discuss state issues, especially the budget. I was the only one of his close advisers who knew much about state government.

Because I had some familiarity with state government, particularly its finances, I became, by default, his principal financial adviser. I trained his first commissioner of Finance and Administration.

The first commissioner was a fine man, with a good head on his shoulders, but highly cautious and careful. The commissioner's job demanded decisions on the spot. As a result, he called me frequently. My secretary referred to him as "Dr. Pepper," because he would call me everyday at 10, 2, and 4.

During that time the legislature established a Tax Reform and Modernization Commission, and Winfield appointed me to it. It consisted of prominent businessmen and lawyers, some legislators, and other government officials. It was then that I got my first real in-depth analysis of Tennessee's revenue structure and its whole fiscal picture. That commission came up with the recommendation that we should pass a flat rate income tax, use part of the money for education, a small portion for general governmental expenses, and the rest to supplement the budgets of local governments, with the proviso that each local government would be required to reduce its property taxes to offset the original amount of the income tax share it received.

I became convinced Tennessee needed to change its revenue structure. At that point, we were heavily dependent upon the sales tax for state revenues and the property taxes for local revenues. Today, it's even worse. Up until the time the sales tax passed, Tennessee had had a state property tax, which was discontinued with the introduction of the sales tax. When someone challenges you to name a tax that was ever discontinued once established, mention the state property tax.

Today the combined state and local sales tax can be as high as 9.75 percent. This is highly regressive in that it falls proportionately much heavier on low-income people than high-income people. It is also inflexible because sales tax revenues do not grow as rapidly as inflation. The sales tax doesn't cover everything, but it does cover most necessities of life. I have been pushing tax reform in Tennessee ever since, without success. During this time I was in Nashville almost weekly.

Because of my increasing visibility, I began to get calls from prisoners who wanted help with their parole. I had never done any legal work like that, was totally unfamiliar with it, and didn't want to get involved. I talked to Winfield and said, "I don't want to do it," and he said, "That's fine." He said, "I've got somebody I'd like to recommend. He's a friend of mine who will handle it." We did that. The calls stopped, but I was appalled at how quickly the word got out that I was the man to see.

Two stories reflect Winfield's integrity and his genuine innocence about the political process. His political involvement was with the Shelby County Republican Party and a race for the state Senate on the Republican ticket, which he lost. Back then, the governor could give out 100 license plates to his friends; he told me one of the hardest things he had to do was give out those license plates. He also said how much he appreciated Bob James and me, his only two friends who didn't want a license plate. One man who came in wanted a license plate and offered Winfield money. Winfield refused: "I am absolutely not going to take that." The guy kept insisting and Winfield said, "I'll give you consideration on the list. I'm not going to assure you you'll be chosen, but I'm not going to accept any funds from you." The fellow said as he walked out, "All the others did."

Winfield and Nelson Rockefeller became friends at an early governors' meeting. Both of them were people persons. Nelson Rockefeller, raised in the lap of luxury as a third generation Rockefeller, had that amazing knack of appearing to be intensely interested in you and what you were saying. It's easy to understand why he was elected so many times as governor of New York. When I met him he was a young presidential aide, I was then chairman of the Republican Association. It was our duty to entertain him, and Jan teased me because I made him walk down to the garage to get the car after he made his speech. Winfield came home from a Nelson Rockefeller event and told me this story: "I met a fellow up at that this thing, and he was pretty drunk, and I have must have been introduced to him three or four times and every time I'd say, 'I'm Winfield Dunn from Tennessee,' he'd reply, 'Oh, Tennessee. I own Tennessee.'" Winfield asked me, "What in the world did he mean?" And I said, "He's a big bond lawyer and he means he has the Tennessee bond business, and what he probably meant was that he'd bought it and paid for it."

Winfield called me frequently for advice on many issues. I usually stayed at the governor's mansion, and I was in Nashville almost every week for four years. Surprisingly, I didn't have many dealings with the legislature. John Wilder, the lieutenant governor and speaker of the Senate, was a friend of mine. Ned McWherter became a client about that time. Bill Jenkins was speaker of the House during the early part of Winfield's administration.

I didn't realize it, but this prepared me for being commissioner of F&A. During the final two years of the Dunn administration, Ted Welch was commissioner of F&A. Ted and I became good friends during that time and have remained close ever since. He rarely called me for advice; Ted knew what he wanted to do and quickly made up his mind.

I got to know a lot of State Troopers, particularly Johnny White and Paul Lane, the two main troopers assigned to the governor. Although I didn't have a governor's license plate, I got preferred treatment from the Highway Patrol. State Troopers treated me with great courtesy, and a couple of times when they stopped me for speeding they apologized. It used make Jan furious, because she didn't believe in any special favors.

During the Dunn administration, a big Constitutional Convention was held. He originally appointed me to the State Tax and Modernization Committee, headed up by the president of Tennessee Eastman. This excellent committee contained politicians and prominent businessmen, had funding, and a strong staff of advisers led by a UT professor familiar with state government. I enjoyed that committee, and we came up with a solid and useful report in 1972 or 1973. We recommended the state adopt a 2 percent state income tax, one-half of the funds would go to the state government to provide additional funds for education, and one-half would go to local governments to allow them to reduce their property taxes. We found that the property tax is one of the most unpopular taxes of all; particularly at that time, many people were frustrated about paying a lump sum at the end of the year. Mortgage companies had not universally adopted the policy of requiring it to be included in the mortgage payment.

The commission got enough attention to cause the Constitutional Convention to consider tax reform, but it was done at the behest of the Farm Bureau to try to prevent the adoption of an income tax and to try to obtain tax preference for farmers. The convention was totally dominated by the Farm Bureau. Out of 99 votes, they had roughly two-thirds at 66. Those of us who wanted consideration of tax reform were not allowed to participate in the proceedings. Their carefully calculated plan was to adopt property classification, which was specifically prohibited by the original 1870 constitution. There would be classifications for farm property and residential homes, and there would be a classification for commercial properties, and then there would be a classification for utilities. A few of us urged the more serious tax reform proposed by the commission, but were easily defeated by the majority.

One time during a discussion about the language for a constitutional amendment that we were adopting, I moved for a recess to discuss wording. My motion was defeated 66 to 33. I asked a friend on the other side to make a similar motion; it passed 99 to nothing.

Later talking to Clyde York, the longtime head of the Farm Bureau, about the matter, he said, "Lewie, you have to understand. I told my people you were smarter than they were, and to vote against anything you proposed." He said, "I was wrong. Property classification did little for the farmers, it only helped a few in Davidson and Shelby counties. In rural counties farms constituted such a large part of the tax base that when you reduce their assessment, and that's what it did, you have 25 percent assessment for farms, 40 percent for business, and 50 percent for utilities, but all it did was require the counties to increase their taxes." I responded, "Clyde, farmers pay so little income

tax anyway, the proposed income tax would have affected them min-
imally, and property tax relief would have more than offset the income
tax." At the time I did not have Clyde York's ear. We became friends
later, and were able to discuss matters in a more rational fashion.

Winfield announced his support for the income tax, but it never got
any traction in the legislature. The state government had begun its
explosive growth. The first billion-dollar state budget was under Governor Dunn. Now it is in excess of $30 billion. A major part comes
from the state's responsibility for Medicaid and Medicare. Also, the
state became much more involved in mental health and child welfare
issues, and the support for education has grown as well. I contributed
to that growth but that will be described in another chapter.

Unfortunately, if you provide an increase for the local school system,
it seems you have to hire a bunch of bureaucrats in Nashville to supervise it. Now, it also seems true for the federal government as well, with
more bureaucrats in Nashville to carry out mandates. Winfield successfully pushed through a sales tax increase to provide kindergartens a
much overdue and important reform because we are now learning the
importance of early childhood education.

We should begin well before kindergarten to get children ready
for school. In Memphis, we have approximately 20 percent of children
coming to school who have never seen a book or been read to. When
you hand them a book, they do not know what to do with it, how to
open it, or which side is up, unless they have pictures. Those children
rarely catch up. The teacher has the responsibility to move along at a
reasonable pace, and some children cannot keep up. The ability of
a young child to learn is remarkable, and some who do not learn in
that period never catch up. Today there is more emphasis on prekin-
dergarten training. Tennessee did not get compulsory kindergartens
until 1972. During Winfield Dunn's term, a governor could not be re-
elected because there was a one-term limit in the constitution. You
could serve again after a lapse. It was incredible to get a compulsory kindergarten approved, quite an achievement for a Republican
governor.

Winfield made an excellent governor, but I saw the danger of the governor being captured by his staff. They constantly said, "You are the governor, you do not have to do this; you are the governor, you ought to do it this way." This did somewhat inhibit Winfield's personal strength, his tremendous ability to deal with people, and his great sincerity and integrity. Sometimes when Winfield called me I would say, "Winfield, here's what I think, but let me remind you, I am a lawyer who represents corporations and a major bank. As a tax-payer I oppose the government and any tax increases. You should talk to people with different points of view to be sure you hear everything you want to know about this subject."

Winfield dealt with Democrat majorities in both houses. In his first years, the technical division favored the Republicans in the House, which was evenly divided with the sole independent voting with the Republicans. It required all of his skills and charm to get his program through and he was able to do most of it. He was smart with absolute integrity and a strong desire to do what was best for the people. You cannot ask for more than that in a public servant. In 1986, I helped persuade Winfield to run again for governor, but his heart was not in it. He did not campaign in the same all-out fashion or show eagerness to serve, nor did he capitalize on his past record. He did not seem to have a real vision of what he proposed to do in a second term. I have found in my public experience that somebody who has to be overly persuaded to run does not end up being a good candidate. I have supported several candidates who should have won but they did not. They really did not want it bad enough. You just do not win statewide offices in Tennessee without campaigning all out and showing that you really want the job.

At the end of the Dunn term, I reduced my political activities some-what, except for the Kuykendall campaigns in 1972 and 1974, and to a lesser extent, the Alexander campaign in 1974. Both 1974 losses could be blamed primarily on Watergate. I briefly assisted Governor Blanton's attempt to pass an income tax, appearing before the State Legislative Joint Committee of Finance and Way and Means. Governor Blanton called me because he could not find anyone to advocate the income tax and needed a supporter to appear before the legislature. While I argued away in my most persuasive manner why an income tax was the solution for the state of Tennessee, a bunch of men in hard hats suddenly came into the room and started shouting and hollering. I thought, "Man, I have really stirred up a storm." It turned out they were working on a construction job across the street, were on strike, and were asking the legislature for support in their strike effort against the contractor.

Blanton asked me to serve on a committee with another lawyer, a Democrat from Middle Tennessee, Ron McFarland, to give an opinion as to whether he could raise the pension payments for judges during their terms. There is a provision in the constitution stating that salaries cannot be changed during that term of office. We gave the opinion that these changes in the pension system could be made without violating the constitution because they did not change income during the judges' terms of office, only at retirement. The legislature adopted the changes he proposed, and they were not contested in the courts.

TWENTY-THREE

POST CITY COUNCIL ACTIVITIES

The years from 1974 to 1978 saw considerable growth of the law firm, and probably represented the peak of my law firm activities. I remained active in city and county political races and state legislature positions. I became good friends with Wyeth Chandler when we served on the council. I advised him and others occasionally. Some members of the City Council called me for advice and for help in their races but it was not a period of major political activity.

In the summer of 1978, in the middle of Lamar Alexander's second run for governor and Howard Baker's last Senate run, I told Howard I would like to be active in that campaign. I had been active in his first campaign, but not subsequent ones because of my involvement with Kuykendall until his 1974 defeat. Howard agreed and I acted as his campaign manager for his final campaign. Politics by then had become much more organized. Having a professional campaign staff meant my job was less hands-on than in the past, but it was a joy to work with Senator Baker. His vote for the Panama Canal Treaty, unpopular in the South, and several significant pro-civil rights votes made him somewhat nervous about the campaign. His opponent, Jane Eskind, had run for several different offices.

During that last campaign, I insisted Howard work some shopping centers in Memphis where face-to-face campaigning was important.

His staff people said that Howard did not do that. Howard told me if I took the job, he would do what I said for the campaign. I got three Memphis shopping centers lined up. We went out to Raleigh Springs Mall and had not gone 10 feet before this pretty young girl, about 16, said, "Senator Baker, my mother thinks you are perfectly wonderful, she just loves you. Would you give me your autograph to give to her? She would really appreciate that." He gave her the autograph and then he walked along another 15 to 20 feet; and two more good-looking young ladies, definitely voter age, said, "Senator Baker, we think you are perfectly wonderful, we love you so much, would you please give us your autograph?" So he signed the autograph and as soon as we walked off, he commented, "This ain't half bad." He did work the three shopping centers and he worked them well. He won that campaign easily.

In the middle of the campaign, while in Jackson, reporters came up to him early in the morning and asked, "Did you hear what Jane Eskind said about you?" He said, "No, I didn't." They told him, then asked, "What do you think about that?" He said, "My policy is never to comment upon what my opponent says about me in a campaign." This went on all day with Jane making ever more shrill comments, and about 5:00 p.m., when they came again, he said the same thing. As they walked away, he added, "Wait a minute, I am going to change my policy. Tell her I said, 'Cool it.'" That was Howard. He did not like campaigning, but he did it superbly and skillfully. His comments were thoughtful, reasoned, and calm, and his rationale, sound.

Senator Baker was a superb public servant. Unusual for a Republican, in every race in Shelby County he got 25 to 35 percent of the black vote, always a sure win in the state. He was involved in the appointment of Ben Hooks as the first black member of a national regulatory commission. His skillful performance and his bipartisan stance on the Senate Watergate Committee established him as a national figure. His able service as minority and majority leader further strengthened his reputation. When he told me that he was not going to run again, I responded, "Howard, as majority leader, you can do so much for Tennessee, you cannot step out now." "No, Lewie, I told you the first time I ran that if I got elected I was going to serve three terms and that would be it, and I am not changing my mind."

In the midst of that campaign, Jan and I vacationed in Alaska, a relaxing and beautiful escape. When we returned, the firefighters and police in Memphis were on strike. It was a huge mess and everybody was calling me saying, "Lewie, what are you going to do about it?" and my standard answer was, "I am a private citizen, what do you mean, what am I going to do about it? It is not any of my business." Well, I got so many requests and so many people talking to me about it, I finally called Wyeth Chandler, then the mayor. I said, "Wyeth, I have told you I was not going to get involved in your business unless you want me to, but would you like me to get involved and try to help settle the strike?" He said, "I will call you back." Well, in two or three hours he called me back and said, "Yes, I would."

I organized a committee with union people, a mix of Democrats and Republicans and prominent business leaders, including Jim McGehee, then chairman of the Chamber of Commerce; Frank Norfleet; and someone from First Tennessee Bank, probably Ron Terry. We wanted to settle the strike. With union representatives, we made real progress. They had access to the firefighters and police, who were not well or-ganized or used to union activity, which caused them to be precipitous in their actions. The committee meeting had opened with an inspiring prayer from Adrian Rogers about the issue's importance to the city. We got close to an agreement. I had a speech to make in Jackson and promised to return by midnight. I called, and they reported an agree-ment. I learned the details and felt the mayor would never agree, be-cause of the long-range fiscal impacts. I called the mayor, who told me how to amend the proposal to gain his acceptance. Chandler got on the phone and talked to other committee members and the strikers, and worked out the settlement. Jim McGehee provided focused lead-ership. I realized one of the committee problems was limited experi-ence in dealing with unions, including union terminology and union techniques to get benefits. Many proposals would not be immediately recognizable as unfavorable to the employer.

A couple of years later, Wyeth, into his third term as mayor, called and said, "Lewie, I am sick of this job, I would like to step down as mayor. Do you think you could get me appointed as a judge? I would love to be a judge." We had become good friends. I told him, "I can get you appointed as judge, but if you are going to be appointed as judge, you are going to have to change your ways. You cannot go around chasing women all over Shelby County." Once when he was somewhere in the mayor's car, a voice came on the police radio saying, "The mayor needs help, the mayor needs help." A humorous and well-reported incident. Wyeth said, "I'm older and I have a new wife. I promise you that if I get on the bench, I'll behave." He did and became an excellent and extremely popular judge.

TWENTY-FOUR

A POLITICAL INTERIM

Lamar Alexander's 1978 election as governor followed my formula for a Republican victory: big majorities in the First and Second Districts; a solid majority in the Third District; losses in Middle Tennessee, including Davidson County, but not too steep; break even in West Tennessee; and capture Shelby County. This formula applied to all his campaigns, two gubernatorial races, and two senatorial races.

Not long after his election, Lamar called and asked me to come to Nashville for a conference. I went to his home, and we talked about cabinet appointments and possibilities. Suddenly, he changed the subject: "I asked you here to urge you to become commissioner of Finance and Administration." When I went up there, I hadn't had the remotest idea of doing that.

I said, "I can't do that. It would take me away from my law practice, and I have no desire for a political career."

Lamar persuaded me by saying, "Lewie, if you are chief operating officer, everybody will report to you and you'll run the state on a daily basis. I'll fix policy and talk to the public and sell my programs and, when necessary, deal with the legislature." He also said, "You've trained for this job with your tax experience, statewide political connections, the advisory position for Governor Dunn, and your friendship with your client, Speaker McWherter. You know of

Tennessee's history and its economic development. You served in the Tennessee Constitutional Convention in 1971 and 1972 and on the Tax Modernization and Reform Commission. Important for me, you know statewide Republican politics." In short, he talked me into it. I did tell him, "Lamar, I will give you three legislatures." That time limit was understood from the beginning.

I remember we were at an apartment with Tom Ingram and his two cats. My eyes began to water and I sneezed and sneezed, discovering an allergy to longhaired cats. We moved into the main house to give me some relief. Jan and I talked about Lamar's offer. Our two older children had left home. Lewie, after receiving a doctorate in Theology from the University of Chicago, was professor of New Testament at Austin Theological Seminary in Austin, Texas, an official seminary of the Presbyterian Church (USA). Janice, married with two sons, lived in Knoxville. Lori had finished college and worked for a CPA firm while planning a spring wedding. During our conversation, I told Jan, "We report our income from the firm on a fiscal year that ends January 31. So my income this year with this job will be less than my income taxes on what I made this year." After Jan and I talked it over, she consented, knowing the job required a move to Nashville and would be very consuming. We decided not to sell our house in Memphis. We rented it out, a disaster. We had three different tenants, the last one did damage to the house. Jan was supportive the entire time. I severed my connections with the law firm and with Memphis.

We enjoyed Nashville thoroughly and made many new friends: Pat Wilson, Nelson Andrews, Dortch Oldham, Ken Roberts, Ted Welch, and many others.

I accepted the job and began immediately to help Lamar develop his first budget. I became his first cabinet appointment.

The Finance and Administration commissioner has wide statutory powers, which extend well beyond the state finances, but Lamar expanded those. All commissioners reported to me. I was a principal spokesman for the governor. I announced all the bad news, and there was plenty of it. Lamar announced all the good news. I was the key person dealing with the legislature. Actually, my friendships with Lt. Gov. Wilder and Speaker McWherter, who had been a longtime client, were tremendous assets to the new Republican administration, which enabled us to hit the ground running.

The job was demanding, about 80 hours a week, but I learned state government from A to Z during my immersion in state finances. I was frequently on TV. I made speeches and appearances all around the state. In subsequent years as a lawyer for clients who were involved with state government, these tools were invaluable.

Lamar was right in saying I had trained for the job my entire career. When I left Memphis, I told my good friend, Frank Norfleet, I would do it for 2½ years and return on July 1, 1981, and I did. Frank was dubious. He said, "You will get up there and do a great job and everybody will tell you that you are indispensable and you will stay on and never come back."

Shortly before I left the commissioner's job, I was talking to Speaker McWherter about an issue in the state budget. He complained and I responded, "Oh, Mr. Speaker, it is only a million bucks." In a flash Speaker McWherter replied, "Lewie, you have been here too long." I answered, "You are exactly right, Mr. Speaker, and that is why I am leaving." When you get swept up in the system, you lose your initial cutting edge. The American system of government encourages citizen participation, and that is part of its genius. If you remain a citizen and do not become a full-time career type government employee, you bring that special outside look that enables you to truly represent citizens and taxpayers.

When I got home I called Frank Norfleet and said, "Well, Frank, I just wanted you to know that I am back," and he laughed and said, "You know, I should have realized, once you said you were going to be back on a certain day, you are so hard-headed you would live up to that."

Those who consider entering public service should keep an exit date in mind. Despite problems with term limits, the idea is sound;

every public servant, particularly elected officials, ought to constantly ask, "Have I served long enough, is it time now for me to go?"

When I served on the City Council, I announced I would serve one term and I lived up to it. If you are not planning to run again you are free to vote your conscience, without fear of reprisal. When someone would say, "I will never vote for you again," I would respond, "You won't get a chance because I do not plan on running again." When I ran for the City Council I hoped to encourage others to take time from their careers, serve one term on the council, give their best ideas, and get a fresh look at government from the inside. Unfortunately, that did not happen.

It worked better with the commissioners of Finance and Administration. A number of people like Ted Welch, Bill Sansom, Hubert McCullough, and John Ferguson came out of the private sector, rendered tremendous public service, and then left. I left state government with a renewed appreciation of the system and recognition that while some people were self-serving, most were dedicated and did their best. Some were outstanding public servants of energy, integrity, courage, and vision. You often wonder how government works, and you find out that in the legislature there are a few outstanding leaders who show the way. In government itself, a few outstanding public servants give their lives to the state government, and without them it could not really work. One of them certainly was Jerry Adams.

I met Jerry when he served as deputy commissioner of Finance and Administration under Dunn, as I mentioned. He continued to serve under Ray Blanton, Lamar Alexander, Ned McWherter, Don Sundquist, and Phil Bredesen. He could draw the budget bill without missing an item. Thoroughly immersed in state finances, he was skilled at estimating revenues more than a year in advance necessary to preparation of state budgets. He handled all the technical details of the bond appropriations and the capital funds budget that provided the capital support for the various projects approved by the legislature. In short, he was indispensable. Without him, the commissioner of F&A would be bogged down in details and unable to handle the duties of the chief financial officer and chief administrative officer of the state. Others who served in state departments in the same way were also invaluable. One in particular was Roy Best in the Insurance Department. He knew insurance law and business, and kept that department going for many years. On his departure, you could tell the difference dramatically.

Lamar, an extremely persuasive person, assembled a superb cabinet, including Clyde York as commissioner of Agriculture, the longtime head of the Farm Bureau; John Neff, commissioner of Employment Security, an insurance executive and successful real estate developer; Bill Sansom, commissioner of Transportation, manager of a large supplier of materials to the transportation industry; and Sammie Lynn Puett, a vice president of UT, commissioner of General Services. Mose Pleasure, commissioner of Welfare, departed quickly. Gene Fowinkle was commissioner of Health; Jim Brown, commissioner of Mental Health.

Bill Jones, my predecessor as the commissioner under Blanton, was most helpful. I had established a friendship with Bill Snodgrass and Harlan Mathews during the Dunn administration. This meant a smooth transition. Both houses of the General Assembly were firmly Democratic. Lamar was anxious to get control of state expenditures, and so was I. We did draconian work on the budget, vitally necessary because the state experienced a recession during Lamar's first two years. Revenues were weak, and, in one year, actually declined. Lamar complained once he wished I wouldn't tell any new commissioners during their first interviews that I planned to abolish their departments.

My years in Nashville began dramatically. During a conference with Lamar to discuss budget issues, Hal Hardin, then the U.S. attorney for the Middle District of Tennessee, called to say the FBI urged that Lamar be sworn in early. The FBI was convinced Blanton planned to issue more pardons before he left office. He had issued 50 pardons on Monday; this was Wednesday. The media had reported the pardons, with suggestions of accompanying bribes.

Thus began one of the most fascinating days of my life. Lamar and I talked about what to do. Should a Republican governor dare to be sworn in early, removing a Democrat from office? I advised not to do anything without the full support of Democrats. We would call McWherter and Wilder. My friendship with both would be critical, because Lamar knew neither. Speaker McWherter, the most powerful Democrat in the state, had been a client of mine. John Wilder from West Tennessee was friends with two of my partners, Ernest and David Williams. I called both and they agreed. Politically seasoned, I responded, "I don't mean to support it, but to attend the swearing in ceremony?" With little hesitation, both agreed. We all agreed the chief justice must swear Lamar in, and again I was chosen to make the arrangements. I went down to Chief Justice Joe Henry's office and told him the story: The FBI and Bill Leech urged the action, and the two Democratic speakers agreed. Chief Justice Henry agreed.

The decision was not easy. As far as we knew, this had never happened before in Tennessee or in any other state. It was not altogether clear the state constitution permitted the governor to be sworn in early. The constitution calls for a four-year term; however, custom had not observed that. The governor was always sworn in on Saturday nearest the actual end of the four-year term and, that set a precedent: A full exact four years were not required. The state legislature fixed the day for the swearing in on Saturday, but this swearing in was going to take place on Wednesday. Lamar felt he should take the risk because if Blanton issued additional pardons we would be rightly criticized. He saw his responsibility to the state clearly. We arranged for the swearing in to be at about 5:00 in the afternoon in the Supreme Court chamber.

When we arrived at the swearing in ceremony, Lamar, an informal dresser, had on a sweater. He called Honey, his wife, to bring a coat, but failed to ask for a tie. He borrowed mine. The two speakers, the constitutional officers, led by the Attorney General Bill Leech, also attended. The press swarmed all over the place, climbing over the bench and on counsel tables, with the Supreme Court clerk having a fit. Finally, order was restored and the chief justice swore Lamar in. With all of us present, the attorney general called Governor Blanton and told him he was no longer governor.

As we started to leave, the FBI agent who initiated the early swearing in said to Lamar, "You should send someone to secure the capitol, because we think Blanton may try to grant some additional pardons despite the early swearing in. Someone should prevent anything being taken out of the building." I learned immediately my new job was to take care of such problems. Lamar said, "I've got this dinner down in Jackson. Lewie, you go up and secure the capitol." I called Jan and told her what I was going to do. I had been late for dinner many, many times in our marriage, but she said that was the wildest explanation ever.

I went up to the capitol. Not sufficiently knowledgeable about state government, I assumed the Capitol Police and Highway Patrol belonged to one organization.

The capitol policeman appeared to be in his mid-60s, was slightly overweight and small. When I told him that our job was to secure the capitol, he looked at me as if I had said, "The Russians are coming." I told him, "I believe we are going to need some more help." And he said, "Yes we are." He said, "I'll call my boss, who is head of the Capitol Police." What I needed was the head of the State Troopers, who was very cooperative and said, "Do you want somebody special?" I responded, "If I could have my choice I'd like to get Paul Lane and Johnny White." I had known them during the Dunn administration and had complete confidence in them. They arrived promptly.

The building was closed and I'd told everybody not to take anything out of the building. All the doors were locked as they always are at night. We used one door where people could exit, and one trooper stood guard over that door.

My wife Jan was watching television. The first thing she heard was, "It's rumored that Commissioner Donelson has nailed up the back door to the governor's office." She said to a friend, "I know that's a lie because Lewie couldn't nail up anything." When one television reporter questioned Paul Lane, who was standing at the door, "What would you do if Governor Blanton showed up?" Lane responded, "I wouldn't let him in. Anyway, he's no longer governor and Commissioner Donelson told me nobody can come in the building. That's what I'm going to do." The reporter said, "Would you shoot him?" He thought for a minute and said, "If Commissioner Donelson told me to, I probably would." What an amazing evening! Technically, I was a private citizen, not yet officially commissioner of F&A.

At one point, I received a call from Governor Blanton's legal counsel who complained, "I understand you won't let me take anything out of the building." I answered, "That's correct, the building is closed, and nobody can take anything out of the building tonight." He said, "I have these papers I want to take out to the governor." I said, "The governor is no longer governor. The new governor has been sworn in, but I'll come down to your office."

I went down to his office and walked in. He said, "I have these papers, 28 more pardons and commutations. I'd be happy for you to look at them if you want to." I said, "No, I don't want to look at them. I don't care what they are, nothing can be taken out of the building." He said, "I'm going to call the governor." He called Governor Blanton, who was in the shower. We sat and stared at each other for many minutes, and finally he said, "I believe I've done my duty, I'm going to leave." Just as he got to the door the phone rang and it was Governor Blanton. "Governor, a fellow here says his name is Lewis Donelson and he's a new commissioner and he says I can't take anything out of the building." I knew Blanton reasonably well and had helped him out of a couple of spots. He said, "Put Lewie on." I got on. "You're telling me you won't let me take anything out of the building." I said, "That's right." He said, "Suppose I come down there." I said, "I won't let you in." He said, "But the press is there," and I said, "Oh, no, I'm not letting the press in. Governor, the building is closed every night." After a moment, he asked, "What am I going to tell everybody?" I said, "Tell them the new governor has been sworn in and your term of office is over." He said, "I can't say that."

We discussed his not serving a full four years. I pointed out only occasionally did a governor serve exactly four years because of the Saturday swearing in. I did not point out that the legislature fixed that date by resolution. Then I emphasized the chief justice of the Supreme Court had sworn in the new governor, the attorney general had been present, and that I had heard the attorney general of the state of Tennessee call him and tell him that he was no longer governor. We had further discussion. He argued, "I can't really tell them that." I suggested, "Governor, I tell you what you do, you tell the press if they ask you that you talked to me and I told you that you were no longer governor and you couldn't get in the building." I had given him good advice in the past and he said, "OK."

Next morning he called and asked if he could come down and get his desk, which he had taken from Congress when he retired. Apparently congressmen are allowed to take their desk as a souvenir of their service. Afterward, everyone agreed the action was essential, that additional pardons that would have been issued without the early swearing in and our securing the capitol.

It gave Governor Alexander's administration a strong start because it showed him as a man of action, willing to rise to the occasion and do whatever seemed to be necessary. No charges were brought against Blanton for those pardons because there was no evidence he received any money. It was proven that several staff members had received money. They were indicted, convicted, and spent time in jail. Blanton was convicted for issuing a liquor license in Memphis for which he received cash directly. He did go to jail for that.

This dramatic beginning helped establish me as leader of the cabinet, improved my relationship with Lamar, and increased his confidence in me. It also consolidated my position with the two speakers because they respected our courage in stepping up to a difficult situation.

Frequently, I went down when other commissioners were being questioned to support them. The governor was the spokesman for the administration. He dealt with the public, tested ideas with his friends and supporters, spoke for the state, and considered his job to sell his programs. Lamar seldom advanced a major program without working it thoroughly with his supporters before presentation to the legislature and then working it carefully with the legislature. He felt it was important to build up a base of support before he tried to push a new program through the General Assembly.

Lamar had a staff meeting every morning. I came 15 minutes beforehand for a private session; I sat in on most staff meetings along with Lamar's weekly breakfast meetings with the two speakers, the majority and minority leaders.

I served on numerous boards. At the first meeting of the Funding Board, they discussed a recently completed bond issue to create a fund for poor counties to draw upon to undertake capital projects. An excellent idea, it provided state interest rates for county projects. I immediately asked, "How many points do you have to pay?" They looked startled and surprised that I knew about points. They somewhat reluctantly said they paid 150 points. I replied, "That's outrageous. I have done bond issues for the Light, Gas & Water division, the First Tennessee National Corporation, and others. They don't pay any points like that. With our excellent state credit we can do much better." They explained how complicated and unique this project was. I was unyielding; we agreed to my calling the guy to tell him the points were unreasonable. If he got all huffy, they could say they had the votes and could outvote me. We got him on the phone and I made my pitch: The state's credit was so good and its bond rating was so good, this was an unfair spread. He replied, "Just a moment," and came back in a couple minutes and asked, "Would 75 basis points be OK?" I agreed. The silence was deafening. No one said a word. That phone call probably amounted to $5 million in saved interest.

After that, they listened with considerable care to my comments. A retired general ran the bond division. In New York to talk about our bond ratings, the general described a problem with one rating agency. He said that he needed to go and talk to them and get the problem straightened out. Bill Snodgrass said, "Would you like for me to go there with you?" And he said, "No, Mr. Snodgrass, I'd like Lewie to go with me."

The Building Commission approved all capital projects, with many contentious issues. I was a member; John Wilder presided when the governor was not present. I had many dealings with the constitutional officers, Comptroller Bill Snodgrass, Treasurer Harlan Mathews, Secretary of State Gentry Crowell, and Attorney General Bill Leech.

When I was chosen as commissioner, I visited at Christmas with a close friend, Helen Allen, who helped build the Republican Party in Shelby County and who worked for Tusculum College in Greeneville, her hometown. It suddenly occurred to me Helen would be perfect as my executive assistant. When I offered her the job, she objected that she was not a financial person. I said, "I don't need you as a financial person. I am commissioner of Finance and Administration. I have many administrative duties that you would handle. I need someone to investigate and report to me." Helen was a tremendous asset; she dealt well with the state bureaucrats and the commissions. She was as bright as she could be and worked tirelessly.

Early in the administration I received a report of state deposits made by Harlan Mathews. After looking over these reports for a couple of months, I said, "Harlan, the state deposits in some of these banks are fully secured by the bonds they owe only because the bonds are valued at face value. The current fair market value is far less than face. I never want to see a situation where state deposits are not fully covered by the current fair market value of the bonds." Harlan took my criticism well and I never saw that situation again.

The commissioner's job was different from what many people understood. You handle the finances, the budget and that sort of thing, but the state law also gave you supervision over much of the administration. Under Lamar, I supervised all of state government's administration. Helen analyzed problems, such as those of the Planning Commission. She carefully reviewed the curricula at the community colleges and technical institutes to determine whether lightweight courses should be in K-12 or in the community colleges. She discovered some community colleges specialized mostly in repairing cars and fixing hair. These had merit in the production of in-demand jobs, but we insisted the curriculum be broadened to include more educational and career subjects. So many of our high school graduates came to college unprepared and needed remedial courses, an expensive way to provide those classes. These needed to be taught by the high schools or by community colleges, not four-year universities. If there was a problem that needed to be solved requiring research and analysis, I could turn it over to Helen because she always did a superb job and relieved me from the responsibility.

Many decisions had to be made on the spot and frequently without sufficient information. If you didn't make them then, you would be swamped. Some of my successors found if you didn't make an immediate decision they pile up and they pile up and they pile up and by the time you get back to them you have forgotten what you knew. I learned very quickly that I would know more that first time than I probably would at any other time, and I might as well call the shot then. This enabled me to stay on top, although I worked about 80 hours a week. All state contracts are signed by the F&A commissioner. In the beginning I went down on Sunday and spent the day reading contracts. With so many, I finally had to categorize those that came to me, and some to subordinates with full authority to sign my name.

An early eye-opening experience came one night when Jan said, "I met this lovely lady today at the Centennial Club and she called us and invited us to dinner Saturday night." I replied, "Who was it?" She said, "Martha Ingram." I laughed and said, "You know what that means. She wants something from the state." Jan replied, "Oh, I thought it was just because she liked me." I said, "You are charming and she probably did like you. She would be a fool if she didn't like you, but I'll bet you she wants something." We went for dinner with some 12 or 15 guests. Butlers waited on the table at the elaborate meal. She introduced the dessert as her specialty, one similar to one of my mother's. Ted Welch spoke up and in his usual straightforward fashion asked, "Martha, do you want me to tell Lewie what we wanted, or do you want to do it?" Jan said she almost fell out of her chair laughing because of my prediction. I had to tell Martha Ingram she was too late; the budget was complete with no room for additions. I couldn't make changes until the following year. This reminded me of the commissioner's power, and people in Nashville were sensitive to the commissioner's control of the budget.

A delegation of scientists from Oak Ridge told me they had developed a system for measuring things from long distances to deal with radioactive materials and thought it commercially feasible. They wanted state assistance in setting up a company to develop it commercially. I asked why they had not gone to the University of Tennessee. Their response bowled me over: They had investigated and there had never been a cooperative project between the University of Tennessee and the Oak Ridge National Laboratory. I found that tragic and difficult to believe. Leading state universities like the University of Tennessee tend to be islands all to themselves. I sent the scientists to UT and a joint project resulted, not successful, but it opened a period of cooperation. The university now is one of the joint managers for the laboratory's operation.

An early problem came from Commissioner James Brown in Mental Health concerning the release of patients from the state mental institutions. Many institutions were warehouses, not treatment centers. Commissioner Brown correctly wanted to get patients back into more normal circumstances. Unfortunately, we did wholesale releases to reduce the number of patients. Many benefited from this; some got out and quit taking their medicine. This created a serious problem. Such action must be done with care and skill, and not wholesale.

Lamar called one day and said, "Marvin Runyon is here and wants to talk about a Nissan plant in Tennessee. He tells me in Georgia his taxes would be $30 million less in the first five years than in Tennessee. I want you to come down here and talk to him." I replied, "It might not do any good because he is right." Lamar was taken aback and he said, "You better come anyway." I walked down there and I remember the press release stating the number of employees and the average wage. I knew the Georgia tax rates. I got down there and said, "Governor, he's right. He would pay considerably less in corporate taxes if he goes to Georgia, but his employees would pay considerably more." Marvin Runyon's answer: "We don't care what our employees pay; we are thinking about what we pay." I suggested, "I could find in the budget, if you promise not to tell, about $15 million to provide you on the front end to equalize the situation." This enabled us to clinch the deal. Marvin Runyon and I became good friends. An experienced automobile executive, he did a great job. He retired and went to TVA to become the chairman of the TVA board. I remember his telling me, "When I first went to TVA, I tried to get things under control. Everything I wanted to do, they said, 'Oh, you can't do that under the act.' Finally I said, 'Give me that blasted act.' So I took it home and read it over two or three nights. I came in and called my staff in and said, 'Ya'll have been lying to me. There is not a word in the act that tells me I can't do all those things.' They said, 'It's custom and we have interpreted the act this way.'" He began to make some changes. He reduced the size of their workforce by 25 percent. He did a magnificent job despite major hostility. He went on to the Post Office where he thought his trouble would be the Civil Service Employee Association, but the high ranking civil service employees took the attitude that they would be there when he was gone. He found them intractable and impossible to deal with and gave up on the problem.

A major difficulty with the state budget was with capital outlays, especially the education budget, but there were many others. It seemed like to me every year I had a raft of requests for new roofs for National Guard armories. We never managed to get a decent roof on any building, only one small portion of my problem. The capital outlay procedure was helter-skelter. People put in their request, fought over it, tried to get it in the budget, and if they failed, they tried to get it stuck on the floor of the legislature. The budget bill had no separate capital budget such as the one I created for the city of Memphis. It never occurred to me that the state did not have one. We created a new capital budget. Charlie Howell, an assistant commissioner, did a fantastic job in developing that first capital budget and creating the procedure to have the capital budget over a 10-year period. Charlie told me one day he had found the deed to Hermitage. He then began to search other state properties and prepared a broad inventory of them. While preparing a five-year capital budget, I talked to all departments about their capital needs and began to make a conscientious effort to prioritize them. Charlie brought some order to the capital budgeting process. Administrators could plan their upcoming projects in a certain forward year, reducing the behind-the-scenes politicking and lobbying to get capital projects. The next step the state should take is a multiyear budgeting process, the procedure used by the United States Congress to project budgets on a 10-year basis to determine costs.

An early decision during Lamar's administration concerned highway construction. Major construction was required to finish the interstate highway system and improve older parts of the system that traffic had outgrown. Lamar came up with the idea to go on a self-funding basis, and he proposed and sold an increase in the Tennessee gasoline tax. For years the highway system remained on a current funding basis, which saved millions and millions of dollars in interest.

The Building Commission, in anticipation of the Tennessee Bicentennial in 1996, had approved the concept that the land immediately north of the capitol, what used to be called Sulphur Dell, the baseball park, would become a state project, Bicentennial Mall State Park. Charlie Freeburg, semiretired from his real estate business and a good friend, took on the task of assembling the land needed for the project. Now this beautiful area enhances downtown Nashville and the magnificent state capitol. A plan is under way to put a new multimillion dollar state museum on this site.

As commissioner of Finance I went many places with the governor, often announcing the opening of a capital project. On one such trip, as we got off the plane, Lamar said to the trooper, "Do you have an aspirin?" Then Lamar turned to me and said, "Do you need an aspirin?" And I said, "Certainly not. You know I give headaches, I don't have them." He laughed.

When I dealt with bureaucrats in various departments and agencies, they liked my being straightforward about their budget proposals. I answered questions directly. Many would say when they left my office they never were in doubt as to my stand.

The commissioner's principal responsibility was preparation of the budget and its presentation to the legislature. I had been involved in preparing budgets for Governor Winfield Dunn, especially the first one, and I knew Jerry Adams, deputy commissioner of F & A, well. Bill Snodgrass and Bill Jones, my predecessors as commissioners of F & A, were most helpful in the budget preparation. Governor Alexander was intent on controlling expenses, and I reduced the size of state government by eliminating a number of unfilled jobs. I also eliminated a few agencies, including the Civil War Commission that did nothing but meet occasionally. Another egregious example of waste hit my desk early in January. All bills for the state came to F & A for payment. One was from *The Tennessean* newspaper for over 850 daily copies. You can imagine my horror. About 400 of them went to the Department of Education. These bureaucrats had the state pay for their daily paper, and then read it on state time. We eliminated virtually all. The state was buying about 100 copies of *The Tennessee Journal*. I canceled them all, but continued to pay my personal subscription at my own expense. Lee Smith, the publisher, complained bitterly.

The commissioners did not need cars for their duties, and the cars were eliminated, except for Transportation and Safety, and the military. A car pool was available when needed. The howl was loud and many complaints came from the legislators in response to the commissioner's requests. The commissioner of General Services, Sammy Lynn Puett, a delightful and able person who ultimately became executive assistant to the president of UT, was responsible. I got a call that she needed my help to explain why the commissioners had their cars taken away. I have this wonderful picture of Sammy Lynn and me before the legislative committee explaining why we did not think the commissioners needed cars.

Six months after I left, all commissioners had their cars back. In government it is so hard to be businesslike. The rationale was government salaries were so low and a car was a reasonable perk; however, those types of things add up and become waste.

Many departments lived off excess funding from vacant but funded positions. I built a vacancy factor into each budget, and I restricted use of funds budgeted for salaries, preventing a shift to another budget line. One example will show how difficult this is. A person whose name or job I do not remember came to defend his position in the budget. I listened carefully, and said, "You'd better look for a job because that job won't be in the budget this year." The next year the same guy appeared again and I complained, "What are you doing here? We wrote you out of the budget last year." He said, "I have a different position now." I responded, "Explain to me what you are doing now." He did and I told him the same thing as the year before. That went on every year while I was commissioner and he remained in some comfy state job that he'd found.

One early complaint from Lamar was I had told the commissioner of Veterans Affairs I saw absolutely no reason for a Department of Veterans Affairs because we provided no financial support for veterans. Lamar said, "I wish you wouldn't tell new commissioners their department's going to be eliminated in your first meeting." I tried to be more restrained, but an all-out campaign was under way to reduce the size of government.

During my tenure I dealt primarily with the comptroller, state treasurer, and secretary of state, and the constitutional officers, partially because of my knowing them and because of our working together on the Funding Board. The commissioner of F&A starts in the fall to prepare the budget for the fiscal year, which begins the next July 1. The upcoming budget is presented in January to the legislature. When you sit down to project revenues in November, the projections extend 18 or more months. Past records and projections of the University of

Tennessee, which includes the Tennessee economic report, provide trends. One year we were able to project available funds within $50 million of the actual figure; $100 million variance was average. Given the billions in the budget, this was not bad.

My first budget presentation to the legislature went on all morning and part of the afternoon. I actually testified before the joint Finance and Ways and Means Committee for seven hours, obviously in great detail. Because I proposed some new and unusual cuts, I thought it necessary to review the budget in great detail with the two finance committees.

During that first hearing, I had put in $100,000 to renovate the governor's mansion, which was in terrible shape. The drapes were in tatters, and the peeling wallpaper gave it a general run-down appearance. When we came to that item, Tommy Burnett, then majority leader, asked, "What fancy interior decorator did you have to determine that it would take $100,000 to fix up the governor's residence?" And I said, "Me." Everybody died laughing, and Tommy told me afterward, "Lewie, the speaker told me you bite." We became good friends in the following months.

Another funny moment involved Burnett. In the middle of the afternoon I was sipping away on my unsweetened iced tea and he said, "Commissioner, if that's bourbon you're sipping, you hold your whiskey better than anybody I've ever seen." I established a precedent for being straightforward about what I proposed without trying to sugarcoat or conceal. That attitude was a major plus for me. My relationships with John Wilder and Ned McWherter gave me significant credibility.

Tommy Burnett had tremendous ability. Smart, attractive, energetic, he was also undisciplined and burned the candle at both ends. He was indicted for filing a false financial statement to obtain a farm loan, and called me to represent him. We brought in a certified public accountant and proved, despite the financial statement's inaccuracies, that it reflected a lower net worth than he had. They dropped the charges. Tommy told me even before the indictment he had not filed a tax return in five years. I lectured him about that and advised him to file something—even a flying estimate on what he owed and get it filed, because if you file before being charged with failure to file, there might be a penalty, but no jail time. I told him, "Once we get you off this one, you know that they'll indict you on that failure to file charge." They did. Again, we got busy and I pushed Tommy as hard as I could. Those tax returns were not filed because he didn't take the time. (There is no defense for failure to file—unless you are unconscious or incapable.) On the day of sentencing, we filed the CPA-prepared returns that showed he owed nothing. I told the judge I had never heard of a case in which a taxpayer had been sentenced to jail for failure to file when he did not owe any income tax. Clearly Judge Miller was surprised; he made some corrections on the bench and Tommy was pleased. The maximum time to serve would be about 60 to 90 days. The DA argued that the judge had made a bigger correction than he intended. We went back and the judge made the correction. Tommy got a sentence of more than one year, which required him to serve almost one full year. In response to comments he served at that "country club place" in Alabama, Tommy said, "Yes, I was at this country club cutting the grass." Tommy was re-elected while he was in prison, finished his prison term, but got into another scandal over bingo legislation and went back to jail. This time he was not re-elected, and he disappeared from the political scene.

I was besieged by requests for government money, but not many appeals succeeded. Linda Thompson (now Prater), my talented secretary who came with me to Nashville, tacked a big sign on the inside of my door: "NO." Lots of teasing resulted, but the message was clear: Government was going to shrink.

Lamar understood that when I cut $250,000 from some item he would say, "You really mean you cut that from the requested increase." Admittedly, that was mostly true. Government feels the effect of inflation as an individual does. State employees needed pay raises to keep even with inflation. Also, new needs arose. Controlling government spending is a continuous battle.

I tried to be open always to legislators, but I strongly positioned myself against pork. That first year, the legislature tacked many items as amendments to my budget. But Tennessee had a process when the conference Committee of Finance, Ways and Means met usually for most of the night: My good friend, Senator Leonard Dunavant, ranking Republican on the Senate Finance Ways and Means and the most knowledgeable legislator about the budget, received tremendous respect from the entire committee. Each amendment was considered separately. As each amendment came up I would turn my thumbs down to reject and Leonard would move to defeat, and usually that happened. If I turned my thumbs up, he would move for it to be approved—and that usually happened.

Another process with which I was unfamiliar included some budget items subject to the commissioner's approval. The commissioner of F&A would determine if there were sufficient funds to provide for that item, and my authority was open-ended and absolute. My disapproval was not subject to overrule as the governor's veto might be. That second year, the budget was extremely tight as our revenues were projected to go down, and did. This was the only year until recently in which the gross state revenues decreased from the prior year. Most years the revenues' increase was smaller than the cost of living. The increase was almost nominal, but it was still an increase. That year, it was not.

Deleting unfilled jobs helped some; some jobs were so important they had to be filled. I put on a payroll freeze and ordered that no one could be hired without my personal signature, a *tremendous* amount of work, but I did review every one of them—proposed new jobs to fill vacancies, or the creation of new jobs. A substantial number of them were approved, but the size of state government was reduced by more than 4,000 people.

In that first year, I found out that some items in the budget, particularly minor capital items, were usually spent at the last minute. This showed that an appropriation for something, even if not needed, was always spent. The next year, on March 31, I put on a freeze: Nothing that had not already been committed in the capital area could be commenced without my personal approval. This stopped the games the departments played with the budget.

In addition to the all-important Building Commission, I also sat on many other boards such as the Purchasing Board, the Aging Commission, the Pension Board, and the Funding Board. In the process I established relationships with legislators who served on those boards, primarily dominated by Democrats. I teased them, saying, "Three to one odds is pretty even." Speaker McWherter had a pithy expression. When I looked around the room and saw the many Democrats there in support of his proposal to which I was opposed, he would say, "Commissioner, I feel a wind blowing." I would respond, "Yes, I feel it too. What is it you're going to do, Mr. Speaker?" I can't remember the board or the issue, but I looked around the room and saw the administration had a majority in the room and said, "Mr. Speaker, I feel a wind blowing." And he looked around the room and laughed. He said, "Yeah, I do too. What are you going to do this time?" Our personal relationship helped to make government work. I believe those of us elected or appointed to office must focus on governing. I was a Republican serving in a Republican administration, but the legislature was dominated by Democrats. Because Republicans were so long in the minority in Tennessee, many Republicans now elected to office feel their principal function is to protest and complain and object, sadly neglecting their responsibility in governing. With the legislature, now controlled by Republicans, this minority mindset persists among some GOP legislators.

In Tennessee government, each department is headed by a commissioner, appointed by the governor, and usually not a longtime government employee, but from the private sector. This provides leaders with different attitudes and approaches, the public's point of view. John Neff, an able commissioner and a successful businessman, was commissioner of Insurance. A proposal from John's department was an example of overregulation and an additional and unnecessary layer of reporting. I called John and asked, "Where in the world is this idea from? I know it didn't come from you." He stammered and said, "You're right. It came from our staff people and I glanced at it and sent it on to you." I teased him. I said, "John, our main function as commissioners is to bring a 'doubting Thomas' cynical attitude from private industry to government. We won't know nearly as much about the issues as the bureaucrats who work for us, but we do have a fresh attitude. And, we ought to always try to preserve that."

Governor Alexander shared my concern for education. Early on, he attacked the higher education system. The Higher Education Commission reviewed and set priorities for all budgets. Its responsibility was to recommend what a higher education program required. No governor had ever funded the recommended amount. This system provided a challenge to the state to evaluate its commitment to higher education. The Alexander administration struggled to meet the challenge. The legislature approved a special committee to review education and provided places for gubernatorial appointments. Lamar appointed me, and I was actively involved in the proceedings. One reporter commented upon my influence and how frequently the committee approved my recommendations.

One excellent idea was establishing Centers of Excellence, with extra funds to hire outstanding professors and staff and create programs to achieve national recognition. The committee also made recommendations about K-12. Through our efforts many of the commission's recommendations were adopted and put into effect. When I urged creation of the Centers of Excellence, I explained that one person could lift a team to excellence; we later found these centers began to lift the whole institution. In later years when I served on the Commission for Higher Education, we were disappointed with some proposals. One commission member with a tart tongue was heard to say, "I often wonder whether some of our colleges and universities know what excellence really is." But it did give higher education a shot in the arm. Lamar came up with another idea, which came out of the committee, for paying for performance among K-12 teachers. This was opposed by the teachers' union. After I left, Lamar finally got that proposal passed, but, in subsequent years, the legislature at the behest of the TEA watered down the plan to nothing. Lamar's actions did lift Tennessee from 49th among the states to something like 39th or 40th in "per pupil" support for K-12 education.

It is interesting to see what happens when a government employee stays too long, especially in the area of contracts. Term limits for elected officials is a different issue, but a disturbing trend in politics today is when families, like the Kennedys and the Bushes, seem to dominate the political process. This is true at the state level as well. If government becomes dominated by a few prominent families with well-known names and wealth passing along special opportunities, the vitality of public life will be sadly diminished. Democratic governments need fresh blood. I have commented previously on my doubts about term limits, and I have observed many officials who served too long. For example, Senator McKellar, who served in the Senate from 1910 to 1952, stayed in office too long. He was not senile, but he was infirm. He was badly scalded in a shower fall and could hardly get around. Yet he could not give up and suffered a humiliating defeat at the end of his career.

During my years in state government, I attended the governors' association meetings and meetings of the financial officers of the states. I met Pete DuPont, a good friend of Lamar's and an extremely able person. He was then governor of Delaware and his wife was a congresswoman. At the finance officers' meetings, I gleaned ideas about cost controls in other states and areas to improve revenue. I promised Lamar not to push for an income tax, although I resumed my support for it after I left state government.

In distribution of public announcements, Lamar announced all good news; I announced all bad news. Given the amount of bad news, most of it budgetary, I received much press coverage. I spoke at a meeting of the Nursing Home Association about its reimbursement under the Medicare formula, perhaps the only speech I ever made without one single clap. They sat there in stony silence. They had been spoiled during the nursing home boom. When it became clear that you could get reimbursed by Medicare for nursing home expenses, many of the legislators got in the nursing home business, including Speaker McWherter. So the legislature tended to be very tender toward them. I learned that the reimbursement for nursing homes in Tennessee was higher than almost every other state, and substantially higher than many. So, we began to bring some reasonable controls over nursing home reimbursement.

After that meeting, a reporter asked me a general question about what happened in the meeting, clearly without any understanding of its purpose. I asked, "Do you know who I am?" He responded, "No, I just know they told me to interview you. You would be the speaker here." I explained, "I am the commissioner of Finance and Administration for the state. And I control the state's budget." Clearly, he had never heard of me and knew nothing about my responsibilities.

"How long have you been here in Tennessee?" I asked. His response: "Oh, about three weeks." That demonstrates the difficulty, especially with television news, of having a reporter with enough knowledge to cover it intelligently. From my years as spokesman for the growing Republican Party and my four years on the City Council, I learned how to deal with the media. I was as open as possible, even when I delivered bad news. The press had few complaints.

Once when proposing something to the legislature, probably a budget item, a member of a legislative committee asked if any other state had done this. I replied, "Not that I know of. Wouldn't it be terrible if Tennessee was the first state to do something?" It brought a few laughs, but probably not that legislator's vote.

I got to know other members of the cabinet well. Bill Sansom, commissioner of Transportation, succeeded me as commissioner of F&A, and we became personal friends, playing golf and dining together with our families. Another close associate and friend was John Neff, commissioner of Insurance. He and his wife became our good friends. John and I played golf several times. He called and asked Jan and me to a husband-and-wife tournament at the Belle Meade Country Club.

Jan had played only a few times. John and his wife were serious. It was an alternate hit. At a short par 3 hole, it was John's wife turn to hit. John advised her, "Don't try to knock it over that water onto the green. You just lay it up short of the green and I'll knock it on the green." She laid it up perfectly in the right position. John walked up and dumped it right in the water. His wife enjoyed it more than Jan and I, but John didn't find it the least bit funny.

I finally became good friends with Clyde York, my adversary in the Tennessee Constitutional Convention, because Farm Bureau people controlled the convention. I described that earlier.

Charlie Howell, my valued deputy commissioner who later became commissioner of Conservation, and I had been political friends before serving in the cabinet together. This was one of many friendships built or enhanced during that time that has lasted, a true benefit of my years in state government.

When I announced plans to leave, one measure in process was a $20 million grant to Memphis for much needed capital projects. I complained to the legislature, particularly to McWherter and Wilder, both from West Tennessee, about how much more gravy Nashville got from the state than Memphis did. Speaker McWherter referred to this grant as Lewie Donelson's going away present. Allocating the funds was an interesting process. We decided to use an existing organization called the Jobs Conference, designed to help produce more jobs in the aftermath of the King assassination, to allocate the funds. The Jobs Conference was made up mostly of community activists with limited business experience. I pushed to use some of the money for the zoo; Abe Plough agreed to match anything up to $10 million. He even sent me to San Diego to see its famous zoo. He had visited the one in Minneapolis and had creative ideas to benefit the Memphis Zoo. Unfortunately, the Jobs Conference types were not interested in zoos, only in urban projects. The money went to Beale Street, the Orpheum Theatre, and similar projects.

Not many years later, Memphis businessman Jim Prentiss and his wife became enthusiastic about the zoo, and with Mr. Plough's help, raised serious money to support it. Memphis now has a first-class zoo, one of the few in the U.S. with pandas.

Perhaps I should have had more control over that money, but Lamar and I felt the public should decide. In retrospect, we chose the wrong vehicle; other public groups might have been better able to select projects of long-range benefit to Memphis.

Upon my departure, I was given a dinner, unusual and extremely complimentary, with many speakers. The funniest one was Bill Sansom, who read a "press release" that said, "Revenues are down," "Alexander cuts away a thousand jobs," and such things. With each line he read, a big smiling picture of me appeared. The audience roared. Lamar paid me many compliments and then concluded, "When there is a difficult problem in state government and I look in this hole and see smoke and fire coming out, I put Lewie down in that hole and it all goes away." He made a classic remark: "You know, Lewie gets up every morning, eats a jar of nails for breakfast, and comes in and gives me my instructions for the day." Jimmy Pidgeon gave me a jar of nails to sit on my desk. I was humbled by this unique event. On the last day, Lamar and I had lunch together. "Lewie, when I told some of my closest advisers that I was going to ask you to be commissioner of F&A, they said, 'You don't want to do that. Lewie is so strong-minded that he would be too hard to control. He will do whatever he wants to do,' but I said, 'No, Lewie has been a lawyer all his life, he understands what it is to represent a client, and he will represent me. I feel comfortable with that.'" He concluded, "I want to tell you, Lewie, I can't remember a single time when you did something and hadn't told me about it that I was sorry that you hadn't told me in advance. I remember many times when you did something and hadn't told me about it and how glad I was not to know. Then I could say, 'Did Lewie really do that?'"

Lamar and I worked together with great success. We understood each other. Lamar knew his role as governor and was clear about my role. Along with that key relationship I worked well with the cabinet, the two speakers, and the chairmen of the Finance Committees. In general, I had good relationships with most legislators. All in all, it was an extraordinary experience. I learned so much; enjoyed myself, especially the accomplishments; and was grateful for the opportunities. I am particularly happy I knew the right time to leave.

TWENTY-FIVE

THE FIRM SPREADS OVER TENNESSEE

U pon my return to the firm, I created a firm with Ogden Stokes and Sam Bartholomew: Donelson, Stokes & Bartholomew. My Memphis partners were not willing to take a risk on a Nashville office, but we obtained a special ruling from the Bar Association that allowed me to do this. I spent five years building up that firm, which was going like gangbusters, partly because of my name and reputation, but mainly because Ogden was a superb lawyer and Sam, a tremendous rainmaker.

After five years, the Memphis firm decided it was willing to merge, but Stokes and Bartholomew decided against it. I left them, and we started over again in 1987 to build a Nashville office. Nashville was a difficult market to penetrate, and many lawyers tried. Richard Byrd, still with us, was the first; but many others have come and gone as we strove to establish that office. The Memphis partners were committed and everyone sacrificed from their own earnings to subsidize the office. It is now a major contributor to our success, after a long, hard effort. I predicted that the Nashville office would become larger than the one in Memphis.

In 1981, Ron Terry complained of unhappiness with the firm's service, not in quality, but in responsiveness. He told them, "Lewie will be back in a few months. He'll get it straight," and he charged me with getting it straight. After four or five months everything had been smoothed out, and he had no further complaints. Then he said, "Lewie, you have got to teach those boys up there that there is 'life after Lewie.'" I was 64 years old, and at that point I began to withdraw from the firm's management.

By 1986, I was almost out of the management of the firm. It took five years to break old habits. I have a strong personality; my older partners were accustomed to my running things. I tried chairman of the board, then member of the board. I finally realized I had to separate myself totally from management. Although the managing partners and CEOs of the firm certainly have consulted me and kept me informed, I have not been a member of the board or held any other management position since then. I consider this management transition one of the firm's greatest accomplishments. This management is one of vision and very well qualified. This is the best assurance that our future is bright.

After several different managing partners, we settled on Charlie Tuggle and adopted a blueprint for growth based on my 1982 plan, my last hurrah as firm leader. Growth, expertise, geographic growth, better organized recruiting, lateral hiring, and regular long-range planning were the major thrusts. I also suggested affiliations, like the then-existing Donelson, Stokes & Bartholomew in Nashville as the first step, then merger as the second. We did not follow that policy, starting from scratch in Knoxville, hiring First Tennessee lawyers in Chattanooga. The lawyer growth plan proposed new hires and laterals, and that happened. Increased emphasis on expertise was certainly our clear policy.

By 1987, we had offices in Knoxville, Chattanooga, and Nashville, with six partners and two associates located in East Memphis. We were close to our long-term goal of a firm with experts in virtually every type of legal matter a business might have. Charlie Tuggle strongly believed in our plan of growth and became a serious student of law firms and their dynamics. His vision, his knowledge of the profession, and his drive led us into unparalleled expansion. Charlie's service as CEO was interrupted by several years during which Ben Adams, Jr., served. Ben was the natural choice. He grew up with the firm and was extremely well connected in Memphis as well as a superb lawyer with a great touch with people. After the interim, Charlie returned. Upon Charlie's departure, Ben took over again and our growth and success has, if anything, accelerated.

Shortly after I left state government, the bank acquired the Knoxville United American Bank. I had come to know the Butchers through politics. Clearly, Jake's brother, C.H. Butcher, was the driving force behind their operation. C.H. called in early February of 1982 and asked to meet with me immediately. He came down the next day and sat down at my desk and said, "How would you like to buy the First American Bank of Knoxville?" I said, "If you mean me, I have absolutely no interest whatsoever. But, if you mean First Tennessee Bank, then I believe they might have substantial interest." This confirmed my visibility as outside counsel for First Tennessee. (Unfortunately, we don't have the same status today.) Ron Terry was out of town, but I got through to him. We alerted the appropriate bank people, and Ron and I flew up to Knoxville on Saturday to try to negotiate the acquisition. It quickly became apparent the Butchers could not sell the bank because it was on the verge of bankruptcy and a state takeover.

We then contacted Bill Isaacs from the FDIC. I got Howard Baker, then majority leader of the Senate, to locate him over the weekend. Howard, his usual modest self, said, "Isaacs won't take my call over the weekend." I said, "I am sure he would take a call any time from the majority leader of the Senate." Isaacs called me and Ron and I began to talk to him. The negotiations went on all day Sunday. We finally made an offer on Sunday night, actually Monday morning at 3:00. We contended the bank should be sold without closing. If you closed the bank, all the associated and affiliated Butcher banks would go down. Bill Isaacs could not seem to understand that problem. He said, "They are separate banks. Why should they just go down because this bank is in trouble?" We tried to explain this to him all on the telephone that in the public's mind, they were all one bank. If you close one, it is going to create runs on the others and you would have to close all of them.

He called us back at 6:00 a.m. Monday and refused our offer. It was too late to get the bank open on Monday morning anyway, because we had not come close to an agreement. He had failed to understand all the details of our offer. We proposed to buy the bank's bonds at par and, at then-current interest rates, the present value of the bonds was considerably under par. He told us at 6:00, "If I had fully understood that, I would have accepted your offer in the first place." This showed the difficulties of telephone negotiations.

We learned later the Butcher banks had a large portfolio of questionable loans floating from bank to bank. When an examination of one bank was likely, all these loans would be transferred to other banks. Some loans were over the limit the bank was allowed to lend. In fact, United American Bank of Knoxville, although only a fraction of the size of First Tennessee, had loans that would have exceeded First Tennessee's loan limit. Most were to a small group of borrowers, cronies of the Butchers.

We spent the next day trying to fashion a bid. The bank was closed; the other Butcher banks followed suit promptly. At 5:00 p.m. we submitted our bid and at 7:00, they called back to say we lost. Ron Terry was disturbed. We had agreed on one offer, but he upped it by $500,000 saying, "I would hate to lose by $500,000."

About a half hour later, when he announced to the employees that we had not bought the bank, a call came from Bill Isaacs. He said to Ron, "If we agree to accept your offer, would you close it tonight?" Neither Ron nor I had been to bed since Saturday morning, but I said, "Yes, we would." The bank got a twin-engine jet and flew me as lone passenger to Atlanta. I managed to negotiate the deal by about 6:30 in the morning, get the contract signed, and fly back to Knoxville to present it to the court at 8:00. So we were able to purchase the bank before it was scheduled to open on Tuesday morning. After I delivered the order to the commissioner of Banking and we officially took over the bank, I went down, and the press was waiting for me outside. Somebody said, "Did you buy the bank?" I said, "Oh, yes." The reporter said, "Well, why isn't it open?" I said, "I don't know." They reminded me, "It is after 9:00." So I went back in. They were frantically looking for the key to the front door. They could not find it to open the bank.

I got into a discussion with a reporter who asked, "What did you pay the stockholders?" I said, "We did not pay them anything." He said, "What do you mean, you bought the bank for nothing?" I said, "Well, we agreed to cover all the deposits so that no depositor would lose a cent. We agreed to take over most of the loans. When you do that, you really do not have anything left for the stockholders. When you have a corporation where the liabilities exceed the assets, the value to the stockholders is zero." Nonetheless, he ran the article, about how in the world could this bank from out of town come in and buy this local bank and pay the stockholders nothing. We did not buy the bank from the stockholders. We bought the bank from the FDIC.

Ron Terry wanted us to open a Knoxville branch of the firm that he agreed to subsidize. We sent John Speer, Craig Donaldson, and John Hicks up to start that office, and selected another lawyer from Knoxville. Unfortunately, we did not select the right local attorney. Ron Terry and Bill Isaacs had worked out an agreement whereby the bank would collect the loans, a major source of revenue for our new law office. The bank and regulators argued continually over which loans the bank would collect. I am confident the bank and the firm could have collected the loans much less expensively and much more quickly than the FDIC. They hired hundreds of people and numerous lawyers and spent a fortune collecting the loans. We could have done a much better job for far less money; FDIC bureaucrats hired more so that they could get raises and promotions because of the number of employees under their supervision. As usual, the taxpayer picks up the tab for empire building.

We had difficulty getting Knoxville established, especially in recruiting good lawyers. The three Memphis lawyers wanted to return, and Craig Donaldson and John Hicks left us. John Speer returned to

Memphis. After several years John Hicks called and wanted to return. I stated, "We will be happy to have you back *once*." That is what I told all deserters. We have violated that rule at least once, to our regret. It took a number of years to get the Knoxville office stabilized. Unfortunately, Knoxville is not a great market for legal services because the principal industries are the University of Tennessee, the Tennessee Valley Authority, and Oak Ridge National Laboratory, all with legal departments of their own. Knoxville is now showing some signs of economic viability, in part because Oak Ridge has been charged with major new tasks.

Several years later Dick Gossett, who was representing First Tennessee in Chattanooga, approached me about joining the firm and creating a Chattanooga office. He was unhappy with his firm and wanted to move the bank's business if he left his old firm. He approached the bank and they suggested he call me. We were happy to have his group to establish a Chattanooga office. In 1993, Gossett recommended we approach the Caldwell Heggie firm to join us. Thomas Caldwell was a distinguished tax attorney with a strong client base and his firm was a perfect fit. It materially strengthened the Chattanooga office with tax, corporate, and transactional business similar to our Memphis office. As anticipated, this merger went smoothly. Tom Caldwell's name was added to the firm, and the Chattanooga office has grown larger and stronger, an integral part of our present operation.

During the eighties we made several successful lateral hires, including Jon McCalla and Henry Doggrell who brought business with them and developed more. Jon went to the federal bench and Henry, to Buckeye as general counsel, then to Pitt Hyde and all of his interests. We kept some of their clients. Sheila Cunningham came with Henry, and followed him to Buckeye. We also took over the remnants of the old Laughlin firm, bringing in Jim McBride, Greg Fletcher, Steve Goodwin, and Ann Stolle, excellent lawyers with a strong client base. Jim and Ann are in Washington. Greg and Steve are in Memphis, and Greg, who heads our litigation group, has begun to include other types of tax and general litigation. Their unique tax practice gives us nationwide recognition; they represent railroads and utilities in state property tax disputes. Jim McBride is a nationally recognized authority in this area. Jerry Stauffer joined us from an in-house counsel position and proved to be a strong rainmaker and a fine lawyer. After a period as managing partner (shareholder) of the Memphis office, he is now chief operating officer located in the Chattanooga office.

During my time as commissioner, one of my best clients, Purnell's Pride, the chicken processor, experienced difficult times. Don Malmo took over the representation from me. When Ray Purnell ran the company, it was successful and grew tremendously. The chicken business is difficult, because with a half-million to a million baby chicks growing, they need 10 weeks to get them ready for market. Market changes in that 10-week period are tremendous; poultry prices move with grain prices. The grain market is notorious for wide price movement. Periods when the market moves favorably, there's profit, but losses are almost inevitable when the grain market moves unfavorably. Ray turned over the operation to his son, Hugh, a bright man, who knew the business thoroughly.

Everybody loved Ray Purnell, and he had the complete confidence of everyone he dealt with. They wanted to help him and to do him favors. Hugh was knowledgeable but he did not have that personal touch. The poultry business is one in which you needed favors, favors from banks, favors from suppliers, and the unwavering support of your growers.

Not long before I became commissioner, Purnell had an inquiry from Cargill about buying the company. Hugh and I flew to Minneapolis and went out to the Cargill headquarters, a lovely private residence on a magnificent site. We had a full day of discussion; Hugh was not anxious to sell, and I agreed with him. I thought the company would continue to grow and command a better price later, a stupid mistake. We waited too long and the poultry business went into a decline. I forgot my Grandfather Donelson's advice, "Never try to sell at the top, just near the top, and don't try to buy at the bottom of the market, just near the bottom."

We traveled on a feeder flight from Minneapolis to Chicago and then home. After Ray Purnell died, the company lost momentum and ended up selling for a song. The family would have been well provided for if it had sold to Cargill.

I learned from that. In addition to knowing when to sell, I was reminded of the difficulty of passing a family business to the second generation, especially a business built upon the personality, ability, and reputation of the founding member. Hugh Purnell disappeared from view; I heard once he was head of the catfish growers of Mississippi. I hear from his sister in Tupelo occasionally, and the company that bought Purnell's poultry operation has disappeared.

Parts, Inc., was sold during the time I was commissioner. Frank Norfleet had discussed selling the firm and had begun serious discussions before I left to go to Nashville. Shortly after, Frank called me and said we were going to New York to finalize negotiations with GKN for the sale of the company and wanted to know if I could go with him. I did. We negotiated with the GKN representatives and reached a price approaching what Frank considered to be satisfactory. We retired to caucus. Herbert Rhea was with us. They both said they thought it was a satisfactory offer and I said I believed we had left something on the table. We discussed whether we should rile the situation with further negotiations and I said, "Why don't we just agree that I can go ahead and say that there are two other people who are not here, Dunbar Abston, Sr., and Dunbar, Jr., who are very interested in this and I believe that they would want more." I thought the company worth more than the offered price. I said, "If this hits them the wrong way, Frank can step in and overrule me and take the offer on the table." I made my pitch for more money; they retired for further discussion and came back with another $1 million. We accepted. You might say that was the result of long experience in negotiating deals.

After the sale, Frank continued to run Parts, finally turning over his responsibilities to Dunbar. Dunbar didn't enjoy the job, and company management passed out of the family. However, GKN was highly satisfied with Frank and finally put him on its advisory board. The company had two lovely flats in London. Jan and I stayed in each one on different occasions. A housekeeper provided us snacks after the theater and orange juice and toast in the morning. It was the perfect way to stay in London.

This was another example of the difficulty of continuing a firm into the third generation. No one in Frank's family was interested in running it. The same was true of Dunbar, Jr.'s, family. Frank had three daughters and Dunbar had children by his first wife and stepchildren with his present wife. None was interested in or qualified to run the company. Even with a willing family member with five or six stockholders, only one active in the business, a serious conflict of interest emerges immediately. How much emphasis should you have on dividends versus compensation? Frequently, this situation is unfair to the family member running the company. This is further complicated when the spouse is the stockholder and the husband only an employee. Even more common is when some family members stay in the company employment drawing salaries and bonuses, and other family stockholders don't receive good dividends. This is an interesting dynamic, and achieving a fair balance is a delicate task.

I had been counsel for Parts, Inc., for most of my career. We worked for the company until it closed down the Memphis operation. During that transaction, we benefited from careful tax planning. When we incorporated the company, we kept the real estate separate. It was owned individually by Frank and Dunbar. After the sale, we rented this property to GKN, obtaining very good rent. This proved to be perhaps the most lucrative part of the deal It provided Frank and Dunbar with excellent income, mostly sheltered by depreciation over many years. Today, all those buildings have been torn down; most of the property sold.

I represented Choctaw, a family owned business, for many years and had begun to serve on its board. When Bill Quinlan, Mr. O.H. Miller's son-in-law who ran the company for many years, died, John Cameron, the chief financial officer, moved up to president. A board reorganization added Frank Norfleet, Herbert Rhea, and Wise Jones.

This group, including me, put Bill Quinlan, Jr., on the board as well. We continued to operate the company, and it continued to prosper. When John Cameron wanted to step down Bill Quinlan, Jr., was elevated to president. I feel that the board provided a great deal of good advice to John Cameron and Bill Quinlan, Jr. The company's situation was difficult. Mr. Miller had nine grandchildren, six Miller girls, two Quinlan girls, and Bill, Jr. One son-in-law was active in the business. The issue arose of how to provide benefits for the grandchildren. So we began to look for sale of the company. With much help from Herbert Rhea and young Bill Quinlan, we arranged an excellent sale and each one of the grandchildren received a substantial sum for their stock.

This gratified me, because Mr. and Mrs. Miller frequently told me to look out for Buddy's little girls. All are well provided for. Young Bill Quinlan operated the company for many years, but finally stepped down from active management. After I became counsel to the family and the company, Mr. Miller depended on me for more and more. I was an important part of the company's decision making process. In Mr. Miller's old age, he wouldn't do anything about the business without my approval. In his latter days Bill Quinlan, Sr., would call about a proposed change in structure or operations. He would ask me to tell "Pappy," as he called Mr. Miller, that it was OK. Once I agreed, Mr. Miller would consent. I know it must have irked Bill to make those calls, but I am sure he was grateful to have me because getting Mr. Miller's consent would otherwise have been very difficult.

During this same period, I became involved with Frank Norfleet, Bland Cannon, and Herbert Rhea in a consulting firm. We advised a number of clients, the principal one being Baptist Hospital during the course of the two years we were in business. I urged Frank and Herbert to start a venture capital firm, which they did. They wanted me to join them but I declined to do so because I recognized that the law is my first love and I did not want to leave the firm. But I invested in their venture capital fund, which did reasonably well, and then in a second fund, which has done extremely well. That firm is now operated by Jim Witherington, Barham Ray, and a couple of other bright young people. They have done a tremendous job.

In the process, I got interested in venture capital funds and urged Ron Terry to start one for First Tennessee. He sent me up to New York to talk to a venture capital lawyer there who was associated with Citicorp. He told me that his first investment for Citicorp was in FedEx, so he didn't have to make many good ones after that. I went on to Boston to talk to a lawyer up there who specializes in venture capital firms. The real key to selecting a good venture capital investment is strong management. Good ideas are not good enough without good management skills, which are needed to grow with the firm and follow the vision. The bank started a venture capital firm, but it got somebody to run it who wanted to be in Alabama. We got no legal business out of the idea; perhaps I should have pushed Ron and insisted we get some of the business. I hinted at that generally, but he responded that the person running that operation should make his own choices. It was inconvenient for us to represent him in Alabama.

TWENTY-SIX

STATE EDUCATION

When I left state government, Lamar asked me which board or commission appointment I would prefer. I said, "The Higher Education Commission." I served for nine years on that commission. I was able to see implemented some changes we recommended for education, such as the Chairs of Excellence program. The Higher Education Commission recommends to the governor the budgets for the various institutions of higher education, basically those under the UT system and those under the Board of Regents. Each institution is treated on a substantially equal basis and gets its money in that way. Before the commission was established, those institutions were dependent on legislative clout and personal contacts for budget approvals. The commission evaluated budget requests by comparing them with institutions in other states. We did not consider any institution in Tennessee comparable to the University of Virginia, the University of North Carolina, or the California system. We did not look at major universities in the Midwest like Ohio State, Michigan, and Minnesota. We made careful comparisons with state institutions in South Carolina, Georgia, Alabama, Mississippi, Louisiana, Arkansas, Missouri, and Kentucky.

We also approved all new degree programs; this authority was designed to prevent creation of graduate programs of limited demand or excessive cost. We required each new program to project a budget for the first five years, an important factor in an approval. Unfortunately, we did not have authority to terminate programs, only to prepare a list of programs considered unjustifiably costly.

As a vocal member of the commission, I read what was given to us in advance. One institution proposed a master's in English literature program requiring 32 hours of credit with a thesis, and 36, without. I asked, "You mean you are giving a master's degree in English literature without a thesis?" The defense: "There will be a lot of writing required." I said, "You won't get my vote." The institution also did not get the commission's approval. It was dangerous to give me something to read because I will read it.

Our process of establishing priorities and funding levels was sophisticated; this included budgets of competing universities. We compared institutions on a tier system, senior, mid-level, and community colleges to similar institutions in the South. We sought to establish funding levels necessary to maintain a competitive position. The examination was carefully put together and carefully considered by the commission. During my tenure, the level of support for the commission's recommendations increased, and during the final two years of Lamar's term, the support was 100 percent.

Publication of that list of academic programs, considered costly and ineffective, did not have tremendous impact, but a few costly programs were eliminated. Many studies related to the number of remedial classes at our universities. At the University of Tennessee, a substantial number were offered; in the regional universities, such as the University of Memphis, Middle Tennessee State University, and East Tennessee State University, even more remedial courses were available. The proportion of the higher education budget appropriated to these "high school" courses was excessively high, something that needed correction. A process is needed to require high schools to raise the quality of instruction rather than depend upon universities. No one should be admitted to college who is not prepared to handle the level of work required.

In our system, many students do not go on to college, but nonetheless deserve a high school diploma. Our emphasis on equal opportunity fosters the assumption that everyone is entitled to a college education regardless of intellectual competence or educational preparation. Summary reports on the amount of remedial education in our colleges were shocking and should have had greater attention from the legislature, from the UT board, and from the Board of Regents. Some progress has been made in reducing the amount of remedial education, but the goal should be zero. European countries understand a certain percentage of their students in public education are not equipped to undertake a college education.

In Tennessee and the United States we provide technical institutes and community colleges for those unable to or uninterested in maintaining the level of a college education. Higher education in Tennessee has suffered heavily in the last 20 years. Governor McWherter's prejudice against the University of Tennessee came from his feeling that UT was too influential in political matters. He lacked appreciation for a college education because he had done extremely well without one. He believed a college education unnecessary or not nearly as important as many people did. During his eight years, the support for higher education in Tennessee was almost static, or perhaps there was less money per student in real dollars, adjusted for inflation, than when he took office in 1989. Because of financial difficulties during the Sundquist administration, Governor Sundquist was unable to catch up from this eight-year lag. My commission term expired around 1990, and Governor McWherter asked if I would like to be reappointed to the Higher Education Commission. I told him yes, but I wanted him to understand I would not be bound by his advice. As his former lawyer and colleague in state government, we understood each other thoroughly. I was not reappointed.

During his administration, the prestige and the influence of the Higher Education Commission declined. I believe the commission was no longer a place where all involved were challenged to provide adequate support for higher education. It became just another tool like the Department of Education to assist the governor in developing his budget for higher education. It did not retain its status as a booster for higher education. In the three state budgets I supervised for Governor Alexander, we did not fully support financially the recommendation of the Higher Education Commission. It was not financially feasible, but we adjusted its recommendations on a pro rata cut. The commissioners understood their major function was to balance the overwhelming political power of the University of Tennessee and the needs of other state universities. It also served to provide a challenge to the state by reflecting on the needs of higher education.

The state Board of Education should perform that same function and not rubber-stamp the governor's plans. They ought to send the governor a public report on needed support for K-12 and remind citizens that Tennessee suffers greatly from the low percentage of our workforce with college degrees. Tennessee is at the very bottom of the states, lower than Mississippi, Arkansas, and Alabama, a frightening statistic. As the United States economy becomes more complex, the ability to compete depends upon an individual's educational skills. This failure to support education is so gradual that it takes 10 to 15 years to see the devastating impact. I remember saying to Governor Alexander, Tennessee's economy was moving along in pace with the national economy. This is no longer true. Tennessee moves at a slower pace in economic growth than the national economy. I feel Tennessee spends much less on education, both K-12 and higher education, than it should. Our support per student is among the lowest in the country. As I often say, nothing in the air and the water down here enables us to provide a good education more cheaply than the other states. Tennessee has a higher proportion of poverty and lower educational achievements in our rural counties than most states. Our urban poverty, while severe in Memphis and a problem in Chattanooga and Nashville, is not proportionally as heavy as in many states. The problems of education are myriad. The first is the federal court's ruling that equal protection applies in the classroom. If there is no discipline in a classroom, there is no learning. Principals no longer support teachers in discipline problems; superintendents don't support principals in discipline problems; and the school board does nothing in many incidences. A main problem in education, not unique in Tennessee, is what I call the dumbing down of America, fostered by the idea of college education for everyone. When you graduate from some college now, you have sort of a slightly post-high school education, carefully adjusted so that everyone can pass. Grades have been inflated and good students no longer really benefit from their hard work. College degrees are handed out to people who can barely read and write; and many cannot write a clear grammatical, correctly spelled paragraph.

We need to establish a system where a high school graduate can read and write reasonably well and know more than the basics of mathematics, including algebra. In Europe, with as much pressure for equal rights as in the United States, they openly established school systems with tracks. Some students are prepared for college and some are not.

A major problem with education in Tennessee: inadequate funding. The cost of education could be reduced by reducing the cost of the State Department of Education and reducing the cost of the superintendents' office in each county and their general overhead nonclassroom expenditures throughout the educational system. There are two reasons why education is inadequately funded in Tennessee. The first is a cultural factor. Higher education gets limited support because too few understand its importance. Anti-intellectualism seems to pervade Tennessee society. That could be expected in the poverty areas of urban communities, but the attitude extends to many middle-class people, most heavily in rural areas. Often people tell me they don't want to give any more money to those sorry schools. I tell them, if you want them to be sorry, that's a good way to make them that way. School will not improve with less money or the same amount of money.

The critical problem is that there really isn't enough money. Because the Tennessee tax structure is almost totally dependent upon general and special sales taxes, it doesn't grow as fast as inflation. Tennessee is constantly in a situation where we pass a tax increase, and, for a few years, have enough money. Then there is a gradual decline in the amount of state revenues until, in desperation, action is taken. Basically, Tennessee, maybe one year out of every five, is fairly flush; in another year, not bad off, but for another three years, hurts for money. We simply don't have enough money to fund education adequately. Funding of education doesn't show an immediate improvement; it takes a whole new generation of schoolchildren, 12 or 13 years, to see a genuine improvement. This makes it hard to drum up support.

As I have mentioned, during my tenure as commissioner of F & A, the General Assembly created a commission to study education. The commission considered many ideas. The idea of basic skills was generally supported, but a far more controversial proposal to pay better teachers for teaching better was not. The TEA fought this to the death. It claimed it was not trying to prevent the reward of quality teaching, but that it was impossible to determine if such a pay scheme would produce favoritism and raise the cost of education without benefit to the students. A professor at the University of Tennessee education school developed an exciting plan to measure the quality of teaching by determining the improvements made by the students in the class each year. It was pretty elaborate, with many subjective elements, but it provided a method to determine who was doing a good job as a teacher, and reward them accordingly. This was the most controversial part of Alexander's proposal, and the governor fought for it all the way. Finally, with some watering down from the TEA, it got passed. Unfortunately, the TEA developed a unique technique to fight this program. They watered down the requirements to such an extent that everyone qualified as a good teacher. It was a great idea that didn't work out in practice. Those who measured subjective progress were inclined to be softhearted on their compatriots. The natural tendency is to want everybody to show improvement. Instead of having some 25 percent of the teachers qualified as outstanding teachers, it ended up that 75 percent qualified, a meaningless result. The basic skills program, however, was adopted, a new education initiative established with new funds raised by new taxes the governor proposed.

Tennessee has a low percentage of postgraduate students in our higher education system. At Virginia and North Carolina, postgraduates constitute around 40 percent of the total student body; when I last looked, Tennessee was well less than 25 percent. Georgia has become a gem and it shows what can be done if funds are provided to raise the quality of the education system. Good teachers and good professors deserve and should get appropriate pay. But unfortunately in Tennessee, all the way through the system, in maintenance, capital outlay, technical support, information systems, and innovative programs, there is regression rather than improvement. As a Republican, I dislike saying it, but more dollars are needed. We could reduce the cost by eliminating at least 25 percent of the employees in the state Department of Education. That ratio might not apply in K-12 education at the local level, but many systems do have topheavy administrative costs. This is tragic because those dollars are so desperately needed in the classroom.

Whatever the source or method, Tennessee education desperately needs an infusion of strong public support and more money.

TWENTY-SEVEN

SOME MAJOR CASES

The highest profile case I ever tried was the "Small Schools case." I served for nine years on the Tennessee Higher Education Commission. The commission met annually with the State Board of Education. The board brought us up to date on their actions, and we updated them on ours. On one of those occasions in early 1988, they reported working on a new allocation formula for K-12 education funding. I interjected, "I can't believe I haven't heard about this. If you think that you are going to come up with a new formula for K-12 education and get it passed with no publicity and no organized political support, you are crazy." Then I added a comment that produced the most interesting case of my career. I said, "As a matter of fact, I'm surprised somebody hasn't sued you already."

Three weeks later, a delegation led by Bill Emerson, superintendent of schools for Crockett County, representing a coalition of small schools, called on me and asked if I had meant what I said at the joint meeting. I responded, "I guess I did." They inquired, "Would you represent a group of small schools (about 75 school systems) against the state to attack the present system of funding education?" I agreed.

Later I heard a rumor that they had called on three other lawyers, who prided themselves on being constitutional lawyers, and were told the case was unwinnable.

In fact, I was uniquely prepared to undertake that challenge. I understood state finances; I understood the education financing; and I had tried many tax cases, some related to the issues in this school finance case. I had established myself as an expert on state finance.

When the suit was filed in July 1988, the first issue was whether the courts would consider it or yield to "legislative prerogative" (the right of the legislature to rule in a state public policy issue). After stalling in answering the complaint, the attorney general finally filed a motion to dismiss on the grounds that financing education was a legislative prerogative.

We gave them two extensions, one 60 and one 30 days; when the motion to dismiss was filed, the hearing was set for the next Friday. I asked for a one-week continuance, because I had promised to take Jan to New York that weekend. The state, following the policy observed throughout the lawsuit of "scorched earth," said, "No." I had to go to the court and get it, which I did. I think the court was somewhat amused.

We argued the motion to dismiss in December 1988. The court took it under advisement and did not render a decision until six months later. The court did have jurisdiction and would decide the case on the merits, holding that the legislative prerogative of the Tennessee General Assembly did not prevent the court from considering the issue of whether the present funding of education violated the state's equal protection clauses.

Tennessee has two somewhat convoluted clauses in the constitution, which have been interpreted by the Tennessee Supreme Court to be the equivalent of the Equal Protection Clause in the federal Constitution. It had actually taken a year from filing to get a ruling on the motion to dismiss. While we were in the process of assembling proof, the state followed its practice to make this trial as expensive as possible for my clients, who were certainly having a difficult time raising the money to proceed. They subjected us to a protracted discovery process. One example: They requested discovery of the minutes of all the school board meetings of all of my 75 clients for the last 10 years.

In some of these small, rural counties, finding the minutes for the last year would be difficult; for the last 10 years, impossible. We assembled boxes and boxes of these records and submitted them. I am sure no one ever looked at them.

A major part of our proof was the state's statistical data. I asked the state's attorney to agree to admit those by consent; she refused. I discussed this with one of my more experienced trial lawyer partners, and he came up with a perfect solution: just subpoena all of the commissioners involved in any of these reports to be there at the hearing. We would call them when we got to them.

I got a call from the attorney general himself who said, "We're going to look rather silly calling the commissioners as witnesses," and I said, "Yes. You are going to look rather silly." And he said, "I guess we could consent to admit those without any further proof."

In October of 1990 we entered into a six-week trial. Two young lawyers assisted me, Joe Conner, who has become one of the finest trial lawyers in our firm, and Buckley Cole, who left us. When I finished my opening argument, they were extremely complimentary and told me I had done a great job. When I questioned my first witness, they again applauded my performance and said, "We got everything in that we needed." I felt good about that until I realized they did not know I could do that. I had done lots of trial work at Canada, Russell & Turner, some on my own, and at Snowden Davis. In fact, I tried numerous tax cases, mostly in Federal District Court, but those days were 30 years back.

It was a protracted trial. Three superintendents testified along with two students. One student testified of her desire to attend a certain college, not Ivy League, however. She could not apply because her high school offered no foreign language. She had to transfer to a school in another county to meet the foreign language requirement.

The other student won a place at the Governor's Science School. When he went, they talked about equipment unknown to him. The lab equipment at his school consisted of a sink and hot water. He was concerned about going to a university to take pre-med courses. He said he had a weak science background, despite having taken every science and math course available at his school.

Our expert witness who had written extensively about equal educational financing for small, rural schools pointed out that in Tennessee, none of the schools we represented had a single Advanced Placement course. Many did not offer the courses required for admission to the major state universities, much less private colleges. An Ivy League school was an impossible reach. He talked about how inequitable funding for textbooks, lab equipment, and other necessary equipment and supplies affected the quality of education in small, rural schools. We introduced one textbook that forecast the possibility of landing a man on the moon. This was 20 plus years after the moon landing.

We also showed a tape from a TV station comparing the schools in Hancock County, a poor rural mountain county, and the adjoining county of Sullivan, home of Tennessee Eastman. The contrast was stark. In Hancock: no foreign language, old dilapidated buildings, no science lab, bare minimum athletic facilities, a pitiful library with a couple of book shelves, and no music program. Over the mountain in Sullivan County, the school had Advanced Placement, several foreign languages, full science labs, a music program, and relatively new buildings.

The state called the commissioner of Education to testify, and he stultified himself saying that the money didn't really matter, and how great things were in rural schools. He was from a small school himself and knew better. Their expert also testified money wasn't important. I enjoyed cross-examining him. He lived in Rochester, New York, and we found out per pupil expenditure in his school district. My clients' school systems spent less than $3,000, some less than $2,500, per pupil. In Rochester, the per pupil spending was over $6,500. He pretended not to know the amount, but when I said, "If I said it was about $6,500 I would probably be about right, wouldn't I?" He admitted it was true.

In July of 1991, after approximately six months, Chancellor High ruled in our favor with an opinion, holding the state responsible for establishment and maintenance of a school system. He ruled the state cannot pass off that responsibility to counties, and when counties fail to support education adequately, the state has responsibility to see that they do so. He held that money does matter, and that every child in Tennessee is entitled to substantially equal access to school financing.

After we won, the state Board of Education proposed a new plan of financing education. Governor McWherter supported it. The key provision called for development of a fiscal capacity index for every county, so that some counties would end up paying considerably more than the average required of a county, and other counties would pay considerably less. The overall division was supposed to be 75 percent state funds and 25 percent local funds, and on capital outlay, 50 percent state funds, 50 percent local funds.

Using the fiscal capacity index on the 75/25 ratios, some counties paid less than 10 percent, and a number of counties paid more than 35 percent. It provided equalization and established a method to evaluate educational costs by 40 or more components to be reviewed each year to make Tennessee competitive in financing education.

Unfortunately, immediately after the plan's proposal in early 1992, the Court of Appeals reversed the chancellor on the issue of legislative prerogative by a 2-1 decision. Then we went on to the State Supreme Court. After my opening statements, the chief justice questioned me for over an hour. Justice Drowota told my partner Buck Lewis my argument was the best he had heard in his many years on the bench.

Meanwhile, the governor proposed a new formula called the Basic Education Program (BEP) to the legislature, and it was rejected. He called a special session, but no agreement was reached. The proposal came up a third time during the general session, but before the legislature acted, the Supreme Court in March of 1993 overruled the Court of Appeals and sustained the chancellor's broad-scale ruling. The court's opinion held the state is required to provide substantially equal educational funding to all students, wherever they live. The Supreme

Court further deemed money a significant factor in educational quality, and reminded the legislature of its ability to require counties, the special school districts, and the municipal (special) school districts to do whatever the General Assembly required them to do to fund education, but with the ultimate responsibility on the General Assembly, not on counties or municipal school districts.

When the plan was finally adopted, the General Assembly eliminated teachers' salaries as a component and stayed with the old plan to determine those salaries. The legislature also phased in the plan over six years. We returned to the chancellor, requesting he strike down the plan as unconstitutional because of its failure to include teachers' salaries and because funding had been stretched over a six-year period. He rejected the motion. I made a direct appeal to the Supreme Court, which held that six years was satisfactory, but that the BEP must include teachers' salaries. Again, the legislature, despite this ruling, chose to make a halfway gesture and came up with a small token adjustment to the lowest-paying school districts. The plan was an absolute mess, which provided little equity.

We returned a third time to the Supreme Court. This time the court made it very clear that salaries must be an integral part of any funding formula, held the existing formula inadequate, and ruled the token adjustment by the legislature insufficient to meet the requirements of equal protection. Governors McWherter, Sundquist, and Bredesen supported the court rulings.

While the funding of salaries by Bredesen was small in the beginning, by 2004 it had gradually increased to bring the small schools substantial equity. Teachers' salaries became a full component of the BEP. Each year teachers' salaries, along with the other 40 plus components, will be reviewed to see whether the cost is in line with actual, competitive costs in other states and in competition with private industry.

The Small Schools case was a great victory and the results were tremendous. It has increased annual state funding from K-12 education by more than $1 billion. Most small school districts now have

Advanced Placement classes; all have at least one foreign language. Physical facilities have improved tremendously. Test scores have risen dramatically. Many rural students now enter elite universities. The BEP has improved public education across the state. When teacher salaries are adequately funded, Tennessee will be competitive again.

A couple of years ago, Bill Emerson, the original chairman of the Tennessee Small Schools System and a former superintendent of Crockett County Schools, called and said, "Lewie, we finally won." I asked what he meant. He replied, "Crockett County just hired a teacher from Madison County (Jackson)." Bill Emerson was a man of strength in the 16 years it took to do this job. He held the group together, begging and scraping to pay the law firm. He provided encouragement to stay the course. Many others also helped, including Larry Ridings, superintendent of schools in Trenton (Gibson County) who succeeded Bill Emerson as chairman of the Small Schools System, and Wayne Quarles, former superintendent in Hickman County, deputy and then commissioner of Education for the state and now the lobbyist for the Small Schools System. Quarles was especially effective in getting Governor Bredesen to include salaries as a component of the BEP.

The urban schools did not join us and missed out on most of this relief. Their significant problems remain unsolved. The case is a source of great pride to me and to the firm despite the financial implications. The small schools group was unorganized when we started. The argument and trial and appeals involved about a $1.5 million in billable time with over $50,000 in unpaid expenses on the books at different times. We initially compromised these fees at about half our normal rate; since the first victory, we have been paid at our normal rates. The pay came slowly, but we received over $1.5 million, remarkable considering the group's very low fiscal capacity. I hope this case sets a tradition for our firm to be involved in other great issues.

One other case came to me, probably because of my service as a city councilman and as commissioner of Finance and Administration. A new state law required all schools boards be elected. In Shelby County, the county executive nominated members of the Board of Education for approval by the County Commission. The small municipalities outside the city of Memphis—Germantown, Arlington, Bartlett, Collierville, Millington, and Lakeland—asked me to represent them in a lawsuit to determine who could vote for the election of the new County School Board; whether the election would be countywide, or whether it would be confined to citizens in those areas who were actually served by the county school system.

The Tennessee Constitution stated all county-elected officers must be elected countywide. I proposed to intervene on behalf of the small cities in the county. The city of Memphis, the city Board of Education, and the Shelby County School Board moved to intervene. The state assistant attorney general came down to oppose my intervention. She said, "We don't mind Mr. Pierce getting in for of the city of Memphis; we don't mind Mr. Winchester getting in for the county school board; we don't mind Mr. Kelly getting in for the city school board; but we don't want Mr. Donelson in this case."

The district judge allowed our intervention. As the state anticipated, I assumed the lead in trying the case. The case was tried on our motions for summary judgment. We won this case before the U.S. district judge, and then in the Sixth Circuit Court of Appeals.

Another complex matter involved representation of a friend and her family. Her father, a struggling farmer with land in Alabama, lost his farm by foreclosure during the Depression. He borrowed $500 from a friend, took that $500, big money in 1930, and bought a peckerwood sawmill and from that, built a timber empire. When he died, he owned 90,000 acres of Alabama timberland free and clear and a large sawmill.

Before and at his death, he gave stock to some employees and relatives, about 20 percent of the company. The balance he put into two trusts, one for each daughter, and designated a large bank in the state as the managing trustee of the trusts. He stipulated one trustee must be an experienced forester, the other trustee, an experienced businessman. The bank dominated the trust. Unfortunately for my client, her sister's husband was a large stockholder in that bank. His uncle had been a director of the bank, one of its largest stockholders, giving my client's brother-in-law much more influence with the trustees than my client. A strong sibling rivalry between my client and her sister exacerbated the situation. Anything my client and her husband proposed was usually rejected. After Congress repealed the General Utilities doctrine taxing corporate dissolutions, there was a six-month window allowing a corporation to dissolve without paying tax on the increased value of the corporation's assets. Most every timber company did just that. My client urged that the corporation be dissolved, but the trustees refused. Then she recommended the trustees should elect Subchapter S for the corporation, particularly desirable because the income from forestry operations is capital gain-type income, taxable at the low capital gain rates. When the corporation receives the profits, it pays taxes at capital gain rates, but then when it distributes dividends, stockholders pay tax on those dividends as ordinary income, a double tax. Again, the board refused; the excuse was that trusts holding stock would not qualify as Subchapter S stockholders. Treasury rulings permitted the Subchapter S stockholder beneficiaries to go to court and have the trust amended so that it could comply with the requirements of Subchapter S, which are simply that there would be only one beneficiary of the trust and that beneficiary would receive all the income from the trust, at least annually.

The company in years past had done excellent tax planning. When the company incorporated, the stockholders retained a large part of the timber as tenants in common. Then a contract was arranged between the tenants in common and the company that provided for the company's purchase of the timber. When I examined the contract, I discovered the minimum annual purchase was insufficient to require the company to purchase all of the timber before the contract expired, and the timber would, therefore, revert to the corporation without payment.

We were anxious to divide the company. My client's brother-in-law was wealthy; they liked to see the trees grow. My client's family and the minority stockholders wanted better returns on their investment with a regular cutting cycle to maximize the return for the property. For a number of years, we were unable to get this done. My client, manager of the tenants in common, was empowered to act for the tenants' in common dealings with the corporation. The contract provided that the corporation could buy a maximum and a minimum amount of timber each year. I took the position that if the company refused or failed to buy the maximum amount permitted, the tenants could sell the timber to others. My argument: Minimum cutting would not exhaust the tenants' in common reserved timber rights, and the timber would, on expiration of the contract, revert to the company, deliberately forfeiting the planned tax advantage. Accordingly, we arranged on December 31 to have a purchaser from the tenants in common buy a tract of timber, move onto the land, and begin cutting timber on December 31. You never heard such hollering and screaming about the illegality, contract violations, and so on. The company never did anything about it, and our action showed the trustees we meant business. The climate changed.

We persuaded the trustees to come to Memphis to meet with my client and me. One trustee, a successful businessman and a friend of my client's brother-in-law, understood business. I pointed out why the company should have dissolved after the repeal of the General Utilities doctrine, why it should have elected Subchapter S, why not cutting the timber sufficiently prevented tenants in common from maximizing their investment in the timber, and why not cutting enough timber annually failed to provide a reasonable return on the investment of the shareholders.

Also, we showed some timber had grown so large that no sawmill within 150 miles could cut it. When I explained all this, the trustee changed his attitude and said, "I am either going to resign as trustee or I am going to get this company divided." A serious discussion of division began.

An experienced forester was hired to develop a plan of what could be done with the company if the cutting was established on a regular

25- to 30-year cycle, how much the return could be increased, and with proper planning, how the cutting could be spaced so that there would be steady income every year based upon the growing timber. It was an impressive result, and after that report, the board did vote to divide the company.

That was just the beginning of the problem. To divide the company, we needed a letter ruling from the IRS that the division would be nontaxable and, in the process, we had to work out an agreement for the division. All the minority stockholders elected to go with my client. Her sister wanted to keep the headquarters, other buildings, and equipment. Fortunately for our side, no substantial value was assigned to hardwood timber intermixed with the pine. We included as much as possible in our share of that division, and they put a very low value on it. The hardwood differential easily offset every other advantage obtained by retaining the equipment and buildings.

At the IRS conference, I raised the issue of Subchapter Selection. The agent in charge suggested that a policy change was under way, but our request for a ruling would create a delay. So she required us to include a statement that we not elect Subchapter S, and agree that we would not do it for five years. This agreement was submitted with the request for a ruling. We did obtain the ruling and divide the company.

The division proved to be successful. The new company then began to set up a system of plantations, which would rotate so a regular amount of timber could be cut annually. Two successful deals greatly increased land holdings. Mature timber ready for cutting was swapped for land with young timber. Thirty thousand acres grew to over 40,000 immediately. Called reverse asset exchanges, these were nontaxable. Profits increased materially, and, ultimately, more timber was purchased in Tennessee.

When election of Subchapter S began, one stockholder refused, and after protracted negotiations, a reverse stock split squeezed him out. Without squeezing other stockholders, one family of the brother-in-law's relatives put all their stock in a voting trust of an eligible Subchapter S stockholder. Under Alabama law, if a reverse stock split was used to squeeze out a shareholder, that person had a right to dissent.

This shareholder did. We were then required to file suit to have the value of the shares determined. This suit had to be filed in the jurisdiction where the company's home office was located. In most states, in such circumstances the valuation standard would be fair market sales, which would include a minority shareholder discount recognizing that a 4 percent shareholder has little leverage and much less marketability, because a 4 percent interest in a closely held company is very difficult to sell. An Alabama Supreme Court decision stated that in cases where a minority shareholder is forced out, the standard should be "fair value" without minority or marketability discount allowed. We contested other discounts. The company, with its low basis on timber, had a large built-in capital gain that would incur as the timber was sold, a complex issue. No Alabama law existed on the question. We cited authority that any purchase of the whole company where virtually all the assets were low basis ones and the company's entire business was selling off those assets, any purchaser of the whole company would insist on adjusting the price for this very large potential tax liability. We also argued you can't sell 40,000 acres of timber all at once; the physical process would take years and an adjustment should be made. We engaged in a protracted battle with that recalcitrant stockholder over the value of his shares. The result was not what we had hoped for. We received some "home cooking" from the small town judge who ruled that the Alabama case permitted no discounts of any kind, although built-in "gain" and the time spent on cutting were not discounts, but adjustments in the value of the whole company. We threatened to appeal and negotiated a slightly better settlement.

In the late 1990s, I represented Medshares, a company in the home health care business that provided visiting nurses. It was in a strong growth mode. Steve Winters, principal stockholder, bought everything available. There were two serious errors. First, he dealt with a "cowboy" finance company; it was accounts receivable-type financing. We learned later this company skimmed the collections. When I first heard about this company, I strongly recommended he discon-

tinue doing business with it, but when we flew up to meet the principal of the company, I allowed him to persuade me he would treat
Medshares properly. I was seriously mistaken.

Second, Medshares purchased from HCA some of its home health
care operations. That required approval from HCFA (the then name
of the federal agency controlling Medicaid and Medicare) for the
transfer within 60 days. HCA was under investigation for fraud, and
although these operations were not involved, some bureaucrat buried
it in his files. The time limit passed, and months went by before we
learned the truth. The results for Medshares were catastrophic. Cash
flow dribbled to almost nothing. Debt from our cowboy financing
source soared. The company was "bankrupt" in the sense that it
couldn't meet its debts as they matured. Despite my warnings, the
company failed to make withholding and Social Security deposits and
fund the pension plan. Chapter 11 bankruptcy seemed the only answer; a huge IRS debt made reorganization impossible. The government, the principal creditor, was intransigent, brazenly unconcerned
about the erroneous and unjustified act of a government employee as
the precipitating cause of the Chapter 11 filing. Steve Winters lost
everything, and was still liable on the huge IRS deficit because of his
responsibility as CEO.

During this period, I also represented Davidson County in construction of a convention center hotel connected to the new convention
center. George Barrett, a close friend of Richard Fulton, associated me
in this matter. Franklin Haney had the contract from the city. We had
met through politics and he called one day to ask why despite his
contract on the convention center hotel, no one in Nashville wanted
to deal with him. I told him to get partners known and respected in
Nashville. I suggested among others Joe Rodgers and Ted Welch. Both
became his partners. Franklin, a true expert in such financial packages,
combined an office building with the hotel. The bonds were Davidson
County bonds, designated for the project. A federal statute authorized
such bond deals and made them tax-free. Exact compliance with the

statute was essential to their tax-free status. Joe Rodgers was an inactive partner, but Ted Welch was an active participant. We couldn't have closed the deal without him. Franklin depended on a section in the Internal Revenue Code, which would expire on December 31 of that year. We spent almost all of December in New York, trying to finalize the deal. We signed the last document at a quarter to twelve.

I told George Barrett I had always wanted to see the ball drop at Times Square. We left the building and ran over there in time. Although George had bragged about running, which I had done regularly for years, I soon left him in the dust. I was only about two blocks away along with thousands and thousands of people, but I got a clear view.

The complex, and sometimes contentious, deal was closed; Franklin Haney and I became friendly. His business since then included the Knoxville Convention Center Hotel and his unsuccessful nuclear power proposal to TVA.

One sidelight of the Convention Center Hotel deal: On December 31, as the day wore on, Ted insisted he needed to leave. Finally, I said, "Why don't you ask her to fly up here?" Ted said, "What do you mean?" I said "You must have a New Year's Eve date or you wouldn't be pushing to leave." He did. Colleen arrived about 1:00 p.m. We all spent the evening together. An attractive and smart dean of nursing at Vanderbilt, she impressed me immediately. The next morning I told Ted, who was single and dated many different girls, "Marry this one." He did. He told her what I had said and Colleen is my good friend to this day.

TWENTY-EIGHT

THE CHANGE OF COMMAND

When Howard Baker decided to step down at the end of his third Senate term, as he promised, I talked to him about merging our firms. I spent the day with Bob Worthington and the other partners in the Knoxville office, but reported to Howard I felt a merger would be difficult because the cultures of the two firms were so different. He asked what I meant. I responded, "The name partners in the Knoxville office take all of the money. The younger partners and the associates do most of the work for nominal compensation." I told him the pay in our firm is based not on seniority or partnership status, but on performance. Those different compensation standards caused us to put off the merger.

About 1992, members of his firm in Nashville approached me about joining us. I indicated we could not take people away from Howard's firm. In the spring of 1994, I read where 20 of his lawyers in Knoxville had left in one fell swoop. I called Howard and said, "Howard, I think it is time now to merge the firms." He said, "I think you are right." After we agreed to merge, I said, "Howard, when we put the firms together, you do what you do best—make rain—and we'll do what we do best—run the firm." That merger was completed in early 1995.

At the time, we had about 125 lawyers, the Baker firm had about

60, and our gross income for fiscal year 1995 was $34 million. The merger gave us over 175 lawyers and moved us into the pre-eminent position in Tennessee. The strong Washington, D.C., office added a new dimension to our practice, national recognition. *Forbes* has listed the Washington office among the top 10 lobbying firms. It also does a lot of international work, mostly on trade matters.

We had a commercial office in Beijing. Larry Eagleburger was responsible for that office. He and Joan McEntee met with the premier of China to secure permission for a client to operate in that country. At the end of the meeting, Larry asked permission to open an office in Beijing. The premier agreed to a commercial office, staffed by two Chinese trade experts. Joan and two other of our Washington lawyers went to China regularly. I cannot resist recounting the conclusion of that meeting. When our business was completed the premier said to Joan, "Will you please step out of the room? I have a message I want Mr. Eagleburger to give to the president." Joan knew she was in high cotton.

We have added two health care policy experts in Washington. Thanks to Howard Baker, former ambassador to Japan, I am confident this office will continue to grow in power, influence, and profitability. The merger also strengthened our Nashville and Knoxville offices and added a strong, small office in Johnson City.

About the time of the Baker merger, Charlie Tuggle talked to me about establishing a health care practice. He found a health care expert in Jackson, Mississippi, in Dick Cowart. I suggested that Charlie tell Dick that we planned to move him to Nashville, a center for health care activity because of Hospital Corporation of America (HCA) and its many spin-offs. I asked Charlie about it. He said, "I mentioned the possibility." That meant I had to tell Dick the news.

In August 1995, he agreed to join us and brought about 10 lawyers with him. The office consisted of outstanding, able lawyers, and was successful from the outset. I persuaded Dick to move to Nashville; from that base he established as fine a health care group as any in the country. With the new addition, our gross rose to over $50 million in fiscal year 1998. We recently ranked third in the country for our health care group, confirming our leadership in that area.

This was a prime example of Charlie's visionary leadership. He also foresaw the field of intellectual property as an important new specialty. The Atlanta office is a product of that foresight, and intellectual property is a growing and strong group in the firm. That office opened in November of 2000, and we have made continuing efforts to expand it. The major barrier seems to be Atlanta pride. No Atlanta firm wants to be a branch of a Memphis firm. We finally persuaded a firm of 35 lawyers who wanted our vision, momentum, technology, and size. With other additions, we now have over 50 lawyers in Atlanta, a strong tax group as well as excellent litigators. Bruce Doeg and Jason Epstein moved to Nashville from the Knoxville office and became experts in computer and IT matters, developing an excellent, growing practice in that explosive arena.

Charlie's last major contribution to the firm was the Birmingham merger. Before we negotiated successfully with the Berkowitz firm, Charlie tentatively arranged a merger with another, the head of which acted unilaterally, negotiating without the knowledge of his other partners. News of the merger leaked out before they were fully informed and the deal blew up. The talks with the Berkowitz firm were carefully conducted. It had over 60 lawyers; we were several times larger. The fit was good. Its practice resembled ours in many ways: small business clients, commercial litigation, some tax and estate planning, strong in construction matters. It needed securities and SEC expertise. We could use the construction expertise. The merger worked well, except for the difficult lead partner. After the first readjustment of his compensation at the agreed time period, he left; however, the merger remained intact and no one left with him. The office is stronger now, more cohesive.

I do not have the financial records available before FY 1986, but there was steady growth from about $600,000 in FY 1965 to $7.6 million in FY 1986. From FY 1987 to the present, the growth continued to up to $116.5 million in FY 2004. In 1991, we had 218 total employees.

In FY 2004 we had 878, slightly less than half of whom were lawyers or consultants. Today we have over 1,100 employees and 600 lawyers, ranking us in the top 75 firms nationally in size.

This ability to look into the future, to be aware of what other firms are doing, and to anticipate trends in law practice is crucial to a great firm. We are fortunate that Charlie and now Ben give us this type of leadership. Our recent addition in Nashville of a group of securities lawyers is another example of seeing a need and responding. That coup (and it was a coup) puts us in the ranks of Nashville's premier firms. To bring on board Gary Brown, a primary lawyer in drafting and passing Sarbanes Oxley, is a major feat.

Almost simultaneously, a group of lawyers, mostly health care specialists from New Orleans, approached us about joining our firm. They knew Dick Cowart and were aware of our strong health care practice, staffed by excellent lawyers. New Orleans was a serious commitment, a civil law state, plus a different culture. The fit was so perfect; we felt confident to proceed. After the new office opened under the Baker Donelson name, we were astounded by the number of lawyers who contacted us. Donna Fraiche, the leader of the health care group, is an active civic leader in New Orleans and has served as chairman of the board of Loyola University. The New Orleans bar was dominated by old-line firms where the senior partners raked in all the profits and the younger partners did all the work. This "tontine" system meant if you outlived your contemporaries, you rose in the firm. As a result of general unhappiness with that culture, many outstanding lawyers joined the New Orleans office. The Louisiana offices have about 60 lawyers in New Orleans, Baton Rouge, and Mandeville. One early recruit, Roy Cheatwood, became managing partner of the New Orleans office and provided leadership for growth. I believe everybody is happy with the results. The two additions are further proof the firm has achieved a stature that allows us to attract such lawyers as those in New Orleans and Nashville.

That long sought acquisition in Atlanta, the Gambrell & Stolz firm with 35 lawyers, brings our presence there to 50 lawyers, a major step. This is Ben's triumph. I only mention it as a bystander.

The Birmingham firm was an ideal fit for us. I anticipate that the New Orleans office will be the same, especially in the health care area discussed. The Atlanta addition is significant, but it is early to judge its full impact.

Now other lawyers call wanting to join; we always seem to have several possibilities under consideration. The key is to make the right additions to fit our overall plan and select those willing to share our culture. Our opportunities are great, but the possibility for mistakes is always present. We have the leadership, the experience, and momentum to continue our successful growth—if we do as well as Charlie and Ben did in the past, and avoid some of my mistakes. Throughout this phenomenal growth, we have maintained a collegiality not present in many large firms. We continue to pay for performance, an important factor in our success.

In a little over 50 years, we grew from a two-lawyer office with one secretary to the largest firm in Tennessee, one of the largest in the South, with a well-respected Washington office. We now provide the broad scale expertise Ben and I visualized at the beginning. Our revenue base allows us to undertake major investments in technology, essential to continuing strength and growth. We upgraded our recruitment program and compete with the larger firms for the best lawyers. We are ready for rapid changes in the law practice with a vision and a plan. Clearly, there is "life after Lewie." I did not quit nor do I plan to retire until I am no longer able to contribute to our quality of legal service. Able leaders have moved the firm ahead to even greater success and prestige. Neither my nor Howard's passing from the scene will hinder the firm's growth as it strives to achieve greatness.

TWENTY-NINE

NEW CHALLENGES

My next major civic initiative involved the Regional Medical Center (The MED), an institution in existence for over 150 years. Memphis had one of the earliest hospitals in this region; perhaps river travelers demanded such care. A facility was established around 1830. The charity hospital was the first and provided care for those without resources; this is the mission of The MED. Medicare and Medicaid altered the system. All such programs start with enthusiasm and that wanes as the pressure of inflation and rising costs and rising expectations outpace the community's ability to provide sufficient tax revenues. The passage of Medicaid had a tremendous impact upon The Regional Medical Center, once the John Gaston Hospital. It permitted people eligible for Medicaid, particularly those marginally at the poverty level, to drift to other hospitals. Before that, they were turned away on the unfortunate presumption that the charity hospital took care of those who couldn't afford to pay. When the Medicaid funds were directed to other hospitals, the charity hospital's population declined. As costs constraints began to bear on the system, it was difficult for the city hospital to provide the care required at the reimbursement level The MED received. The Medicaid system assumed the hospital would offset those costs by increasing charges to paying patients; particularly the insured. At The MED there weren't enough paying patients to overcome those costs.

When Governor McWherter decided to establish what was called TennCare, a plan designed to greatly increase the percentage of the population actually covered by Medicaid and Medicare, the state obtained a waiver from the federal government for the new system. During those negotiations for the waiver, those who could not pay were not well represented at the table and got the short end of the stick. Soon The MED had serious financial problems. It did not make enough money from trauma and burn and a few other profitable centers, nor from Medicaid funds to provide care for those nonpaying patients. They experienced a year of substantial deficits and the prospect of another.

The county mayor, Jim Rout, an old friend whom I had recruited into politics, called and asked me to chair a committee to study the financial condition of The MED. I agreed. The reimbursement system for its disproportionate share of nonpaying patients was totally unfair and inadequate. The federal government matched the costs of free care offered by Tennessee hospitals with an additional appropriation, but our state waiver did not add it to the hospitals' payment. This money went directly to the state; state officials did not divide the money in the same proportion as when free care occurred. The MED provided approximately one-half or more of all the free care in Tennessee by public hospitals and received only about 20 percent and sometimes less money than the federal government provided. Tennessee provided about $10 million of free care to Mississippi patients and $10 million of free care to Arkansas patients with no reimbursement from either state. We brought those problems out and suggested the necessity of additional support from the state and the county if The MED was to continue its existence. After I made a report, Mayor Rout called and said, "Lewie, you need to go on the board of The MED." I agreed. He called back the next day and said, "I am appointing almost a new board and you ought to be the chair." I had been lured gradually into a task where I spent the next 10 years struggling with the problems of The MED, which was always in danger of financial disaster.

The president of The MED, a fine man, wasn't tough enough to deal with the hard problems. Shortly after my arrival, we discovered the provision of free care for people indirectly associated with The MED who were not entitled to care and whom we couldn't afford to serve. I directed the president to stop that. Six weeks later I asked him if he had done so, and he had not. I concluded he couldn't run this institution which required a strong leader willing to step up to the hard problems. He departed.

We hired a health care consultant, Quorum Health Resources, to do a survey of the hospital, and it agreed to the need for new leadership. Quorum also suggested a reduction in the administrative staff. Some had limited qualifications and could not be transferred to other jobs. It also recommended a reduction in staff of about 450, which was about 25 percent. We created an early retirement plan, and we had more applicants than we were able to accept. This was difficult because most retiring employees were union members, and that union was the American Federation of State, County and Municipal Employees (AFSCME). As described earlier, during my previous dealings I had established a good working relationship with union leaders. Bill Owens, an organizer when I was on the council and who became the union representative in Memphis, was now the national secretary/treasurer and a veteran leader. When I explained the situation, I asked him, "Would you rather have 450 fewer employees, or none?" He understood and came to Memphis and helped us sell the plan to the union. He did it graciously, and everything went smoothly.

The next step was to find a new president. Bruce Steinhauer, who had just retired from the Lahey Clinic in Boston and had been a longtime staff member of the Henry Ford Hospital in Detroit, was an excellent choice. A Harvard Medical School graduate, he understood medicine and the American health care system. The MED's dealings with government were a major part of the day-to-day operations. Bruce had a low-key style, but more than anything else, he provided The MED with credibility and an expert voice in the councils of government. Now we were able to produce believable figures. When I first talked to the state about The MED figures, I found out they were totally wrong and I was terribly embarrassed to present figures that were not supportable. Bruce was there during the downsizing. We then together tried to build an able and credible executive staff. Our first chief operating officer didn't stay long because of his inability to work with the nurses and other staff. We then hired a woman who did a good job for several years. She gave up the position because she didn't want to undertake the responsibility of the president's job, and we wanted a COO who could move up when Bruce retired. We had some excellent people. The head of nursing was outstanding, the head of human relations was also a competent person, and the chief of staff was dedicated to the institution. He and the medical staff were provided by the University of Tennessee.

We had virtually no private practice doctors when I arrived. We did develop some as the years went by. The service provided by UT doctors was strong in some areas and weak in others. Given the financial crisis the University of Tennessee medical school faced, the doctors were heavily dependent upon income from their private practices. Their time for The MED was limited by the need to work with paying patients to provide additional income, essential to a reasonable standard of living.

Next we undertook the Mississippi/Arkansas problem. I suggested no more service for out-of-state people. That was impossible. When they arrived, the hospital had to care for them. I was taken aback for a few weeks; then I realized that although unable to refuse care, we could refuse to send the helicopter. I had learned that many who came to the trauma center would not have survived if they had come by car or ambulance. The helicopter was crucial in treating trauma cases. This got attention, particularly in Mississippi. They struggled around and got a proposal from the state to provide us $6 million. Then we discovered the federal government wouldn't approve of their sending the money. We went to Washington and, with much help from Harold Ford, Jr., got a meeting with the head of the Health Care Financing Administration, the man in charge of the interstate transactions. He reported provisions for out-of-state patients in the Medicaid system called for 5 percent of the patients to be from out-of-state. This was entirely inadequate to cover The MED situation. Then he said, "We don't permit and don't allow Medicaid money to cross state lines." My comment was, "I thought that is why we had a federal government." It made no impression on him. He was adamant, and gave me a highly bureaucrat look. It read, "I am going to be here when you are gone, so don't mess with me, buddy. Nothing you can do about it." But there was something we could do.

We got legislation that specifically permitted those dollars to cross state lines. We did a lot of finagling, with assistance from Congressman Ford and primarily Senator Bill Frist, then majority leader. Bill explained that since he appointed the members of the conference committee, he could say, "I want this provision in the conference report." It would almost always get in there. That way the bill passed, permitting reimbursement from Arkansas and Mississippi for a limited period. This has been renewed now for an unlimited period. While The MED doesn't receive the $6 million from Mississippi every year, it gets some help. It also got help from Arkansas. Arkansas was able to provide much less because of a poor formula for reimbursement from the federal government. With Bill Clinton as president for eight years, Arkansas should have been on top of the list in getting reimbursement from the federal government. Nonetheless, the money from Arkansas and Mississippi was an important factor in keeping The MED financially viable.

My next venture was spectacularly unsuccessful. When Baptist Hospital announced plans to move to East Memphis and close its midtown hospital, Bruce Steinhauer and I contacted Steve Reynolds, chairman of the Baptist system, and asked if he would be interested in giving us the building. He was; it seemed like a dream. We could unite all The MED operations in a magnificent building. We could have greater visibility and a more attractive appearance. We hoped to persuade some Baptist doctors with practices concentrated in Midtown to continue to practice in the new facility. This appeared to be an outstanding solution to The MED's problems. The move would free up existing buildings for the county to sell and invest the funds to help provide some capital to spend on bringing The MED up to snuff, particularly its trauma center and its emergency room. The value of that gift is difficult to estimate, but it was somewhere between $75 million and $100 million, at minimum. Baptist agreed to the proposal and promised to encourage some doctors to stay with The MED, which would build up private practice doctors. We did a survey of doctors to determine how many might be interested, and the response was encouraging. Although we showed millions of dollars in savings by being in one fairly new building, we had to secure approval of the County Commission. The mayor had to approve the deal, but that was not a stumbling block. There may have been some behind-the-scenes opposition bad-mouthing the deal, concerned it might be detrimental to their interests. Other hospitals were concerned that The MED might become more of a competitor than a resource. The hearing before the County Commission was appalling. First, the opposition thought the deal was going to help the University of Tennessee, and therefore they were against it. Second, some people hated Baptist Hospital because it was a "rich people's" hospital. A totally erroneous impression arose that the arrangement would benefit Baptist. Baptist Hospital would get no financial benefit from giving its buildings away because it could be sold or torn down, and the land sold. The opposition would do nothing that indirectly benefited that "rich people's" hospital.

During my years on the City Council and in dealings with the County Commission, I had never seen such a negative atmosphere. It was apparent we didn't have the votes for approval. One commissioner had the gall to say that Baptist wasn't giving enough. I responded that I knew of no other charity hospital in the United States that had received a charitable contribution of $100 million. That had absolutely no impact other than to draw some insulting comments. In retrospect, I failed to prepare the ground adequately in the beginning, and I was totally unprepared by the reaction. I knew that when you present a controversial item to a legislative body, you need to prepare the ground. No matter how good your presentation is, officeholders need an opportunity to air their views beforehand. We should have visited them all and handled their resentments in private to get the proposal approved. We failed. I consider it my own personal failure, which ranked next to my failure to settle the garbage strike, as the two the great failures of my public career. My interest in The MED declined at that point. I was in a holding pattern after that.

We had a strong and resourceful board, supportive of The MED's work, including Bruce Steinhauer, Barbara Holden, Allen Boyd, Travis Smith, Harry Smith, and Dr. Blackmon. We made progress in making The MED more acceptable to the general population and changing its image. We publicized the trauma center as one of the finest in the United States, and the newborn center as an outstanding facility in the area. The burn center was the only serious one of its kind in the Mid-South. The obstetrics service was good and helped a tremendous number of people.

Part of this improvement was increased visibility and effectiveness of The MED Foundation, which operated for a number years raising money from employees and a few other sources, and providing $350,000–$500,000 per year to support the hospital—highly needed assistance. We did even more under the leadership of John T. Fisher. We received four gifts of $1 million. Particularly heartwarming was an anonymous gift in honor of Jan and me. We aired two effective television programs to publicize the importance and quality of service at The MED. We received tremendous support from people in North Mississippi. Penn Owen was the leader; we raised the level of confidence in The MED. Although about the time I left, difficulties arose with regulating authorities about some incident that could harm the institution's reputation. All were the kinds of things that happen in all hospitals. When there were threats to close The MED, I said to tell them to go ahead and take the flack. The MED is always experiencing a new financial crisis with grave discussions about what should be done. I believe The MED's status as an independent hospital should be preserved. If taken over by Methodist, for example, competition between the two would arise with an almost inevitable conflict of interest, drawing away from The MED the paying patients and giving it the non-paying ones. Not to my surprise, securing a replacement for Bruce Steinhauer was much more difficult than anticipated. Some talk suggested employing a management company to take over The MED rather than an having an individual who would be totally dedicated to the task. They found a fine replacement.

I stepped down from the board in August 2006. Harry Smith resigned before I did because he joined the Baptist Hospital board and felt that could be a conflict. Allen Boyd and Barbara Holden followed me shortly, resigning from the board. Jack Morris took over for me as chairman, but his term was brief. Gene Holcomb succeeded him; Gene is an intelligent man experienced in the medical industry from many years at Blue Cross. Travis Smith remains on the board and provides serious financial supervision and advice. I hope everything possible is done to preserve this asset to the community. Proper support for Arkansas and Mississippi is one key; the other, to get a bigger and fairer share of the funds provided for disproportionate share. Tennessee must provide support because of The MED's service to counties in West Tennessee. If The MED got its fair share of the funds that are provided for the free services that hospitals in Tennessee provide, it would be in a comfortable financial situation, roughly $50 million to $60 million of those funds. It gets only a fraction of that, and the amount varies from year to year with the whims of state and federal governments. That ought to be stopped as well. There ought not to be a statutory formula that requires the state to give The MED its share of these funds based upon the proposition of free care The MED provides. This would be at least 50 percent. There ought to be a clearly defined formula for determining The MED's share from the federal funds that Tennessee receives for free care. The present system, giving the state total discretion, invites political game playing. The MED is now receiving a much larger share of these funds. The new president has finally been able to get a fair share of the disproportionate share funds and the finances are in better shape.

A survey of The MED showed that nurses and doctors received

good marks from the patients, but administrative personnel did not. Admissions and discharge staff, particularly, were viewed as rude and inconsiderate. Their attitude seemed to be if you weren't paying, you didn't deserve to be treated with respect. An intensive campaign began to improve this. Some improvement was apparent. In some cases, doctors in some areas provided excellent service, but others were somewhat cavalier in their responses to the patients. The trauma center, though, is probably one of the nation's best. Everyone in the Mid-South has learned that if you are in a severe accident, seriously wounded in some way, you should say, "Take me to The MED." Those patients, particularly the paying patients, want to be transferred as soon as possible to another hospital. The physical facilities at The MED are not bad. The quality of the medical team is excellent. The leading physicians and surgeons on the UT faculty give generally excellent medical care.

I would say that The MED was my last major contribution to the community in a nonprofit capacity. I remain active at St. Jude, in my church, and in Republican affairs. I no longer serve on the National Rural Schools Trust, to which I was elected in the aftermath of my victory against the state of Tennessee. I hope to continue to be of service because I am healthy and in full possession of my faculties.

I have been honored by my community beyond any justification. Receiving awards from the Civitan Club as an outstanding citizen, from the Rotary Club as an outstanding community servant, from the National Conference of Christians and Jews as a humanitarian, and the Ladies Hermitage Association, which established the Lewis R. Donelson Award in my honor. I was the first recipient of the award. The Choate School, my prep school, honored me with the Alumni Seal Prize as did Southwestern (Rhodes) with an honorary degree and a Distinguished Service Medal. Memphis gave me a dinner when I departed for service as commissioner of F&A, and Nashville also gave me a farewell dinner. In recent years I received the Multiple Sclerosis Society Distinguished Service Award, the Boy Scouts of America Outstanding Citizenship Award, and have been recognized by the Republican Party as an outstanding contributor. These last honors were in the form of dinners, attended by many people. It humbles me to think about how much I have been honored. Former Senator Fred Thompson came to Memphis to speak at the Boy Scouts Award dinner. In response to all this, I say not only have I enjoyed community service, but have benefited by it. I got much more out of it than I gave; a satisfactory experience, and I recommend it to everyone. These honors suggest that I have achieved what I started out to do: to use my talents to help my community to be a better place.

Since the early 1980s. Bill Morris and I have been friends from his years as sheriff and as county mayor. I even tried to convert him to the Republicans and run for governor. An excellent campaigner with a solid record as Shelby County mayor, he had an excellent chance to win. If he had listened to me, he said recently, he might have been governor.

Bill put me on a committee called Free the Children, a well conceived project, to pick an area of poverty in North Memphis, 20 to 30 blocks, and to experiment with how to help lift people out of poverty and into productive citizens. An eye-opening experience! First, we had a big job fair and got jobs for 60 young men. When the social worker reported back two months later, more than half of them had moved on. When we asked them why they had lost their jobs, the answers were distressing: "The job was boring," or, "I was late all the time." How did you get to work? "I got up in the morning and I looked for a ride." Did you ever take public transportation? "No, I never thought about that." Did you ever plan the night before for who was going to take you? "No, I didn't. I just looked for a ride."

The social worker explained these young men thought of a job as they did a used car. You could either take care of it or you could abuse it. It was yours to do with as you saw fit. Basically, they lacked any concept of work, of how to hold, succeed, and advance in a job. The social worker told us many families in that area of Memphis had four generations without anyone who had ever worked. A daunting task, and we made little progress. The mayor, in an effort to balance the committee, named several black members, who felt their only purpose was to stir up racial discord. The committee disintegrated from misdirection and I resigned.

Shortly after my return from Nashville, Sam Cooper called and said St. Jude was threatening to leave Memphis, move to St. Louis, and associate with Washington University, and we were trying to keep them here. He asked if I could get the St. Jude people an appointment with Governor Alexander to help persuade them to stay. I set up an appointment with Lamar and brought up a delegation from St. Jude, including most of the crucial players. Lamar always handled such matters with finesse. He met first with me and discussed what I considered to be the problem. St. Jude had a troubled relationship with the University of Tennessee because a former St. Jude executive had been fired and went to the University of Tennessee, where he poisoned the well. The relationship with the University of Tennessee was important because many researchers missed the academic atmosphere and needed that connection and the opportunity to serve as adjunct professors or on research projects. We met first with Ed Boling, then president of UT. Lamar cautioned him to be sure UT indicated its readiness for full cooperation with an understanding of the reasons for the existing relationship, and to underline that UT was anxious to expand its limited medical school research with St. Jude. Ed Boling resisted that assertion and talked about the amount of research at the UT med school. Lamar said, "Ed, I don't want to hear any of that bull." We wanted to convince St. Jude to stay in Memphis.

In the middle of the meeting, Ed Boling began talking about all their medical research. A conflict erupted because St. Jude found little ongoing research at UT, at least in terms of St. Jude's interests. Lamar, following his usual practice, said, "Gentlemen, I'm going to step out of the room and you're going to get this problem resolved. And when you get it resolved, Lewie will come and tell me, and I'll come back." He stepped out of the room. I made some plain statements. Ed Boling backed down and began to cooperate, and we made some progress. I called the governor back into the room and he handled it superbly. He told the St. Jude delegation what they wanted to hear and how he would insist UT work them to the maximum extent possible. He also reminded them he was chairman of the UT board. Then, he pulled his masterstroke, and said, "I'm going to call a special session of the legislature and we will make Danny Thomas an honorary citizen of Tennessee." They ate that up and it cinched the deal. Sure enough, Lamar did call a special session; many St. Jude board members came up. The General Assembly passed a formal resolution making Danny an honorary citizen. As they thanked the governor for his generosity and kindness, Lamar said, "You ought to put Lewie on your board because he knows how to handle UT." That remark ultimately got me elected a member of the St. Jude board. I didn't realize how difficult that was to do until after I became a member. The charter of St. Jude requires that more than 60 percent of the board be people of Syrian, Lebanese, Palestinian, and Middle Eastern descent, with a limited number of slots for non-Arabs. It is a large board, but hyperactive. I thought I would not like working under a board that's too involved in the day-to-day hospital management and fundraising. It works remarkably well because of so many dedicated people striving to do what's best for St. Jude. Despite strong arguments, they always seem to settle them and move on, focusing on the success and development of St. Jude Children's Research Hospital.

My first year on the board, I was quiet and listened during some tumultuous meetings. Al Josef, at almost every meeting, would storm out saying that he would never return, but he always did. He was one of the original people with Danny Thomas, and he was totally devoted to its welfare. Dick Shadyac was another one of the original people also totally devoted to the hospital and very influential in running it. Not long after I joined the board, he quit his law practice to become head of the fundraising arm. Although he had been a successful trial lawyer all his life, he did a superb job as a fundraiser, lifting the hospital to completely new heights. I think that when I got on the board, we were probably raising something around $40 million per year. By the time he retired, we were raising over $400 million a year (and now $700 million per year).

The hospital experienced fantastic growth, but clearly the chief financial officer was out of his depth. Financial statements and the interrelationships between ALSAC (the American Lebanese Syrian Associated Charities, the St. Jude fundraising arm) and St. Jude were complex, and someone with greater experience and expertise was needed. I approached Paul Simon, then chairman of the Finance Committee, and he agreed with me. Surprisingly enough, he promptly suggested the chief financial officer resign, and we replaced him with another more able person. Then it appeared the chief operating officer was also beyond his capabilities. I talked about that. Finally, they appointed me chairman of a special *ad hoc* committee to reorganize the administrative side of the hospital and find a new chief operating officer. We did an amazing job in getting the hospital more adequately staffed to deal with its growing size and complexity. I served on the Finance Committee, the Legal Committee, the Human Relations Committee, the Building Committee, and the Special Committee on Staffing. Also, I became a resource in interpreting Memphis and Tennessee politics, helping with the hospital's relationship with state government, and continuing to smooth out the relationship between St. Jude and the UT medical school.

After several years, the hospital director moved on. Art Nienhuis was named the new director, and we became good friends. I served as the interpreter of the board to Art. He provided a different and tremendous lift to the hospital because of his connections and respect in the world research community. He had been with the National Institutes of Health and recruited an amazing array of outstanding scientists. Our superb fundraising allowed the hospital to offer substantial enticements to Art's recruits. As head of the hospital, Art moved St. Jude into the forefront of international child research institutions. St. Jude initially had a policy that no one would pay. That rule was slightly misleading, because we used the funds from those who had Medicaid or payments from those who had insurance; no one paid out of their own pockets. If they didn't have insurance or Medicaid, everything was free. That included not just hospital stay and care, but also room and board at the hospital. In the process, the hospital went from renting hotel rooms for patients and their families to providing a marvelous facility at Target House, another at the Ronald McDonald House, and then the Memphis Grizzlies House, which is on the campus. Patients and their families who come are provided with free room and board. Regardless of your ability to pay, you get the absolute finest care available anywhere in the world with the best and latest techniques and treatments.

The hospital does not keep any new discoveries secret. They broadcast them to their connections around the world with similar institutions—even one in Beirut; others are taught to use the St. Jude techniques. It's an amazing outreach and so much in line with Danny Thomas' attitude that the hospital should be dedicated to the goal that "no child should die in the dawn of life." Everything that is developed through perhaps some of the greatest research teams in the world is made available to the general public.

Not long after I joined the board, they decided on a $1 billion expansion program that has exceeded that amount with the completion of the Chili's building. The campus is a scintillating example of the latest in research and health care and one of the city's great prides. I'm now an emeritus board member but still active, attending most meetings, and I remain a member of the Legal Committee. At one retreat, I mentioned my surprise that an institution of St. Jude's size did not have a Human Relations Committee. One was promptly created. I was made the first chairman and I still serve on that committee, as well as on the Building Committee. It's been a joy and a privilege to be a board member. I tease them by saying they treat me with such great respect and affection that they've made me an honorary Arab.

Of course, I continued my political activities. I worked with Senator Howard Baker on his presidential campaign and went on his tour of New England. On that fateful trip, he decided to stop his quest for the presidency. Howard was brilliantly prepared for the job. He knew everyone of significance in Washington. He was greatly respected on both sides of the aisle. A Senate vote would have shown him to be the Senate's choice for president, and that vote would have included Democrats as well as Republicans.

The day began with a successful visit to Brown University in Providence. There was a strong turnout. On to Boston, where we were a little less successful. We made two or three stops in New Hampshire. We went onto Portland, Maine, which proved to be the conclusion of the trip. Senator William Cohen was strong supporter of Howard's bid for the presidency, and Howard expected to get the endorsement of the Maine convention. When Howard got up to speak, I had never heard him as flat. He was totally ineffective. He failed to win the support of the Maine delegates and after some consultation, withdrew from the race.

Howard's relationship with his first wife, Joy, was tempestuous, but he never said anything negative. He supported her through all of their difficulties. It was so unfortunate that Joy, daughter of Senator Everett Dirksen, was timid and found political campaigning extremely difficult. Howard said one time, "You know, Lewie, it's getting difficult to handle Joy's travels because she's refused to fly anymore, and getting around the country is extremely hard to do." That's the only thing I ever heard him say the least bit negative about Joy. He, apparently, was wild about her.

Talking to Lamar one day during Howard's campaign, he asked me, "If Howard gets to be elected president, how would you like for me to appoint you to the United States Senate?" I said, "Lamar, I don't want to be a freshman senator." (I think I was 64 at that time.) "It takes years to get established in the Senate and I wouldn't have time to do that. Now, if you could work it out where you could be senator and I could be governor, I'd be in favor of that because a governor is effective from the day he takes office." Lamar has gone on to be a senator, and an excellent one.

Lamar continued as governor until 1986. I tried to get him to work for us, but he said, "I really don't like practicing law." I said, "You wouldn't do much law if you came with us. You've got so much to offer: a good mind, mixing politics with excellent judgment." One day he called and said, "Lewie, I'm going to be president of the University of Tennessee." I objected, "Lamar, you don't want to do that." He said, "What do you mean?" I answered, "They don't want to do what you will want to do with that university. What do you want with that job?" He would tell you now I was right.

The University of Tennessee at Knoxville is an incredibly ingrown institution with a limited interest in the graduate school. Almost everything that Lamar proposed was resisted by the UT community and the board. The final straw was when Lamar was invited by President Reagan to a lunch at the White House to discuss higher education with a small group. He attended. The luncheon was on a Saturday when UT had a football game. The newspapers named him the first president in the history of the university to fail to attend one of the team's games in Knoxville—the unforgivable sin. He was able to exit gracefully and become secretary of Education under President Bush.

Lamar ran for president in 1996 and 2000. In 1996, he lost to Bob Dole on the absurd basis that it was Bob's turn, that he had earned the right. Lamar, an immensely able person, has proven his executive ability and his visionary approach to governmental problems. Unfortunately, he doesn't like to speak in sound bites, because of his extremely thoughtful and carefully analytical nature. He knows the United States faces problems too complex to be characterized with a quip. In 1996, when running against Dole, it looked like he might win New Hampshire and be on his way. The opposition came out with an ad alleging that Lamar had advocated an income tax as governor. This was a total falsehood. Not even I, who had been his commissioner of Finance and Administration, advocated an income tax while in state government. We discussed buying advertising on television for denial of the malicious lie. Lamar decided not to spend the extra money, and expected to win anyway. Unfortunately, he didn't, and his campaign never regained momentum. The attitude in 2000, when he ran against George W. Bush, was that he had had his chance and now it was someone else's turn. Lamar told me in the year before he ran the second time that he had attended more than 250 fundraising events. He described it as like walking across the country on your hands and knees. I'm not sure the present primary system does a better job of candidate selection than the smoke-filled rooms. Then, the candidates were picked by those who knew their strengths and their weaknesses. Today, it's a popularity contest and dependent upon the ability to speak in sound bites, raise tremendous amounts of money, and please as many people as possible. Perhaps Lamar could not have beaten Bill Clinton running for his second term, but he would have made it a lot better race than Bob Dole did. Bob Dole was the tragic victim of overhandling by so-called professionals. He had a very witty side that was sometimes acerbic. His handlers were frightened of his making an off-the-cuff remark that could be turned against him. They had him so toned down that the real Bob Dole—an able and attractive man— was invisible. These pros are the curse of modern campaigns, taking daily polls and trying to have candidates say only what the polls reflect.

CHAPTER 30

CONCLUSION

I have been privileged to live in Memphis virtually all my life except for my time in law school and in Nashville with the Alexander administration. I have been active in the community since the 1940s and active in political affairs since 1952. I have seen many, many changes.

When I returned from law school in 1942, Mr. Crump was at the zenith of his power. Memphis won repeated awards as the quietest and the cleanest city in the United States. Its park system was a model and the envy of many cities our size. While the cotton and lumber businesses began to decline in influence, they were still important economic forces. Mr. Crump had succeeded in bringing in considerable industry: Firestone, Dupont, Kimberly-Clark, International Harvester, to name a few.

Unfortunately, Mr. Crump did not promote the air transportation industry. Chicago and Southern, our original airline, became Republic, which ultimately became a part of Northwest, now Delta. Memphis did not play a major role in the tremendous aviation revolution. The demographics in Memphis have been negative in the long range, with a significant brain drain as many of our most able people leave for better opportunities.

Memphis has been greatly influenced by its tremendous entre-

preneurial spirit. In my lifetime the self-service grocery store origi-
nated in Memphis, and during my career the motel business and the
overnight air transport of packages were created in Memphis. Unfortunately, the grocery business lost its major connections in Memphis.
Holiday Inn, which was the bellwether for many years, was sold and
is now part of a British company, with its gambling operations run
by another hotel company. Thus, two of those three industries are no
longer centered here. Fortunately, FedEx remains. While the cotton
industry has shrunk and cotton's presence in the community has diminished, Memphis is still the center of most cotton shipping. All the
large cotton shippers have offices here; many are headquartered here,
including Dunavant, the largest. The hardwood lumber industry has
likewise diminished, although Anderson Tully remains and is a major
player. E.L. Bruce has disappeared, along with other smaller hardwood
flooring companies.

Memphis was very progressive in dealing with segregation in the
fifties and sixties. The sanitation workers' strike and the death of Martin Luther King set us back and tarnished our image nationally. Nonetheless, the community maintains a vitality uniquely its own. Our
airport is the busiest freight airport in the world. Our barge and truck
traffic remain strong. Memphis is served by five railroads, and only a
handful of cities can claim this.

On the social side, the revival of downtown with more than 30,000
people living there is an amazing development, a sign of strength in
the community. The University of Memphis, formerly Memphis State,
has emerged as an excellent university with promise for even greater
achievements. Rhodes College, formerly Southwestern, has become
an outstanding liberal arts college, one of the best in the country. And
Christian Brothers is a fine, small university here. We have plenty of
water despite recurring lawsuits raising some questions as to who
owns it. Our location is unequaled. We are a true transportation hub,
and we are the largest city nearest to the center of the United States.

We have not dealt adequately with poverty in the community. The
state of Tennessee has few programs to deal with the problem, and
the city of Memphis and Shelby County have done little except par-

ticipate in available federal and state programs. The MED, our public hospital, is our shining example of help for the poor. This problem of poverty extends into the school system with its dropouts and inadequately prepared students; our workforce is short of high school and college graduates.

Unfortunately, our governmental system does not provide the leadership and vision necessary to sustain and propel a great city. I describe Memphis as a place with blacks in the majority and the whites in the minority, but blacks act as if they are the minority and whites act as if they are the majority. We do have two good mayors now but it is hard to get anything done. We desperately need more black leaders willing to govern, to get in there and do things for the city, not think about complaints or past disadvantages but about what to do now to make this city a better one. The whites need to demand that of them and support them in doing so. It might not be the city that white leaders would develop, but it would be a city that represents the community and looks at the future, planning for it and daring to face those challenges unafraid.

One of the smartest things I did was to run for the City Council and serve only one term. You are free to do courageous things that you sincerely believe to be in the best interest of the whole community when you are not worrying about your political future. That is the tradition I hoped to create in Memphis. It has not happened, but leaders must come forward from both communities, active leaders who are going to serve, to sacrifice themselves to help this city. I know they are out there. I know some of them personally. We have to create an atmosphere in this community where these people know they can serve and be elected in an atmosphere that supports such leadership. It will require leaders who take some risks. We cannot continue to operate with a standpat attitude. Memphis needs change. It needs dynamic new leadership to maximize our strengths. That takes leaders who will take risks, will try new ideas, and who will begin to face our challenges with creative thought to show us how to work together for the present and the future.

I love Memphis and the state of Tennessee. I have discussed my many Tennessee ancestors and their service and devotion to this state. I have tried to live the creed I was taught: Those who are privileged should use their skills and opportunities to give back to the community. I have attempted to do this without sacrificing my law career or my family. I hope I have made a contribution to this community.

I would be remiss if I did not mention again my dear wife, Jan. I recently lost her after more than 65 years of happiness. She was a strong influence on me throughout our relationship, but more than that, she was a great influence for good in this community. Her joyful and loving spirit lifted everyone she knew. I added to these memoirs the obituary my son and I wrote at her passing. I hope it expresses in some inadequate but sincere way how wonderful she was.

I am proud of my children. They have been wonderful children. We were very close to them and have a loving relationship, made somewhat difficult because they do not live in Memphis. They are fine people, and they all in their own way contribute to their community. Yes, I have a blessed life. I have been favored with a great wife, wonderful parents, fine children, a superb education, opportunity, and good health. I am truly blessed.

JANICE OST DONELSON

Janice Ost Donelson died September 22, 2010 at Baptist Memorial Hospital. It would be a mockery to state her age. She believed that you were as young as you felt and she was always young in spirit. She had a busy, fruitful, and victorious life. She loved life, the world, her family, her friends, and her God. She was active in the Story Tellers League for many years, serving as its President and telling stories to young students and senior citizens. She was a great story teller. In the 1950s Jan was among the group of young Memphians who created a new Republican Party in Shelby County and the state of Tennessee. She served as president of the Republican Workshops, which used a technique of neighborhood meetings in homes to bring members into the Republican Party. Her tireless efforts and her warm personality helped to build a countywide organization, not of fat cats, but of ordinary people who became involved in politics, to build a two-party system and a powerful grassroots organization that grew from a handful of supporters to become a dominant political force in Shelby County in the 1970s and '80s. She sought no glory, nor office, but only to create a better community. She served on the State Republican Committee for 10 years. She loved Rhodes College and enjoyed participating in its activities. She was predeceased by her father Louis G. Ost; her mother Myrtle Stewart Ost; and her brother Louis G. Ost, Jr., a Memphis architect. She is survived by her husband of 65 years, Lewis R. Donelson, III, founding partner of Baker, Donelson, Bearman, Caldwell, and Berkowitz; her son, Lewis R. Donelson, IV, ordained minister and professor of New Testament at Austin Presbyterian Seminary; her daughters, Janice Donelson Goddard, for many years Operations Director of a Montessori School in Knoxville, TN; and Katharine Loring Donelson Daniel, a bankruptcy analyst for the Department of Justice; five grandchildren,

Donelson Howell, Mason Howell, James Martin Donelson, David Daniel, Jr., and Sarah Donelson; and her brother, Jerry Ost. Memorials can be sent to the Third Church of Christ Scientists, Rhodes College or the charity of the donor's choice. Memorial service will be 1 p.m. Friday, September 24, at Idlewild Presbyterian Church, with visitation to follow in the T.K. Young Fellowship Hall. Canale Funeral Directors 901-452-6400.

INDEX

INDEX